SSSP

Springer
Series in
Social
Psychology

SSSP

Language and Social Situations

Edited by
Joseph P. Forgas

Springer-Verlag
New York Berlin Heidelberg Tokyo

Joseph P. Forgas
School of Psychology
University of New South Wales
Kensington, N.S.W. 2033
Sydney, Australia

With 14 Figures

Library of Congress Cataloging in Publication Data
Main entry under title:
Language and social situations.
  (Springer series in social psychology)
  Includes bibliographies and index.
  1. Psycholinguistics—Social aspects. 2. Social
interaction. I. Forgas, Joseph P. II. Series.
BF455.L273 1985   153.6   84–26805

Typeset by Ampersand, Inc., Rutland, Vermont.
Printed and bound by R.R. Donnelley, Harrisonburg, Virginia.
Printed in the United States of America.

9 8 7 6 5 4 3 2 1

ISBN 0-387-96090-2 Springer-Verlag New York Berlin Heidelberg Tokyo
ISBN 3-540-96090-2 Springer-Verlag Berlin Heidelberg New York Tokyo

To Teeshie, Peti, and Pono

Preface

Most of our interactions with others occur within the framework of recurring social situations, and the language choices we make are intimately tied to situational features. Although the interdependence between language and social situations has been well recognized at least since G. H. Mead developed his symbolic interactionist theory, psychologists have been reluctant to devote much interest to this domain until recently. Yet it is arguable that a detailed understanding of the subtle links between situational features and language use must lie at the heart of any genuinely social psychology. This volume contains original contributions from psychologists, linguists and philosophers from the United States, Canada, Europe, Israel, and Australia who share an interest in the social-psychological aspects of language. Their work represents one of the first concentrated attempts to chart the possibilities of this exciting field.

It is perhaps in order to say a few words about the origins of this book. The need for a volume integrating research on language and social situations first emerged during the 2nd International Conference of Language and Social Psychology at Bristol University in 1983, at which I was convening a symposium with a similar title at the request of the organizers, Peter Robinson and Howard Giles. When they first approached me with this idea in 1982, I gladly accepted, since my own research on cognitive representations of social episodes seemed eminently relevant to a symposium on language and social situations. It was only after several months of intensive reading in this field that I fully realized the difficulty of my task. Depending on the way one looked at it, there was either no such field as research on language and situations, or alternatively, large parts of social psychology, sociolinguistics, sociology, and ethnography consisted of little else but studies of situated language use. This impression was confirmed as the contributions for my symposium began to arrive, ranging from cognitive-information processing studies to sociological and philosophical treatises on the social nature of language.

By that time, I was already convinced of the importance of my topic for cognitive social psychology, but still very much in the dark as to where its boundaries lay. The Bristol conference was something of a catalyst. It gave me an opportunity to meet researchers from many countries and many disciplines, who shared my interest in this domain. During many discussions, the need for a volume of this kind slowly emerged, and I met some of the contributors to this volume for the first time. Yet I would like to emphasize that the resulting book is in no way a collection of conference papers. Only some of the original symposium participants are represented, and their contributions are not identical with their conference papers. Many others were invited to join the project later.

I am of course well aware of the recent preponderance of edited volumes among academic psychological publications, a trend I certainly do not applaud. Why contribute to the deluge? It seemed to me that the topic at hand could not at present be handled in any other way, yet I was convinced that the time for such a book had truly arrived. I found my task of ensuring the integrity of the volume difficult at times, given the heterogeneity of interest in language and social situations. It was harder than I expected to find chapters which succeeded in focusing on this theme while at the same time adequately retaining the original flavor of their different orientations. I had to occasionally reject contributions not on the basis of any qualitative short-comings, but simply because they strayed too far from the central theme of the book. My aim here was to fully represent the rich variety of approaches available to explore the links between language and social situations, at the same time pointing the way to the convergence of these orientations toward an integrative cognitive social-psychological model. As all editors must, I also hope that the book that has resulted is more than its constituent parts, in that it makes a point over and above the intellectual contributions of the individual chapters.

The substantive contributions to the book are organized into four complementary parts, concerned with the (1) developmental, (2) psycho-logical, (3) socio-cultural, and (4) clinical and pathological aspects of language and social situations. My first chapter is intended as a general review and introduction to the field, which should help the reader appreciate the chapters that follow. Part I is concerned with the role of situational factors in language development. Chapter 2, by Jerome Bruner, presents a model of language acquisition in which knowledge about interaction situations, the shared "formats" of child and caretaker, lie at the heart of that almost miraculous feat, the learning of a language. As distinct from essentially asocial nativist or environmental language acquisition models, Bruner's model is a genuinely social account of that crucial aspect of development. Chapter 3, by Harry Levin and Catherine Snow, presents a model and empirical evidence demonstrating the situational fluidity of "baby talk."

In Part II, we turn to the role of psychological factors in situated language use. Teun van Dijk, in Chapter 4, describes a model of discourse production which is based on cognitive situation models in memory, and illustrates its consequences by an analysis of prejudiced talk. Chapter 5 summarizes the achievements of the ongoing research project at Mannheim by Theo Herrmann, Siegfried Hoppe-Graff and their associates, who developed one of the few truly psychological models of situated language use and collected a great deal of experimental evidence to support it. Raymond Gibbs, in Chapter 6, discusses the role of situational factors in the use and interpretation of that most problematic language category, requests.

Part III is concerned with the more complex social and cultural aspects of language and social situations. In Chapter 7, Shoshana Blum-Kulka and her collaborators at the Hebrew University describe a cultural analysis of situational variations in the language of requesting in Israel. Patricia Wetzel, in Chapter 8, analyzes the way situational conventions are involved in the use of words denoting giving or receiving in Japanese culture. Chapter 9, by Cynthia Gallois and Victor Callan, presents intriguing data about the way situational contexts influence the interpretation of accents in a multicultural society, Australia. The last contribution in this section, Chapter 10 by Rom Harré, offers a most stimulating and perhaps even controversial account of the way rhetorical language use by football fans, psychiatrists, or indeed, social psychologists, follows subtle situational conventions.

The fourth and final part of the book contains contributions dealing with situational influences on communication problems and communication pathology. Janet Bavelas, in Chapter 11, describes her situational model accounting for the use of evasive, "disqualified" messages, presenting some elegant experiments to prove her point. Chapter 12, by Hannele Heikkinen and Maarit Valo, presents a thought provoking analysis of the situational genesis of what they term "interaction slips." In Chapter 13, Günther Bergmann and I seek to develop a preliminary situational model accounting for speech dysfluencies (in particular, stuttering) in interpersonal communication. My aim in the final chapter is to review and integrate the foregoing chapters, and to provide some pointers as to the future development of this promising field of research.

The book should be of interest to academics and researchers working in fields such as social psychology, sociolinguistics, and sociology as well as to clinicians and practitioners concerned with the diagnosis and therapy of speech disorders and social-skills deficiencies involving language problems. The contributions are organized in such a way that the book should also be readily suitable for use as a core textbook in advanced undergraduate or postgraduate courses in social psychology or sociolinguistics concerned with the social parameters of language use.

Before concluding, I must acknowledge the various sources of help I received during the preparation of this book. Research grants received from the German Research Society (DFG) and the Australian Research Grants Scheme were a considerable help in carrying out some of our own studies described here. I did much of the work on this volume while occupying the Chair of Social Psychology at the University of Giessen, West Germany, and during my stay at Stanford University in 1984. I am grateful for the facilities and support I received at both institutions. Mrs. Pfanschilling at the University of Giessen has helped a great deal in preparing and typing the various chapter drafts, and Stephanie Moylan helped with the preparation of the index. Most of all, I must thank my wife, Letitia Jane Forgas, who has read and re-read all of the chapters several times, and offered many constructive stylistic, grammatical, and substantive suggestions from which my own chapters benefited greatly. I hope that this book will indeed be successful in focusing interest on the links between language and social situations, and thus will help to establish this domain as one of the central themes in the emerging field of cognitive social psychology.

Giessen, November 1984   Joseph P. Forgas

Contents

Part II. Psychological Factors in Situated Language Use

Part III. Social and Cultural Aspects of Language and Social Situations

Contributors

Janet Beavin Bavelas, Department of Psychology, University of Victoria, Victoria, British Columbia V8W 2Y2, Canada.

Günther Bergmann, Department of Psychology, University of Giessen, 6300 Giessen, Federal Republic of Germany.

Shoshana Blum-Kulka, Department of Communications, Hebrew University, Jerusalem, Israel.

Jerome Bruner, The Graduate Faculty, New School for Social Research, New York, New York 10003, U.S.A.

Victor J. Callan, Department of Psychology, University of Queensland, St. Lucia, Queensland, 4067 Australia.

Brenda Danet, Department of Communications, Hebrew University, Jerusalem, Israel.

Joseph P. Forgas, School of Psychology, University of New South Wales, Kensington, N.S.W. 2033, Sydney, Australia.

Cynthia Gallois, Department of Psychology, University of Queensland, St. Lucia, Queensland, 4067 Australia.

Rimona Gherson, Department of Communications, Hebrew University, Jerusalem, Israel.

Raymond W. Gibbs, Jr., Clark Kerr Hall, University of California—Santa Cruz, California 95064, U.S.A.

Rom Harré, Sub-Faculty of Philosophy, University of Oxford, Oxford, England.

Hannele Heikkinen, Department of Applied Linguistics and Speech, University of Jyväskylä, SF-40100 Jyväskylä 10, Finland.

Theo Herrmann, Department of Psychology, University of Mannheim, 6800 Mannheim, Federal Republic of Germany.

Siegfried Hoppe-Graff, Department of Psychology, University of Mannheim, 6800 Mannheim, Federal Republic of Germany.

Harry Levin, Department of Psychology, Cornell University, Ithaca, New York 14853, U.S.A.

Roland Mangold, Department of Psychology, University of Mannheim, 6800 Mannheim, Federal Republic of Germany.

Catherine Snow, Department of Psychology, Harvard University, Cambridge, Massachusetts 02138, U.S.A.

Teun A. van Dijk, Department of General Literary Studies, Section of Discourse Studies, University of Amsterdam, 1012 VT Amsterdam, The Netherlands.

Maarit Valo, Department of Phonetics and Speech Communication, University of Jyväskylä, SF-40100 Jyväskylä 10, Finland.

Patricia J. Wetzel, Department of Modern Languages and Linguistics, Cornell University, Ithaca, New York 14853, U.S.A.

Peter Winterhoff-Spurk, Department of Psychology, University of Heidelberg, 6900 Heidelberg, Federal Republic of Germany.

Chapter 1
Language and Social Situations:
An Introductory Review

Joseph P. Forgas

This book is about the role that common social situations play in the way people use language in everyday life. Verbal communication is the essence of social interaction: Most of our encounters consist of talk. Exchanging greetings and morning pleasantries with your colleagues at the office, discussing the price of meat with a familiar shop assistant, or asking your children about the day's events at school are examples of recurring verbal exchanges that are almost completely routinized.

Once entering a familiar situation, appropriate verbal messages seem to automatically "roll off" the mysterious mental production line where language is assembled. Other kinds of situations call for very different language strategies. At times, we are almost tangibly aware of the numerous verbal choices available to us to accomplish a particular social move. The selection of the most suitable request form, a speech act that often involves the possibility of loss of face for one or both partners (Brown & Levinson, 1978), usually requires such high-level situation-contingent processing.

The link between language and social situations is formed very early in life. An implicit understanding of the rules and requirements of interactive situations is not only one of the earliest foundations of language acquisition (cf. Bruner, this volume, Chapter 2), but every utterance we produce, and every utterance produced by others that we understand, is similarly dependent on people's shared knowledge of the surrounding social situation. As Rommetveit (1983) recently proposed, "My making sense of the world by means of ordinary language is an inherently other-oriented activity" (p. 101), in the sense that both the meanings of utterances, and shared definitions of social situations, are the result of collective, and not individual, cognitive activity (cf. Forgas, 1983c.)

Social psychological processes and language use are thus inextricably tied to each other. Yet despite growing emphasis in recent linguistic research on the pragmatic aspects of language use (cf. Smith, 1983), attempts to link language with the psychology of social situations are still in an embryonic state. The contributions to this volume reflect the richness and variety of the data relevant to this enterprise. The material on language and social situations presented here should be of interest not only to social psychologists, but to every student and researcher involved in the study of language and social interaction processes. The relevant evidence comes from a variety of fields: Psychology, linguistics, philosophy, sociolinguistics, anthropology, and ethnography can provide us with many exciting insights into the intricate patterns of language as a situational communication device.

This volume, then, seeks to contribute to research on the social psychology of human interaction by drawing together for the first time research from various disciplines dealing with the relationship between language and social situations. Before embarking on this enterprise, it will be necessary first to consider some of the conceptual issues associated with this line of research, and to review some of the work so far accomplished. This is the task of this introductory chapter.

The Background to the Study of Language and Situations

For some decades now, linguists have been increasingly aware of the necessity to take into account situational influences on language use, as illustrated by what Grice (1975) called conversational postulates governing discourse. The speaker is expected to be relevant, speak to the point, not speak too much, be truthful, give sufficient but not too much information about the context, and so on. Of course, even these very abstract "maxims" are themselves culturally relative, reflecting the shared mores of Western cultures. Other cultures have different ways of regulating conversations. The Apache culture, for example, seems to include a conversational maxim stating that you should "remain silent when the situation is unpredictable or ambiguous" (Basso, 1970).

These very general and global maxims and expectations will of course become more and more specific and prescriptive as the consensual definition of the situation between the interactants becomes clearer (cf. Thomas, 1966). Just as the shared background of the partners promotes the indexicality of verbal messages, more detailed definitions of situations hammered out in the course of repeated interactions (Goffman, 1974; Mead, 1934) by necessity lead to the evolution of more and more specific, if implicit, communicative maxims (Giles & St. Clair, 1979). Acquaintances use language differently from strangers: "By virtue of their privately shared social knowledge, [they] can construct orderly dialogue with less moment-to-moment guidance" (Kent, Davis, & Shapiro, 1981, p. 197).

It is thus clear that there are at least two levels at which situational influences on language use can be studied: the individual-psychological and the sociocultural, represented in Parts II and III of this volume, respectively. Definitions of situations also reflect this duality: On the one hand, our culture and society provides us with a situational repertoire which is in some sense "given." On the other hand, every one of us develops unique shared situation definitions with each of our interaction partners, by virtue of our ability to abstract and symbolize our encounters, as symbolic interactionists so clearly emphasize (cf. Mead, 1934).

But what exactly is it about situations that guides our communication strategies? Numerous linguists have attempted to construct (usually speculative) models of exactly how, and through which features, situations might influence language behavior. Their focus on ad hoc taxonomies of objective situational features is curiously similar to early attempts by psychologists to describe situations (cf. Ekehammar, 1974; Forgas, 1979). Firth (1957) was an early proponent of such an approach, suggesting that the "context of situation" consists of components such as features of the participants, relevant objects, and the effects of the verbal action. A further elaboration of this model was suggested by Gregory (1967), who identified three situational features: the medium (or communication channel), the role (or topic), and the addressee (interpersonal relationship). Mode, field, and tenor of discourse are dimensions along which linguistic choices may respectively vary in response to situational features such as these.

Such conceptual, descriptive analyses of situations are of course heavily dependent on the shared, taken-for-granted norms of the larger culture regulating acceptable forms of interaction. As Poyatos (1976) proposed, "If we consider culture as a series of habits shared by members of a community, [then] any portion of cultural activity sensorially or intellectually apprehended in signs of symbolic value" (pp. 313–314) may be analyzed as a unit of culture. Just as the smallest meaningful unit of language is a morpheme, Poyatos labeled the smallest meaningful unit of a culture a *cultureme*. At an intermediate level of analysis, such culturemes consist of behavior settings (e.g., school, home, office, classroom, restaurant, etc.) that symbolize culturally sanctioned ways of interacting (cf. Barker, 1968).

This idea found its most powerful expression in Dell Hymes's proposals for a new field to study the "ethnography of speaking." As conceived by Hymes, the ethnography of speaking is primarily concerned with the patterns and functions that organize the use of language in social life, and the study of situations that regulate speaking. Perhaps not surprisingly, Hymes (1967, 1972) used the 'SPEAKING' mnemonic to summarize the various situational factors influencing conversations, such as Setting and scene, the Participants, Ends (outcomes and goals), the Act sequence, the Key (or manner of communication), Instrumentalities, Norms and the appropriate linguistic Genre.

Hymes's list shows surprising similarities to recent social psychological characterizations of social situations (e.g., Argyle, Furnham, & Graham, 1981). However, Hymes's (1967, 1972) situational taxonomy was still based on the implicit assumption that objective situational characteristics in some way directly determine language behavior—in other words, similar objective situational features would lead to similar language behaviors across a wide range of possible encounters. This assumption may be open to serious doubt, as language choices are more likely to depend on the perceived than on the actual situation: "People act under the impact of a situation which they themselves perceive . . . the social world is broken down into situational experience" (Leodolter & Leodolter, 1976, p. 325–326). In Kurt Lewin's terms, it is the perceived rather than the actual "life space" which will ultimately determine our choice of words.

The situation classification scheme constructed by Hymes (1972) became quite influential and eventually exerted a considerable impact on the developing field of sociolinguistics. However, this was only one of a number of attempts to develop taxonomies of situations. Ervin-Tripp (1964, 1972) suggested the need to develop a situational hierarchy as a prerequisite for developing what she called a *social grammar*. A more recent such descriptive taxonomy was proposed by Brown and Fraser (1979), who thought of situations as composed of the scene (including the setting, and the purpose of the interaction) and the participants (individual features of the partners, and relationships between the participants). Almost identical features of situations (i.e., the setting, and the relationship between the partners) were found to be important by social psychologists interested in situation perception (Forgas, 1979; Wish, 1975).

The Brown and Fraser (1979) taxonomic system has some advantages over earlier schemes, such as the implicit emphasis on social roles, the acknowledgment that it is subjective representations of situations that ultimately influence language behavior, and the suggestion that the choice of language code both determines and is determined by the situation. These ideas were further developed by Giles and Hewstone (1982), who take a more social psychological orientation, and argue that a crucial feature of communicative situations is whether the participants construe it as an intergroup or an interindividual encounter (cf. Tajfel & Forgas, 1981). They suggest that other crucial features of situations are formality, involvement, perceived tension, and cooperation, characteristics that were found important by judges by empirical research on situation taxonomies (Forgas, 1979, 1982, 1983a, 1983b; Pervin, 1976; Wish, 1975; Wish, Deutsch, & Kaplan, 1976). This classification scheme clearly points to the necessity of studying interaction situations psychologically, in terms of the social actors' perceptions of them.

Descriptive schemes of this kind naturally focus on abstract, general schemes of situations. Can such schemes adequately describe what happens in the myriad unique encounters that constitute our social lives? General situational categories, such as "eating in a restaurant" or "having a lovers' quarrel" are of course empirical abstractions, prototypical configurations of features that may never be enacted in exactly this idealized way in any actual encounter (Rosch & Lloyd, 1978; Schank & Abelson, 1977). Pike's (1967) now classic emic-etic distinction is relevant to this problem. The overtly distinct, or "etic," features in an actual situation do not necessarily change the prevailing meaning of the event for the participants, while the structurally distinct "emic" aspects of a situation, being part of the cultural, normative system, do. Classifications of situations are thus invariably based on the emic characteristics of the idealized interactions they seek to describe. It is reasonable to assume that such abstract cognitive schemes, and not unique situational features, have the greatest influence on our language-processing strategies.

The Psychological Tradition

Interest in situational influences on behavior also has a long tradition in psychology (Brunswick, 1956; Lewin, 1951; Murray, 1951; etc.), as well as in sociology (cf. Mead, 1934; Thomas, 1966; Wolff, 1964; etc.). Using a psychological orientation, one might study situations at the level of individual representations (e.g., Heider, 1958; Lewin, 1951). Taking a sociological perspective, we may study situations at the level of a group, a subculture, or an entire society. We shall briefly consider both of these traditions here.

Psychological approaches to situational influences on behavior evolved from the early atomistic, external, and physicalistic conceptualisations of the Stimulus-Response theorists to more recent holistic, internal, and cognitive models (Barker, 1968; Brunswik, 1956; Heider, 1958; Lewin, 1951; Murray, 1951). External, situational regularities in behavior were of major interest to early learning theorists (cf. Guthrie, 1952; Watson, 1913). Paradoxically, in their preoccupation with atomistic stimulus-response sequences, radical behaviorists never showed any interest in developing taxonomies of situations. Their conceptualization of language as simply reinforcement-contingent "verbal behavior" has been similarly inadequate (cf. Bruner, this volume, Chapter 2). Although Kantor (1924), in his "interbehaviorism," proposed over sixty years ago that an individual should be studied as "he interacts with all the various types of situations which constitute his behaviour circumstances" (p. 92), this proposal was only taken up by some social-learning theorists relatively recently (Mischel, 1968, 1979), and then only in a programmatic rather than an empirical manner.

Conceptualizations of situations eventually became more realistic with the advent of Gestalt psychology. Koffka's (1935) distinction between the external, objective, or "geographical" situation, and the internal, subjective, or "behavioral" situation is echoed by recent calls for a similar distinction in the social psychology of language (cf. Giles & Hewstone, 1982). Lewin's (1951) field theory represents a major attempt to place a social actor's internal, subjective representations of the surrounding situation, his "life space," in the focus of psychological analysis. "The situation must be represented as it is 'real' for the individual in question, that is, as it affects him," insists Lewin (p. 25).

Lewin's approach continues to be particularly relevant to the analysis of language. The research program on disqualified messages by Bavelas (this volume, Chapter 11) relies on an explicitly Lewinian theory. Indeed, it is surprising that field theoretical analyses of language behavior are still relatively rare in the literature. Other psychologists, such as Murray (1951) and Brunswik (1956), have placed similarly strong emphasis on situational variations in behavior. Brunswik's insistence on "representative design" based on the careful sampling of situations is equally valid today as a model for sociolinguistic research. These traditional psychological approaches to situations serve as the foundation for recent cognitive conceptualizations (Forgas, 1979, 1982) which made their appearance in the literature during the past decade or so.

Cognitive Approaches

Parallel with the recent "cognitive" revolution in social psychology (Fiske & Taylor, 1984), there has been a growing interest in situations in various branches of the discipline. These more recent cognitive approaches to situational variations in behavior represent a development on the earlier, Gestalt tradition of Asch, Lewin, Heider, and others. In *personality research* in particular, situational variables are increasingly seen as major determinants of behavior (Ekehammar, 1974; Frederiksen, 1972; Mischel, 1979). Yet the "development of adequate taxonomies of person-situation interactions remains in most areas a promissory note yet to be paid" (West, 1983, p. 279). The advent of cognitive learning therapies in *clinical psychology* (Mahoney, 1977) has similarly highlighted the need for research on subjective representations of situations. *Social psychologists* have also shown growing interest in studying interactive situations, or "social episodes" (Argyle, Furnham, & Graham, 1981; Forgas, 1979, 1982), with promising empirical results.

Representations of recurring behavior routines, variously labeled "scripts" (Abelson, 1980), action plans, or event schemata (Lichtenstein & Brewer, 1980), are also of increasing interest to *cognitive psychologists*. Such cognitive models of situations influence memory as well as inferences (Bower, Black, & Turner, 1979), and the application of the information-processing approach to the domain of language behavior is a promising possibility. Recent theories by van Dijk (this volume, Chapter 4) and Herrmann (1983; see also Chapter 5, by Hoppe-Graff, Hermann, Winterhoff-Spurk, and Mangold) make explicit use of such cognitive situation schemata.

Environmental research on situations or "settings" provides another alternative. Barker's (1968) exhaustive taxonomy of behavior settings is also relevant to analyzing variations in language behaviors. His idea of physical behavior settings as places impregnated with cultural norms and expectations is very close to the way that many linguists prefer to think about situations (cf. Firth, 1957; Hymes, 1972). Others, such as Moos (1968), have developed instruments such as the Setting Response Inventory for analyzing reactions to situations, which showed that evaluation, self-confidence, involvement, and friendliness were the major underlying situational dimensions.

During the past ten years in particular, several studies analyzing cognitive representations of situations have appeared. Wish (1975; Wish et al., 1976) used multidimensional scaling to represent the implicit structure of communicative situations. Forgas (1976, 1978) defined social episodes as consensual cognitive representations about recurring interaction routines, and showed that such cognitive representations can be reliably quantified. Episode perception style was dependent on a person's subcultural background, group membership, and personality characteristics. More recent studies (Forgas, 1979, 1983b) also indicate a link between episode perception and a person's social skill, and by implication, linguistic skill. Some examples of such empirically obtained models of episode spaces are illustrated in the following figures.

Figure 1-1 shows the way in which common social episodes practised by university students were cognitively represented. Four implicit psychological dimensions—self-confidence, evaluation, seriousness, and involvement—defined the subjects' implicit views of these encounters (Forgas, 1983a). Figure 1-2 illustrates the perceived episode space of members of a college rugby team at the University of Oxford, England. These people possessed an interaction repertoire that consisted of sport-related as well as other social encounters. The 15 members of the team developed a consensual, shared model of their interaction episodes, defined by characteristics such as friendliness, intimacy, and activity (Forgas, 1981a). In both studies, there were also significant differences between individuals in their episode representation styles, which could be empirically explained in terms of personality, demographic, and attitudinal differences among them, as well as differences in social skills.

Other researchers, such as Battistich and Thompson (1980), found that the connotative episode dimensions reported by Forgas (1979), Pervin (1976), and others have considerable validity across different cultures and groups. Perceived episode characteristics such as self-confidence, involvement, evaluation, formality, and task vs. socioemotional orientation provide a useful way of relating situations to likely language behaviors (Giles & Hewstone, 1982). Most of these characteristics have little to do with the objective nature of the encounter, and mainly reflect the judges' subjective perceptions and reactions to a situation.

The study of these implicit cognitive representations of episode domains is not only of heuristic interest. Once episode representations become quantifiable, the empirical links between such situation models and social skills, personality traits, demographic variables, attitudes, and even language choices can be established (Forgas, 1982). We are now on reasonably firm ground in concluding that the a priori classifications of situations developed by linguists (e.g., Brown & Fraser, 1979; Firth, 1957; Gregory, 1967; Hymes, 1967) do not necessarily tap those aspects of situations that are psychologi-

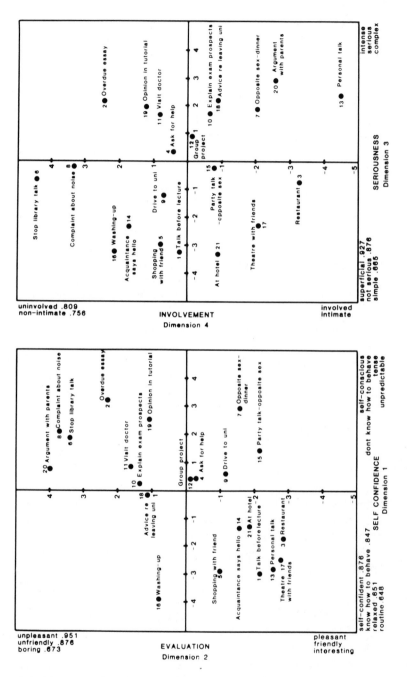

Figure 1-1. The perception of social episodes in a student milieu. The figure shows the way a "typical" university student cognitively represents this group of episodes relative to one another.

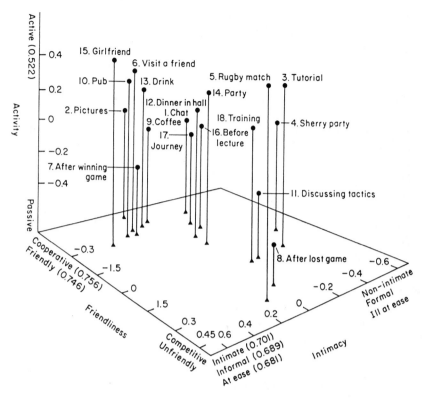

Figure 1-2. The perception of social episodes by members of a rugby team.

cally significant from the speaker's perspective, and best predict his or her language choices. It appears that situational taxonomies based on empirical research are far more likely to yield connotative, rather than denotative, characteristics as the basis for everyday situation perceptions. It is reasonable to conclude that language behaviors are dependent on such subjective representations, rather than on the objective situational features predominantly studied so far.

The Sociological Tradition

Interaction situations are among the most important building blocks of a culture: "All societies recognise certain communicative routines which they view as distinct wholes, separate from other types of discourse, characterised by special rules of speech and nonverbal behaviour and often distinguishable by clearly recognisable opening and closing sequences" (Gumperz & Hymes, 1972, p. 17; see also McCormack & Wurm, 1976). People are constituted as a society with a certain *culture* to the extent that they share the same means of social communication. Kroeber (1963, p. 33) suggested that "cultural activity, even of the simplest kind, inevitably rests on ideas or generalisations; and . . . ideas, in turn, human minds seem to be able to formulate and operate with and transmit only through speech."

Both language and social situations are cultural products (Mead, 1934; Stone & Farbermann, 1970). The roots of a sociological approach to language and situations that takes the actions and cognitive representations of individuals seriously may be found in the cultural sociology of Max Weber, who maintained that "action is social . . . by virtue of the subjective meaning attached to it by the individual . . . it takes into account the behaviour of others, and is thereby oriented in its course" (1968, p. 248). It was in this vein that W. I. Thomas and Florian Znaniecki made situational analysis one of the cornerstones of their monumental work on cultural adaptation. Thomas (1966) argued that "prior to any self-determined act . . . there is always a stage of examination or deliberation which we may call the definition of the situation" (p. 41), a statement that also applies to every form of verbal communication.

Thomas also recognized that cultural "schemes" provide a guiding pattern to situation defininition: "The individual, in order to control reality for his needs, must develop not a series of uniform reactions, but general schemes of situations" (p. 29). Language use is of course dependent on such cultural situation schemes. Anthropologists such as Sumner used the term "folkways" to describe such standardized and culturally sanctioned patterns of behavior.

Anthropological analyses of small-scale social systems provide us with many clear illustrations of the links between language and culture, as several influential volumes on the "ethnography of speaking" indicate (Gumperz & Hymes, 1972; McCormack & Wurm, 1976). Research on the social customs and speech behaviors of small communities, such as Norwegian villagers (Blom & Gumperz, 1972), Burundi tribesmen (Albert, 1972), or suburban Americans (Garfinkel, 1972), offer impressively detailed descriptions of the interdependence of language and situations. Many ethnographic analyses of language make explicit use of anthropological descriptions of the relevant "folkways" of the particular culture (cf. Ferguson, 1959; Gumperz & Hymes, 1972; Platt, 1977). Chapter 7 in this volume, by Blum-Kulka, Danet, and Gherson, is a good example of how cultural values, cognitive situation representation strategies ("folkways"), and, ultimately, language choices are related in a particular society: Israel. Wetzel's work in Chapter 8 is another illustration of how the value placed on group identification—in this case, in Japanese society—influences the way that situations are interpreted and language choices are made.

Mead's (1934) social behaviorism also assigns a central role to symbolic representations about social situations. The ability of human beings to abstract and store schematic representations of their social encounters is the basis on which both cultural systems and individual personalities rest.

Communication was of particular interest to Mead; the problem of situational variations in language is readily accessible to symbolic interactionist analysis. As Farr (1981) as well as Forgas (1983c) recently argued, the symbolic interactionist model provides perhaps the largest untapped reservoir of theoretical ideas in the social sciences. Mead's notion of meaning as a negotiable social product also underlies many recent criticisms of Cartesian linguistics (cf. Rommetveit, 1983).

Many other sociologists, such as Waller, Wolff (1964), Goffman (1974), and Garfinkel (1967), followed Mead in relying on situational analysis as a central aspect of their work, and the microsociological analysis of situation-contingent communication developed by Goffman (1961, 1974) in particular represents a rich observational data base of direct interest to our enterprise. Harré's ethogenic theory goes beyond traditional microsociological concerns in suggesting that the "moral order" of a community plays a crucial role in strategic self-presentations. His chapter in this volume (Chapter 10) looks at the effects of such situated moral systems on language use by members of such subcultures as psychiatrists and academic psychologists.

Both representations of situations and language are aspects of culture—created, maintained, and revised in the course of our daily interactions with one another. Neither situations nor language can be understood at the level of individual behavior alone (Forgas, 1981b, 1983c). "The culture itself is a semiotic system, a system of meanings and information that is encoded in the behavior potential of the members, including their verbal potential—that is, their linguistic system. The linguistic system is only one form of the realization of the more general semiotic system which constitutes the culture" (Halliday, 1976, p. 122). The sociological approach of looking at situations and language remains a lively and stimulating source of ideas on this issue (cf. Moscovici, 1981), with every promise that such cultural representations may eventually be incorporated into cognitive models of situation-contingent linguistic choices. Having so far considered the various roots of interest in studying the links between language and social situations, we will next turn to a brief outline of existing empirical research on this issue.

The Evidence for Links Between Language and Social Situations

There are of course many studies that show situational influences in language use. Indeed, the potential domain to be reviewed could include almost the entire field of sociolinguistics, and parts of social, cognitive, and developmental psychology as well. In this review, however, we shall only focus on research that directly deals with situational influences on language. Given the heterogeneity of the approaches and methods, it seems best to organize the material in terms of the particular kinds of language behaviors that were investigated.

Situational Effects on Choice of Communicative Strategies

Situations exert considerable influence on global communication intentions, and people often select and construe interaction situations in ways to suit their interactional purposes. Furnham (1982) carried out a simple experiment to illustrate this point. Adult subjects were asked to indicate on a questionnaire how likely (or unlikely) it is that they would choose to communicate 16 different possible messages (refusing a request, talking about their own life history, etc.) in each of 16 possible factorially manipulated situations (others present/not present; other activities/no other activities carried out in situation; situation open/closed to new entrants, etc.).

The experimenters found that situational features had a significant effect on communications. Certain messages (e.g., confronting a friend about previous behavior, important self-disclosure, and imparting bad news) were much more situation dependent than others (e.g., refusing an unreasonable request). Despite the ad hoc nature of the situations manipulated, research of this kind is of considerable promise, and could be readily extended to the study of a broader and more ecologically valid range of situations. In a more recent study, we (Argyle, Forgas, & Trimboli, 1985) asked subjects to indicate their communicative preferences toward a range of possible partners and in respect of a number of possible discussion topics. Results indicated highly situation-specific communicative preferences: Apparently, people have very clear implicit ideas about how suitable certain messages are to particular people in given situations. It is clearly important to replicate the results of such self-report studies in more realistic encounters.

Situational Variation in the Use of Language Codes

Perhaps the paradigmatic example of situationally regulated language use is the ability of people who are competent in two or more languages or dialects to adapt their language code to the situation (polyglossia). When one of the codes is clearly and consistently associated with a particular situation, we may speak of "situational shifting" (Ervin-Tripp, 1972). Occasionally, more than one language code may be used within a single interaction. Diebold (1962, p. 56) defines such code switching as "the successive alternate use of two different language codes within the same discourse; it implies that the speaker is conscious of the switch." In the simplest case, the choice to be made is between two languages or dialects. Often, a simpler, low-status code may be used in common everyday domestic episodes, and the more elaborate high-status code may be used in official, formal, or administrative situations (Ferguson, 1959).

Fishman's (1971) well-known study of bilingual Americans demonstrated the situation-contingent use of English (in education and employment) and Spanish (in family, neighborhood, and religious situations). There are many other empirical studies demonstrating such situation-contingent language choices (cf. Giles & St. Clair, 1979; Robinson, 1972). Uyekubo (in Hatch, 1976) described a common form of code switching, when bilingual Japanese changed from Japanese to English and back again to accommodate the arrival and subsequent departure of an English-speaking partner. Barber (1973) showed that in the trilingual Yaquie Indian community, language codes were dependent on the behavior setting (cf. Barker, 1968): Different code combinations were permissible at ceremonial meetings, in the store, and at work.

In my own experience, such code switching may be very finely tuned indeed, with automatic adjustments for the shifting proportion and relative status of individuals preferring one code or the other in a given interaction, even in a large and fully bilingual group. At the German university where I worked, all Germans in our research group spoke English, and all Americans and Australians spoke German. Yet at our usual morning coffee meetings, switches in language use could often be observed, reflecting the fluctuating relative numerical- and status-composition of the group, as individuals joined or left this loosely defined social encounter.

Sometimes, communicative content may also occasion code switching. Rayfield (1970) describes many examples of code switching even within the same sentence in a Yiddish/English bilingual community in Santa Monica. Yiddish may be used when referring to family, and English for the rest of the sentence. This form of message-contingent code switching may indicate the very deeply internalized associations that speakers develop between language codes and "suitable" situations. Another illustration of topic-contingent code switching is offered by Blom and Gumperz (1972). In the small Norwegian community they studied, a local dialect and a standard dialect were the two codes used: "At the community administration office, we noticed that clerks used both standard and dialect phrases, depending on whether they were talking about official affairs or not. Likewise, when residents step up to a clerk's desk, greeting and enquiries about family affairs tend to be exchanged in the dialect, while the business part of the conservation is carried out in the standard" code (p. 425).

Code switching is not always a reaction to situational changes—it may be used as a rhetorical device, or as an attempt to define a situation. Sections deemed to be important may be repeated in both codes, or the "low" code may be selectively used for joking, swearing, or to emphasize a friendly, informal situation definition (Hatch, 1976). Sometimes, our language choices serve to elicit and affirm chosen social identities. In one study, Bond (1983) showed that the language code chosen by a questioner has wide-reaching consequences for the respondents' behavior, and may even cause situational fluctuations in his or her self-reported attitudes and values. Bilingual Chinese subjects in Hong Kong were asked either in English or in Cantonese to indicate on the Rokeach value survey the typical positions occupied by the Chinese (autostereotype) and by Westerners (heterostereotype). The language of the question had a significant effect in activating different auto- and heterostereotypes in the subjects.

This study complements the extensive research on polyglossia, suggesting that sociocultural processes both determine, and are determined by, the choice of language codes. There is considerable scope for further experimental studies on this interrelationship in multilingual societies. The simple subdivision of language codes into high and low varieties is of course often insufficient, and the preponderance of predominantly a priori classifications of communication situations is also a serious limitation. Platt's (1977) notion of polyglossia has been the answer to the first problem, and research on subjective representations of situations has sought to address the second issue (cf. Fishman, 1971). Ultimately, models of episode cognition may be linked to language choices using cognitive models successfully developed in related domains (e.g., Forgas, 1982).

Situational Variations in Semantic Choices

The same message may be expressed by speakers using a multiplicity of semantic alternatives. Which one they choose is one of the core issues in research on situated language use. Herrmann (1982; Herrmann & Deutsch, 1976) suggests that the two major choice alternatives are usually *standard* words and *nonstandard* words such as slang, jargon, intimate speech, etc. Small social distance between the partners and small topic distance (much shared knowledge about the subject) may result in the greater use of nonstandard words. Empirical research by Herrmann (1982) confirmed that in naming objects relevant to two fields (football or discotheques), adolescent subjects used more nonstandard terms when the partner was similar in status (same-age friend vs. adult), and topic distance was small (i.e., much shared knowledge about the field).

A related, and especially interesting question is how we choose the words we use to address one another. Enduring cultural conventions, often reflecting underlying social and economic structures, play a major role in the regulation of address forms, as Brown and Gilman (1960) showed. But situational variables may also be important, as some ethnographic studies have demonstrated. Tyler (1972) studied the use of kinship terminology in the Indian Koya people, and reported that "the appropriate use of Koya kin terms cannot be predicted solely on the basis of a formal analysis . . . of genealogical reckoning. There are many contextual factors to be taken into consideration. Among these are social setting, audience composition, sex and age of speaker/ hearer, linguistic repertoires of speaker/hearer, and—most difficult of all— something that might be called the speaker's intention" (p. 268).

Situational variations also exist in the use of binary address forms (e.g., the formal "vous" and informal "tu" in French) in European languages. Friedrich (1972) analyzed the situation-contingent use of address forms in 19th-century Russian in the works of writers such as Tolstoy, Lermontov, Gorki, and

Pushkin, and found that although the use of the Russian "vy" and "ty" supposedly parallels the French vous and tu, there were many situation-dependent deviations from the pure status norm. The formal-reciprocal "vy" is normally used by the aristocracy, but may be used by peasants during formal episodes, such as between matchmakers and peasant parents during marital negotiations and at weddings. Reciprocal informal address between intimate friends of the aristocracy would be "switched to formal terms during the challenge and execution of a duel." It seems that address forms are indeed dependent on situational factors such as "the cultural matrix of social statuses and group categories" (p. 298).

Situational Effects on the Choice of Requests

Usually, it is when we ask others to do something for us that we are most acutely aware of situational influences on our verbal behaviors (cf. this volume, Chapter 6, by Gibbs). Such requests, or "mands," are among the most directly instrumental verbal moves we can make, eliciting goods, services, and information (Skinner, 1957). Soskin and John (1963) classified varieties of "mands," ranging from direct requests, or "regnones," such as "Shut the door," through more indirect forms such as "structones" ("It is cold today") or "signones" ("I feel cold"). Perhaps the most salient feature of mands is their explicitness versus neutrality. The neutralization of requests by using indirect forms depends on situational features such as the status relationship between requester and target. According to Ervin-Tripp (1972), "Within some families, mands were neutralized between equals most of the time, less than half of the time from seniors to juniors, and in a minority of cases when juniors spoke" (p. 246).

In a work environment, requests are most frequently neutralized when oriented toward non-peers, or toward acts that are not normally part of the other's duties. The preference for direct or indirect request forms may also be an important cultural characteristic. Blum-Kulka et al. (this volume, Chapter 7) analyzed social influences on the use of request variants in modern Hebrew. Situational variables such as the age, sex, and relative status and power of the speakers and listeners regulated the request strategies and mitigating devices used in naturalistic settings. Such analyses may also provide relevant data about enduring cultural generalizations based on linguistic choices, in Blum-Kulka et al.'s case, for example, why do outsiders often see Israelis as arrogant and abrupt in social interaction?

Request choices have also been studied experimentally. Laucht (1979) describes a study in which subjects role play a two-person detective game, during which they are forced to request a partner (a confederate of the experimenter) to relinquish a gun (see also Hoppe-Graff et al., this volume, Chapter 5). In accordance with Herrmann's (1982) theory, situational manipulations such as shared or nonshared definitions of the situation, willingness or nonwillingness to comply, and legitimate or nonlegitimate requests influenced the semantic choices of the 144 adolescent subjects. In a related study, subjects had to state appropriate forms of requests that other people should use in specific situations presented on film. Results were once again consistent with the theory. The techniques used by Gibbs (this volume, Chapter 6) represent another example of a similar experimental strategy.

Ethnographic studies provide an alternative to the experimental or linguistic analyses of requesting strategies. Albert (1972) describes how varieties of petitioning styles were determined by situational and role demands in Burundi. Petitioners were found to switch speech and behavior patterns with apparent ease in reaction to well-developed codes of situational definition in that culture. For instance, the "notion of a social call without a definite purpose is not entertained . . . visiting is categorized according to the visitor's purpose and is subject to a variety of formulas which must be learned" (p. 79). Each possible such visiting episode in turn included specifications of sanctioned forms of requesting or petitioning. It seems that requesting is a speech act that is perhaps most likely to endanger the interactants' "face" (Brown & Levinson, 1978), and is thus most closely associated with strategic language choices. The chapters in this volume by Gibbs, and Blum-Kulka et al., bear witness to the special importance of this topic.

Social Situations and Language Acquisition

Adults are not the only ones who are sensitive to the situational requirements of language. The same sensitivity to situational routines is already present in pre-verbal infants, and their knowledge about interaction routines is an important prerequisite to acquiring language. As Bruner (1978) suggested, "Many of the conventions that underlie the use of language are learned prior to the onset of articulate phonetic speech . . . A close analysis of the first year of an infant's life provides not only a catalogue of the joint 'formats' in which communicator and recipient habitually find each other, but also provides a vivid record of how roles developed in such formats become conventionalized" (p. 22). This exciting research program is summarized in Bruner's Chapter 2 in this volume.

Until recently, the role of pragmatics in language acquisition (Morris, 1946) has received considerably less than its due share of attention (Bruner, 1981). Yet at least since the pioneering work of Brown (1973), it has been abundantly clear that "language acquisition is enormously aided by the child's pre-linguistic grasp of concepts and meanings that make it easier for him to penetrate grammatical rules" (Bruner, 1978, p. 43). Bruner's research at Oxford has provided convincing evidence for the importance of learning about communicative contexts as a precursor of language acquisition. His views provide a highly plausible third alternative to the hitherto predominant nativist (Chomsky) and environmentalist (Skinner) views of language acquisition. Furthermore, it is only in this kind of social interactionist model that the crucial importance of the intricacies of mother-child interaction in language learning is finally accorded its due share of attention.

Very early mother-infant communication routines show a gradual evolution and increasing sophistication, parallel with an increasingly subtle awareness of situational conventions. Bruner (1978, 1981) suggests that this evolution may be charted as progressing from a *demand* mode through a *request* mode to an *exchange* mode, finally reaching the stage of *reciprocity*. Once the child is able to use language as a means of effective social communication, his or her implicit understanding and representation of situational rules develops in mutual interdependence with his or her language skills.

It seems than that the development of knowledge about interactive frames or situations proceeds hand in hand with the development of linguistic skills. The evidence for the interdependence between episode representation strategies and linguistic skills in children points to the much more general links that exist between social situations and language: "Language acquisition occurs in the context of an 'action dialogue' . . . The evolution of language itself, notably its universal structures, probably reflects the requirements of joint action and it is probably because of that evolutionary history that its use is mastered with such relative ease" (Bruner, 1978, p. 44). This conclusion is indeed applicable to the entire field of research on situated language use: Human beings are able to think about and represent social situations because such cognitive situation schemes reflect an optimal way of dealing with functionally important action routines (Mead, 1934).

Situational Effects on Talking to Children

Adults typically communicate with young children by using "baby talk," a special communication register characterized by slow delivery, syntactic simplicity, redundancy, and semantic concreteness. Such baby talk may manifest very fine situational variations indeed. In a review of the literature, Wells and Robinson (1982) conclude that baby talk "facilitates linguistic development, and . . . it is contingently related to the child's own behavior— either to his preceding utterance or utterances, to his current activity, or to his [presumed] focus of attention" (p. 62). There is thus a parallel between how infants come to understand and discriminate between situation scenarios as an aid to language acquisition, and how adults can vary baby talk in communicating with infants and children. Brown (1973) proposed that baby talk varies in terms of two distinct and independent dimensions: communicative clarity and affection/nurturance. Such variations accommodate the goals that adults seek to achieve and the requirements of the situation. There is indeed growing evidence suggesting the importance of situational factors in influencing the characteristics of baby talk.

Levin and Snow (this volume, Chapter 3) analyzed baby talk by parents toward their four-to-nine-year-old children before and after a minor surgery.

Coders looked at parents' utterances in terms of predefined categories, and found that parents used more supportive and nurturant communication in the postoperative session. Almost by definition, speakers are particularly sensitive in their language behaviors when addressing children—an immature, dependent audience with limited communicative competence. The description of such situation-contingent shifts is of considerable promise, as the study by Levin and Snow suggests. It is quite remarkable that an already highly specialized speech register, such as baby talk, can thus be still further modified to reflect situational requirements. The use of situational shifts in baby talk is likely to play an important role in the children's developing sensitivity to situations.

Situational Variations in Paralanguage

Language is more than the words we speak. Situational variables clearly affect not only *what* we say, but also *how* we say it. Increasingly sophisticated investigations of paralinguistic characteristics helped to clearly establish a situational dimension in these cues. Von Raffler Engel (1976) looked at the communication behavior of black and white subjects in a welfare office in the American South, recording their behavior while informally conversing in the waiting area and while being formally interviewed by the staff. Speech tempo was slower and pauses fewer in the formal interview. Code switching was also accompanied by kinesic variation, particularly in the older subjects. Klaus Scherer (unpublished) at the University of Giessen recorded and analyzed the paralinguistic quality of the speech of bureaucrats executing various communication tasks. The situation and goals of the interaction were again found to have a significant effect on paralinguistic performance under these more carefully controlled laboratory conditions.

Not all paralinguistic variables, however, are readily changeable. Some, like accent, are likely to accompany a person possibly for a lifetime. Does the interpretation and perception of such stigma-like paralinguistic cues depend on situational factors? As interethnic and intercultural communication becomes a more and more common feature of our lives, questions such as these will take on increasing importance. The study described by Gallois and Callan (this volume, Chapter 9) suggests that reactions to accents are very finely tuned indeed. The speaker's and the listener's sex and status, and the communication situation and the social identity of the partners, all interact in determining how a particular accent will be perceived. Investigations of this kind provide us with growing evidence of the importance of situation schemata in the way we evaluate paralinguistic cues.

Situational Effects on Communication Difficulty

Not just language use, but also language misuse is intimately linked to situations. Our encounters can sometimes be so ridden with conflicting requirements that straightforward messages become impossible. Bavelas shows (this volume, Chapter 11) that avoidance-avoidance conflicts in particular are likely to result in evasive, "disqualified" communication. Her Lewinian theoretical analysis of situations is a particularly stimulating example of the continued applicability of this approach. Empty, confusing, or equivocal messages need not be "pathological" communication, according to this study; often, situations inevitably generate such messages.

Another kind of communication difficulty occurs when people say the wrong thing without intending to. Heikkinen and Valo (this volume, Chapter 12) analyze a large sample of such "interaction slips," and show that these too are situation contingent. The problem lies in situations that generate under- or overmonitoring of our messages. Both highly routinzed and highly problematic encounters can lead to such interaction slips, albeit of different kinds.

More serious communication difficulties, such as stuttering, also have a clear situational background. It is remarkable that until very recently, theories of stuttering were largely focused on the motor difficulties and the assumed emotional and cognitive problems of stutterers (see also Bergmann & Forgas, this volume, Chapter 13). The social etiology and situational characteristics of stuttering were largely ignored: "Many theories of stuttering are still asocial insofar as they do not take into consideration the social background of speech" (Krause, 1982, p. 78). Cross-cultural research tends to show that the incidence of stuttering is a significant comment on the culture that produces it (Bloodstein, 1975). Stuttering tends to be more common in competitive, achievement-oriented societies, which emphasize status and prestige.

There is also some evidence that parental attitudes, values, and behavior play some role in the etiology of stuttering. Competitive, aggressive, or dissatisfied parents more often have stuttering children. Apart from these enduring social influences, stuttering also depends on the features of the particular social situation: "Situations producing great communicative pressure can be considered as stimuli eliciting the disturbed behavior... Status differences between the stutterer and his partner, unfamiliarity of the interactors, and audience size are some of the well-known social releasers of stutterer spells" (Krause, 1982, p. 116). Recent research developed this approach further, placing major emphasis on social situational variables in the analysis of stuttering, as outlined in the chapter by Bergmann and Forgas.

Language Use and Situation Definition

Until now we have concentrated on the effects of situations on language. The relationship works both ways, however, because language use often serves to define and negotiate sometimes ambiguous interaction situations: "For interaction to succeed, participants must essentially agree in their social situation definition" (Leodolter & Leodolter, 1976, p. 327). A study by Handelman (1976) illustrates this approach nicely. Handelman documents a lengthy and unfocused interchange in the lobby of an Israeli migrant absorption hostel between two residents who are seeking to develop shared situation definitions that will enable a focused interaction to proceed. Alas, they fail: Their conversation is analyzed as "an instance of interaction in which negotiations between participants do not result in a basis of discourse upon which a congruent definition of the 'situation' can be further negotiated" (p. 308).

The detailed analysis of the verbal steps leading to this result offers an insightful, if somewhat atheoretical, account of this process. We are all familiar with the kind of hesitant, exploratory verbal moves that are characteristic of such a search for a shared situation definition, without which continued interaction is impossible. Various microsociological analyses by Goffman (1974), Garfinkel (1967), and others offer similar insights, but without the corresponding emphasis on linguistic variables. The work of Harrè (this volume, Chapter 10) includes several interesting illustrations of the strategic uses of language to define situations and identities. It seems that the study of language use in the absence of shared situation definitions should ultimately provide us with most interesting insights into the role that situations play in our discourse strategies. This is a technique that eminently lends itself to controlled experimental analysis.

People often use alternative language codes as situation definitional devices, a strategy particularly common in bilingual societies. The already mentioned study by Blom and Gumperz (1972) describes an ethnographic analysis of a small Norwegian community using two language codes, a local dialect (R) and the standard code (B). In this community, "teachers report that while formal lectures—where interruptions are not encouraged—are delivered in (B), the speakers will shift to (R) when they want to encourage open discussion among students" (p. 424). Even in monolingual communities, most teachers and university lecturers should be able to report similar linguistic ploys used to impose desired situation definitions on their students. I am quite certain that the language I use in a lecture or a seminar varies a great deal depending on the preferred situation definition I wish to impress upon my students: Formal or informal, interactive or one-sided, friendly or unfriendly are some of the alternatives.

The use of linguistic choices as tools of situation definition is also documented by Mitchell-Kernan (1972), who describes the rich verbal code of black Americans. She describes a "rapping" episode in which two black males (her informants) were trying to "pick her up" in a park. The stylistic dissonance of using "black" and "standard" English expressions within the same dialogue is used to define the situation as a put-on, signifying that the male speakers' apparent sexual advances are not to be taken literally. Building on such descriptive analyses, empirical studies of the definitional functions of language choices in social episodes offer a most promising topic for further research.

Summary and an Outline of the Volume

As this necessarily brief review of the conceptual antecedents and empirical approaches to research on language and social situations suggests, the field is of crucial importance to an adequate understanding of social interaction processes. At the same time, it is also clear that research on this important topic has suffered from the unnecessary theoretical and methodological fragmentation of the various social science disciplines concerned with its study. Linguists, psychologists, anthropologists, and sociologists have been the main contributors to our knowledge about situational influences on language, yet these contributions rarely amounted to an integrated framework or model. Only in the last few years has a cognitive-representational approach to situations emerged in social psychology which offers some promise of integrating these various strategies. The present volume should help to clarify the pathways leading to the emergence of such an integrated model of situated language use.

In the meantime, the selection of the chapters included in this book must of course reflect the heterogeneity of interest in how social situations and language are interrelated. The chapters were selected and organized in such a way that they may be readily used as core discussion topics in a lecture or seminar course concerned with the use of verbal communication in social interaction. The contributions should be of interest not only to social psychologists, but to any researcher or student concerned with the study of how human beings use language in their daily lives.

The chapters are organized into four interrelated sections. The first part (Chapters 2 and 3) discusses the role of shared situation definitions in language development, and in the use of "baby talk." Part II is concerned with the role of psychological factors in situated language use (Chapters 4, 5, and 6). Part III (Chapters 7, 8, 9, and 10) looks at the role of social and cultural influences on the use of language in different situations. Finally, in Part IV we turn to the role of situational variations in communication difficulties (Chapters 11, 12, and 13). The first and the last chapters are devoted to, respectively, an introductory survey of the antecedents of research on language and social situations, and a review of some of the most critical issues in this field.

Part I begins with a chapter by Jerome Bruner, summarizing his research on language acquisition. It is indeed eminently suitable for introducing this volume. The cumulative empirical evidence presented by Bruner showing that an implicit understanding of situational regularities in interaction is the foundation upon which language acquisition is built is a most persuasive illustration of the importance of our topic. The second chapter in this section, by Harry Levin and Catherine Snow, offers a complementary view to Bruner's, demonstrating that the characteristics of the "baby talk" register used by parents in talking to children is also significantly dependent on the situational context. It is indeed quite remarkable that such a highly specialized speech register as baby talk is nevertheless subject to further major situational modifications, reflecting the functions of the encounter.

Part II deals with more general psychological influences on situational language use. The next two chapters, by van Dijk, and by Hoppe-Graff, Herrmann, Winterhoff-Spurk, and Mangold, describe strongly theory-based research programs on situational influences on language. Van Dijk's work on the role of situation prototypes in communication about ethnic minorities is an excellent example of the balanced treatment of cognitive and social-psychological concerns. His work draws not only on recent cognitive research on discourse processing, but also on the increasingly topical social psychological work on episode representations and on prejudice and discrimination against minorities.

The chapter by Hoppe-Graff and his colleagues clearly summarizes the research program on language and situations carried out in Theo Herrmann's Mannheim laboratory. Herrmann uses logical principles to construct a theoretical model which then serves as the basis for a series of experiments looking at situational effects on the use of various language categories, such as naming, requesting, etc. The model is rooted in cognitive psychology, and it also shows strong affinity with recent artificial-intelligence approaches.

In the final chapter of this section, Gibbs summarizes his research on the situational aspects of requesting, a question that was also of interest to Herrmann. Gibbs undertakes a careful situational analysis of requests, using an experimental psychological approach. It has long been assumed that the directness of requests is an intrinsic quality, readily associated with certain linguistic forms. Indeed, this assumption is the local reflection of the more general Cartesian notion of "immanent meanings," much criticized by Rommetveit (1983) and others. In a series of experiments Gibbs establishes something like a "situational semantic" model of requests, showing that these complex and often problematic verbal moves are direct or indirect, polite or impolite, only in the context of certain situations.

In Part III, we move on from the cognitive-psychological level of analysis to the socio-cultural. Blum-Kulka, Danet, and Gherson collected a large number of everyday requests in Israel, and analyzed the variations in request use as a function of numerous situational variables. The project is an excellent illustration of how cultural values are reflected in situation definitions and language use, and provides a nice complement to the previous two chapters, also concerned with requests. Blum-Kulka and her colleagues find that direct-request forms are indeed unusually common in Israeli parlance, although they are still modulated by subtle situational variables. They suggest that the "pioneering" Israeli cultural tradition, with great emphasis on equality and solidarity, is reflected in the preponderant use of direct rather than indirect request forms. Whether this is indeed due to "solidarity" politeness as distinct from "conventional" politeness is a challenging interpretation of these data.

In the next chapter, Wetzel's analysis of situational variations in the use of the verbs of giving and receiving in Japanese takes a more linguistic orientation. The heavy emphasis on group identification in Japanese society is shown here to be clearly reflected in language use, where the speaker's group identification takes precedence over individual identity in his or her choice of words. The study is an intriguing illustration of how cultural values influence situation definition strategies and, ultimately, language use.

The following chapter by Gallois and Callan is concerned with situational variation in reactions to accents in a highly heterogenous country, radically different from the homogenous Japanese culture studied by Wetzel: Australia. In this multicultural society, Gallois and Callan show the subtle and often surprisingly complex way that situational features, sex, and several other variables interact to influence judgments of particular accents. As interethnic interaction is an increasingly common feature of our everyday lives, studies of this kind should prove of considerable importance in explaining how we use situational and other representational information to evaluate the language characteristics of our partners.

The final chapter in this section is by Rom Harré, who applies his ethogenic theory, itself a development of the microsociological analyses of Goffman and Garfinkel, to the analysis of situational variations in language as a self-presentation device. He selects four situations for analysis: the language of "football hooligans," or "aggro-talk," the language of situational control, or gossip, the language of character description, or "file-speak,"and finally and most intriguingly, the language of social scientists, or "psych-speak." Harré suggests that in each of these examples, language is used not so much to communicate meanings, but as a means of strategic self-presentation, revealing the speaker as a worthy moral character within the accepted situational definitions of the relevant subculture. Although the chapter is largely programmatic, except for Harre's description of his study of psychiatric file-speak, it contains many stimulating and controversial ideas about the manipulative use of language.

The last section in the volume, containing three chapters, concerns itself with the situational genesis of various communicative difficulties. Bavelas describes her research program, which takes as its point of departure the extensive clinical research on "double-bind" communication, for example, in families of schizophrenics. She shows that such evasive, amibiguous messages can represent the most "rational" communication strategies in certain conflict situations. We all use such messages, of course. After reading her chapter, we should all become much more aware of the situational antecedents that often force us to adopt such strategies.

Heikkinen and Valo address another issue in communication problems: the reasons for the various verbal "interaction slips" that have already proven so fascinating to Freud in his "The psychopathology of everyday life." Heikkinen and Valo offer an insightful analysis of the varieties and etiology of such messages, and suggest that cognitive processes, such as over-monitoring or under-monitoring of our communications, may explain such slips. In the final chapter, Bergmann and Forgas turn to a much more serious problem in verbal communication: speech dysfluency and stuttering. These are quite severe and debilitating language problems, which have been mainly dealt with in terms of a medical model in the past. The chapter surveys extensive evidence that suggests that features of social situations probably play a major role in both the etiology and the frequency of stuttering. Finally, the volume is concluded by a brief epilogue which seeks to integrate some of the major themes of the book.

Each of these chapters, of course, may be profitably read on its own, although the integrative aims of the book would be best appreciated by a more consistent approach. I hope, as do all editors, that this collection will indeed prove to be more than the sum of its parts. This is a critical time in the study of language and social situations, and the recognition of the complementary interests and skills of psychologists, linguists, and sociologists should help our enterprise considerably. I certainly hope that this book will contribute to such an integration of the field, and that it will prove a useful and stimulating tool for students and researchers alike interested in the intricacies of everyday social interaction.

References

Abelson, R. P. (1980). *The psychological status of the script concept.* (Cognitive Science Technical Report No. 2). New Haven, CN: Yale University.

Albert, E. M. (1972). Culture patterning of speech behaviour in Burundi. In J. J. Gumperz & D. Hymes (Eds.), *The ethnography of communication.* New York: Holt, Rinehart & Winston.

Argyle, M., Forgas, J. R. & Trimboli, C. (1985). [Situational variations in communication strategies]. Unpublished data.

Argyle, M., Furnham, A., & Graham, J. (1981). *Social situations.* Cambridge: Cambridge University Press.

Barber, C. G. (1973). Trilingualism in an Arizona Yaquie village. In P. R. Turner (Ed.), *Bilingualism in the Southwest.* Tucson, Arizona: University of Arizona Press.

Barker, R. G. (1968). *Ecological psychology.* Stanford, CA: Stanford University Press.

Basso, K. (1970). To give up on words: Silence in Western Apache culture. *Southwestern Journal of Anthropology, 26,* 213–230.

Battistich, V. A., & Thompson, E. G. (1980). Students' perceptions of the college milieu. *Personality and Social Psychology Bulletin, 6,* 74–82.

Blom, J-P., & Gumperz, J. J. (1972). Social meaning in linguistic structures: Code-switching in Norway. In J. J. Gumperz, & D. Hymes (Eds.), *The ethnography of communication.* New York: Holt, Rinehart & Winston.

Bloodstein, O. (1975). *A handbook on stuttering.* Chicago: National Easter Seal Society.

Bond, M. (1983). How language variation affects inter-cultural differentiation of values by Hong Kong bilinguals. Unpublished manuscript. *Hong Kong: The Chinese University.*

Bower, G. H., Black, J. B., & Turner, T. J. (1979). Scripts in memory for text. *Cognitive Psychology, 11,* 177–220.

Brown, P., & Fraser, C. (1979). Speech as marker of situation. In K. R. Scherer & H. Giles (Eds.), *Social markers in speech*. Cambridge: Cambridge University Press.

Brown, P., & Levinson, S. (1978). Universals in language use: Politeness phenomena. In E. Goody (Ed.), *Questions and politeness*. Cambridge: Cambridge University Press.

Brown, R. (1973). *A first language: The early stages*. London: Allen & Unwin.

Brown, R., & Gilman, A. (1960). The pronouns of power and solidarity. In T. Sebeok (Ed.), *Style in language*. Cambridge: Technology Press.

Bruner, J. S. (1978). From communication to language: A psychological perspective. In I. Markova (Ed.), *The social context of language*. Chichester, England: Wiley.

Bruner, J. (1981). The social context of language acquisition. *Language and Communication, 1*, 155–178.

Brunswik, E. (1956). *Perception and the representative design of psychological experiments*. Berkeley, CA: University of California Press.

Diebold, A. R. (1962). Code-switching in Greek-English bilingual speech. *Monograph series on languages and linguistics, 15*, 53–69.

Ekehammar, B. (1974). Interactionism in personality from a historical perspective. *Psychological Bulletin, 81*, 1026–1048.

Ervin-Tripp, S. (1964). An analysis of the interaction of language, topic, and listener. In J. Gumperz & D. Hymes (Eds.), *The ethnography of communication*. New York: Holt, Rinehart & Winston.

Ervin-Tripp, S. (1972). On sociolinguistic rules: Alternation and co-occurrence. In J. J. Gumperz & D. Hymes (Eds.), *The ethnography of communication*. New York: Holt, Rinehart & Winston.

Farr, R. (1981). An historical look at social cognition. In J. P. Forgas (Ed.), *Social cognition: Perspectives on everyday understanding*. London: Academic Press.

Ferguson, C. (1959). Diglossia. *Word, 15*, 325–340.

Firth, J. R. (1957). *Papers in linguistics*. London: Oxford University Press.

Fishman, J. (Ed.) (1971). *Advances in the sociology of language*. The Hague: Mouton.

Fiske, S., & Taylor, S. (1984). *Social cognition*. Reading, MA: Addison-Wesley.

Forgas, J. P. (1976). The perception of social episoddes: Categorical and dimensional representations in two different social milieus. *Journal of Personality and Social Psychology, 33*, 199–209.

Forgas, J. P. (1978). Social episodes and social structure in an academic setting: The social environment of an intact group. *Journal of Experimental Social Psychology, 14*, 434–448.

Forgas, J. P. (1979). *Social episodes: The study of interaction routines*. London: Academic Press.

Forgas, J. P. (1981a). Social episodes and group milieu: A study in social cognition. *British Journal of Social Psychology, 20*, 77–87.

Forgas, J. P. (Ed.) (1981b). *Social cognition: Perspectives on everday understanding*. London/New York: Academic Press.

Forgas, J. P. (1982). Episode cognition: Internal representations of interaction routines. In L. Berkowitz (Ed.), *Advances in experimental social psychology*. New York: Academic Press.

Forgas, J. P. (1983a). Episode cognition and personality: A multidimensional analysis. *Journal of Personality, 51*, 34–47.

Forgas, J. P. (1983b). Social skills and the perception of interaction episodes. *British Journal of Clinical Psychology, 22*, 195–205.

Forgas, J. P. (1983c). What is social about social cognition? *British Journal of Social Psychology, 22*, 129–144.

Frederiksen, N. (1972). Toward a taxonomy of situations. *Amerian Psychologist, 27*, 114–123.

Friedrich, P. (1972). Social context and semantic feature: The Russian pronomial usage. In J. J. Gumperz & D. Hymes (Eds.), *The ethnography of communication.* New York: Holt, Rinehart & Winston.

Furnham, A. (1982). The message, the context and the medium. *Language and Communication, 2,* 33–47.

Garfinkel, H. (1967). *Studies in ethnomethodology.* Englewood Cliffs, NJ: Prentice-Hall.

Garfinkel, H. (1972). Remarks on ethnomethodoly. In J. J. Gumperz & D. Hymes (Eds.), *The ethnography of communication.* New York: Holt, Rinehart & Winston.

Giles, H., & Hewstone, M. (1982). Cognitive structures, speech and social situations: Two integrative models. *Language Sciences, 4,* 188–219.

Giles, H., & St. Clair, R. N. (Eds.) (1979). *Language and social psychology.* Oxford: Blackwell.

Goffman, E. (1961). *Encounters.* Indianapolis: Indiana University Press.

Goffman, E. (1974). *Frame analysis.* Harmondsworth, England: Penguin.

Gregory, M. (1967). Aspects of varieties differentiation. *Journal of Linguistics, 3,* 177–198.

Grice, H. P. (1975). Logic and conversation. In P. Cole & J. L. Morgan (Eds.), *Syntax and semantics: Vol. 3. Speech acts.* New York: Seminar Press.

Gumperz, J. J., & Hymes, D. (Eds.) (1972). *The ethnography of communication.* New York: Holt, Rinehart & Winston.

Guthrie, E. R. (1952). *The psychology of learning.* New York: Harper Bros.

Halliday, M. A. K. (1976). Early language learning: A sociolinguistic approach. In W. C. McCormack & S. A. Wurm (Eds.), *Language and man.* The Hague: Mouton.

Handelman, D. (1976). Components of interaction in the negotiation of a definition of the situation. In W. C. McCormack & S. A. Wurm (Eds.), *Language and man.* The Hauge: Mouton.

Hatch, E. (1976). Studies in language switching and mixing. In W. C. McCormack & S. A. Wurm (Eds.), *Language and man.* The Hauge: Mouton.

Heider, F. (1958). *The psychology of interpersonal relations.* New York: Wiley.

Herrmann, T. (1983). Language and situation: The pars pro toto principle. In C. Fraser & K. Scherer (Eds.), *Advances in the social psychology of language.* Cambridge: University Press.

Herrmann, T., & Deutsch, W. (1976). *Psychologie der objektbenennung.* Bern: Huber.

Hymes, D. (1967). The anthropology of communication. *Social Research, 34,* 632–647.

Hymes, D. (1972). Models of the interaction of language and social life. In J. J. Gumperz & D. Hymes (Eds.), *The ethnography of communication.* New York: Holt, Rinehart & Winston.

Kantor, J. R. (1924). *Principles of psychology.* Bloomington, Indiana: Principia.

Kent, G. G., Davis, J. D., & Shapiro, D. A. (1981). Effect of mutual acquaintance on the construction of conversation. *Journal of Experimental Social Psychology, 17,* 197–209.

Koffka, K. (1935). *Principles of Gestalt psychology.* New York: Harcourt.

Krause, R. (1982). A social psychological approach to the study of stuttering. In C. Fraser & K. Scherer (Eds.), *Advances in the social psychology of language.* Cambridge: Cambridge University Press.

Kroeber, A. L. (1963). *Anthropology.* New York: Harcourt Brace.

Laucht, M. (1979). Untersuchungen zur sprachlichen Form des Aufforderns. In W. Tack (Ed.), *Bericht uber den 31. Kongress der Deutschen Gesellschaft fur Psychologie.* Gottingen: Hogrefe.

Leodolter, R., & Leodolter, M. (1976). Sociolinguistic considerations on psychosocial socialisation. In W. C. McCormack & S. A. Wurm (Eds.), *Language and man*. The Hague: Mouton.

Lewin, K. (1951). *Field theory in social science*. New York: Harper.

Lichtenstein, E. H., & Brewer, W. F. (1980). Memory for goal-directed events. *Cognitive Psychology, 12*, 412–445.

Mahoney, M. J. (1977). Reflections on the cognitive learning trend in psychotherapy. *American Psychologist, 32*, 5–12.

McCormack, W. C., & Wurm, S. A. (Eds.) (1976). *Language and man*. The Hague: Mouton.

Mead, G. H. (1934). *Mind, self and society*. Chicago: University of Chicago Press.

Mischel, W. (1968). *Personality and assessment*. New York: Wiley.

Mischel, W. (1979). On the interface of cognition and personality. *American Psychologist, 34*, 740–754.

Mitchell-Kernan, C. (1972). Signifying and marking: Two Afro-American speech acts. In J. J. Gumperz & D. Hymes (Eds.), *The ethnography of communication*. New York: Holt, Rinehart & Winston.

Moos, R. (1968). Situational analysis of a therapeutic community milieu. *Journal of Abnormal Psychology, 73*, 49–61.

Morris, C. (1946). *Signs, language and behavior*. Englewood Cliffs, NJ: Prentice-Hall.

Moscovici, S. (1981). Social representations. In J. P. Forgas (Ed.), *Social cognition: Perspectives on everyday understanding*. London: Academic Press.

Murray, H. A. (1951). Toward a classification of interaction. In T. Parsons & E. A. Shils (Eds.), *Towards a general theory of action*. Cambridge, MA: Harvard University Press.

Pervin, L. A. (1976). A free response description approach to the study of person-situation interaction. *Journal of Personality and Social Psychology, 34*, 465–474.

Pike, K. L. (1967). *Language in relation to a unified theory of human behaviour*. The Hague: Mouton.

Platt, J. (1977). A model for polyglossia and multilingualism. *Language in Society, 6*, 361–378.

Poyatos, F. (1976). Analysis of a culture through its culturemes: Theory and method. In W. C. McCormack & S. A. Wurm (Eds.), *Language and Man*. The Hague: Mouton.

Rayfield, J. R. (1970). *The languages of a bilingual community*. The Hague: Mouton.

Robinson, P. W. (1972). *Language and social behaviour*. Harmondsworth: Penguin.

Rommetveit, R. (1983). Prospective social psychological contributions to a truly interdisciplinary understanding of ordinary language. *Journal of Language and Social Psychology, 2*, 89–105.

Rosch, E., & Lloyd, B. B. (1978). *Cognition and categorization*. Hillsdale, NJ: Erlbaum.

Schank, R., & Abelson, R. P. (1977). *Scripts, plans, goals and understanding*. Hillsdale, NJ: Erlbaum.

Scherer, K. [Interaction between civil servants and their clients]. Unbpulished data.

Skinner, B. F. (1957). *Verbal behaviour*. New York: Appleton-Century-Crofts.

Smith, P. M. (1983). Social psychology and language: A taxonomy and overview. *Journal of Language and Social Psychology, 2*, 163–183.

Soskin, W. F., & John, V. (1963). The study of spontaneous speech. In R. Barker (Ed.), *The stream of Behaviour*. New York: Appleton.

Stone, G. P., & Farbermann, H. E. (Eds.) (1970). *Social psychology through symbolic interaction*. Waltham, MA: Ginn-Blaisdell.

Tajfel, H., & Forgas, J. P. (1981). Social categorisation: Cognition, values and groups. In J. P. Forgas (Ed.), *Social cognition*. London: Academic Press.

Thomas, W. I. (1966). Situational analysis: The behaviour pattern and the situation. In M. Janowitz (Ed.), *W. I. Thomas on social organisation and social personality*. Chicago: Chicago University Press.

Tyler, S. A. (1972). Context and alternation in Koya kinship terminology. In J. J. Gumperz & D. Hymes (Eds.), *The ethnography of communication*. New York: Holt, Rinehart & Winston.

von Raffler Engel, W. (1976). Linguistic and kinesic correlates of code switching. In W. C. McCormack & S. A. Wurm (Eds.), *Language and man*. The Hague: Mouton.

Watson, J. B. (1913). Psychology as the behaviourist views it. *Psychological Review, 20*, 158–177.

Weber, M. (1968). *Economy and society*. New York: Bedminister.

Wells, C. G., & Robinson, W. P. (1982). The role of adult speech in language development. In C. Fraser & K. Scherer (Eds.), *Advances in the social psychology of language*. Cambridge: Cambridge University Press.

West, S. G. (1983). Personality and prediction: An introduction. *Journal of Personality, 51*, 275–285.

Wish, M. (1975). Subjects' expectations about their own interpersonal communication. *Personality and social Psychology Bulletin, 1*, 11–20.

Wish, M., Deutsch, M., & Kaplan, S. (1976). Perceived dimensions of interpersonal relations. *Journal of Personality and Social Psychology, 33*, 409–420.

Wolff, K. H. (1964). Definition of the situation. In J. Gould, & W. K. Kolb (Eds.), *A dictionary of the social sciences*. New York: The Free Press.

Part I

Situational Factors
in Language Development

Chapter 2
The Role of Interaction Formats in Language Acquisition

Jerome Bruner

Learning a native language is an accomplishment within the grasp of any toddler, yet discovering how children do it has eluded generations of philosophers and linguists. I would like to take this opportunity to ask anew some puzzling questions about what it is, beyond a splendid nervous system, that makes it possible for the young child to acquire language so swiftly and so effortlessly. Perhaps they are no longer puzzling questions save to those of us who have spent a great deal of time working and brooding over whether the acquisition of knowledge about the social world and about the world generally is in some sense constitutive of language.

The awkward dilemma that plagues questions about the original nature and later growth of human faculties inheres in the unique nature of human competence. For human competence is both biological in origin and cultural in the means by which it finds expression. While the *capacity* for intelligent action has deep biological roots and discernible evolutionary history, the *exercise* of that capacity depends upon man appropriating to himself modes of acting and thinking that exist not in his genes but in his culture.

I shall argue in this chapter that language acquisition "begins" before the child utters his[1] first lexicogrammatical speech. It begins when mother and infant create a predictable format of interaction that can serve as a microcosm for communicating and for constituting a shared reality. The transactions that occur in such formats constitute the "input" from which the child then masters grammar, how to refer and mean, and how to realize his intentions communicatively.

The child, however, could not achieve these prodigies of language acquisition without, at the same time, possessing a unique and predisposing set of language-learning capacities—something akin to what Noam Chomsky has

---

[1]Masculine pronouns are used throughout this chapter to refer to the child; feminine pronouns refer to the mother.

called a Language Acquisition Device (LAD). But the infant's Language Acquisition Device could not function without the aid given by an adult who enters with him into a transactional format. That format, initially under the control of the adult, provides a Language Acquisition Support System (LASS). It frames or structures the input of language and interaction to the child's Language Acquisition Device in a manner to "make the system function." In a word, it is the interaction between LAD and LASS that makes it possible for the infant to enter the linguistic community—and, at the same time, the culture to which the language gives access. The remainder of this chapter is an amplification of how this process works.

Two Conflicting Views of Language Acquisition

Saint Augustine believed that language acquisition was quite simple. Allegedly recollecting his own childhood, he said: "When they named any thing, and as they spoke turned towards it, I saw and remembered that they called what one would point out by the name they uttered. . . . And thus by constantly hearing words, as they occurred in various sentences, I collected gradually for what they stood." But a look at children as they actually acquire language shows Saint Augustine to be far, far off target. Alas, he had a powerful effect both on his followers and on those who set out to refute him.

Developmental linguistics is now going through rough times that can be traced back to Saint Augustine as well as to the reactions against him. It is one of the mysteries of Kuhnian scientific paradigms that this empiricist approach to language acquisition persisted in psychology (if not in philosophy, where it was overturned by Frege and Wittgenstein) from its first enunciation by Saint Augustine to its most recent form in B. F. Skinner's *Verbal Behavior*. It would be fair to say that the persistence of the mindless behavioristic version of Augustianism finally led to a readiness, even a reckless readiness, to be rid of it. For it was not only an inadequate account, but one that damped inquiry by its domination of "common sense." It set the stage for the Chomskyan revolution.

It was to Noam Chomsky's credit that he boldly proclaimed the old enterprise bankrupt. In its place he offered a challenging, if counterintuitive, hypothesis based on nativism. He proposed that the acquisition of the *structure* of language depended upon a Language Acquisition Device that had as its base a universal grammar or a "linguistic deep structure" that humans know innately and without learning. LAD was programmed to recognize in the surface structure of any natural language encountered its deep structure by virtue of the kinship between innate grammar and the grammar of natural languages. The universal grammatical categories that programmed the LAD were in the innate structure of the mind. No prior nonlinguistic knowledge of the world was necessary, and no privileged communication with another speaker was required. The only constraints on rate of linguistic development were psychological limitations on *performance*: the child's limited but growing attention and memory span, for example. Linguistic *competence* was there from the start, ready to express itself when performance constraints were extended by the growth of requisite skills.

It was an extreme view, but in a stroke it freed a generation of psycholinguists from the dogma of association-cum-imitation-reinforcement. It turned attention to the problem of rule learning, even if it concentrated only on syntactic rules. By declaring learning theory dead as an explanation of language acquisition (one of the more premature obituaries of our times), it opened the way for a new account.

George Miller put it well. We now had *two* theories of language acquisition: One of them, empiricist associationism, was impossible; the other, nativism, was miraculous. But the void between the impossible and the miraculous was soon to be filled in, albeit untidily and partially.

Initial Cognitive Endowment

If we are to consider the transition from prelinguistic communication to language, particularly with a concern for possible continuities, we had better begin by taking as close a look as we can at the so-called "original endowment" of human beings. Might that endowment affect the acquisition and early use of language?

Let me begin with some conclusions about perception, skill, and problem-solving in the prelinguistic infant, and consider how they might conceivably predispose the child to acquire "culture" through language.

The first of these conclusions is that much of the cognitive processing going on in infancy appears to operate in support of goal-directed activity. From the start, the human infant is *active* in seeking out regularities in the world about him. The child is active in a uniquely human way, converting experience into species-typical means-end structures.

To say that infants are also "social" is to be banal. They are geared to respond to the human voice, to the human face, to human action and gesture. Their means-end readiness is easily and quickly brought into coordination with the actions of their caretakers. The pioneering work of Daniel Stern and Berry Brazelton and their colleagues underlines how early and readily activated infants are by the adults with whom they interact and how quickly their means-end structuring encompasses the actions of another. The infant's principal "tool" for achieving his or her ends is another familiar human being.

Infants are, in a word, tuned to enter the world of human action. Obvious though the point may seem, we shall see that it has enormous consequences for the matter at hand. This leads directly to the second conclusion, which concerns infant "endowment."

An enormous amount of the child's activity during the first year and a half of life is extraordinarily social and communicative. Social interaction appears to be both self-propelled and self-rewarding. Many students of infant behavior, like Tom Bower, have found that a social response to the infant is the most powerful reinforcer one can use in ordinary learning experiments. Conversely, withholding social response to the infant's initiatives is one of the most disruptive things one can do—an unresponding face, for example, will soon produce tears.

While the infant's attachment to the mother (or caretaker) is initially assured by a variety of innate response patterns, there very quickly develops a reciprocity that the infant comes to anticipate and count on. For example, if during play the mother assumes a sober immobile face, the infant shows fewer smiles and turns his head away from the mother more frequently than when the mother responds socially, as Edward Tronick and his colleagues have shown. The existence of such reciprocity—buttressed by the mother's increasing capacity to differentiate as infant's "reasons" for crying as well as by the infant's capacity to anticipate these consistencies—soon creates a form of mutual attention, a harmony or "intersubjectivity," whose importance we shall take up later.

In any case, a pattern of inborn initial social responses in the infant, elicited by a wide variety of effective signs from the mother, is soon converted into a very complex joint anticipatory system that converts initial biological attachment between mother and child into something more subtle and more sensitive to individual idiosyncracies and to forms of cultural practice. *The third conclusion is that much of early infant action takes place in constrained, familiar situations and shows a surprisingly high degree of order and "systematicity."* Children spend most of their time doing a very limited number of things. Long periods are spent in reaching and taking, banging and looking, etc. Within any one of these restricted domains, there is striking "systematicity." Object play provides an example. A single act (like banging) is applied successively to a wide range of objects. Everything on which the child can get his hands is banged. Or the child tries out on a single object all the motor routines of which he or she is capable—grasping the object, banging it, throwing it to the floor, putting it in the mouth, putting it on top of the head, running it through the entire repertory. There may be differences of opinion concerning the "rules" that govern this orderly behavior, but there can be no quarrel about its systematicity.   ˙

It is not in the least surprising, in light of this conclusion, that infants enter the world of language and of culture with a readiness to find or invent systematic ways of dealing with social requirements and linguistic forms. The child reacts "culturally" with characteristic hypotheses about what is required and enters language with a readiness for order.

There are two important implications that follow from this. The first is obvious, though I do not recall ever having encountered the point. It is that from the start, the child becomes readily attuned to "making a lot out of a little" by combination. He typically works on varying a small set of elements to create a larger range of possibilities.

The second implication is more social. The acquisition of prelinguistic and linguistic communication takes place, in the main, in the highly constrained settings to which we are referring. The child and his caretaker readily combine elements in these situations to extract meanings, assign interpretations, and infer intentions. A decade ago there was considerable debate among developmental linguists about whether in writing "grammars" of child speech one should use a method of "rich interpretation"—taking into account not only the child's actual speech but also the ongoing actions and other elements of the context in which speech was occurring. Today we take it for granted that one must do so. For it is precisely the combining of all elements in constrained situations (speech and nonspeech) that provides the road to communicative effectiveness. It is for this reason that I shall place such heavy emphasis on the role of "formats" in the child's entry into language.

A fourth conclusion about the nature of infant cognitive endowment is that its systematic character is surprisingly abstract. Infants during their first year appear to have rules for dealing with space, time, and even causation. A moving object that is transformed in appearance while it is moving behind a screen produces surprise when it reappears in a new guise.

Objects explored by touch alone are later recognized by vision alone. The infant's perceptual world, far from being a blooming, buzzing confusion, is rather orderly and organized by what seem like highly abstract rules.

It is *not* the case that language, when it is encountered and then used, is the first instance of abstract rule following. It is not, for example, in language alone that the child makes such distinctions as those between specific and nonspecific, between states and processes, between "punctual" acts and recurrent ones, between causative and noncausative actions. These abstract distinctions, picked up with amazing speed in language acquisition, have analogues in the child's way of ordering his world of experience. Language will serve to specify, amplify, and expand distinctions that the child already has about the world.

These four cognitive "endowments"—means-end readiness, transactionality, systematicity, and abstractness—provide foundation processes that aid the child's language acquisition. None of them "generates" language, for language involves a set of phonological, syntactic, semantic, and illocutionary rules and maxims that constitute a problem space of their own. But linguistic or communicative hypotheses depend upon these capacities as enabling conditions.

Such sensitivity grows in the process of fulfilling certain general, non-linguistic functions—predicting the environment, interacting transactionally, getting to goals with the aid of another, and the like. These functions are first fulfilled primitively if abstractly by prelinguistic communicative means. Such primitive procedures, I will argue, must reach requisite levels of functioning before *any* Language Acquisition Device (whether innate or acquired) can begin to generate "linguistic hypotheses."

Support for Language Acquisition

We can say, I think, that the last decade of research strongly supports the view that language acquisition *is* aided by the acquirer gaining world knowledge concurrently with or in advance of language, and is aided also by maturation and by a privileged social relationship between the child and an adult who is moderately well tuned to the child's linguistic level. If there is a Language Acquisition Device, the input to it is not a shower of spoken language but a highly interactive affair shaped, as we have already noted, by some sort of an adult Language Acquisition Support System.

The view that acquisition depends upon interaction as the clue-giving source for language acquisition has several variants. The most recent grows out of speech-act theory. Its central argument is that prelinguistic infants already know, say, how to delare and demand (e.g., Clark & Clark, 1977) by means other than language—by gesture and intonation, for example. Mastering the more conventional linguistic forms for carrying out these acts is a matter of a substituting new linguistic procedures for old nonlinguistic ones with the aid and/or modeling of an adult who already knows the language and its social conventions. Much of the literature on Motherese deals with how this is presumably brought about (e.g., Snow & Ferguson, 1977). Two of my own studies are typical of this approach (Ninio & Bruner, 1978; Bruner, Ratner, & Roy, 1982). The question that such studies pose, to out it baldly, is whether the prelinguistic communicative functions that the child can fulfill before the development of language proper are either constitutive of the language that he is about to learn, or whether they even provide any clues to the aspiring learner about the formal structure of language.

To this point we have been presupposing that the child is operating pretty much of his own initiative, even in social interaction and certainly in use of previously acquired world knowledge as a guide. Insofar as the adult partner has come into the picture, it is rather as a model from whom the child can get an input of the language in order to make his or her own inductions, piercing discoveries, or intuitive recognitions, depending upon what view you may take of the process. But may not the adult herself arrange the environment and her encounters with the child in ways that *scaffold* language input and interaction to make it better fit the child's "natural" way of proceeding? She, after all, *knows* the language that the child is trying to master and she probably has an implicit and practical theory about how to help the child learn it. There may, in a word, be a Language Acquisition Support System that readies or that formats the input of language to the child in a way that makes its rules more transparent to the child's Language Acquisition Device. *LASS*, so to speak, helps *LAD*. We shall want to reexamine the fine-tuning hypothesis later with this in mind.

One final point before turning to a more detailed consideration of those already introduced. Beyond early world knowledge and social interaction as aids to the acquisition of language, there is one other possibility, one particularly well developed in a recent paper by Shatz (1982). Might it be the case that, though language is a problem space of its own, there are certain *general* cognitive processes developed in the child's early years that can also serve him or her in cracking the linguistic code? This is not the same as Piaget's argument that cognitive development *produces* language as one of its spinoffs or symptoms. Rather, it asserts that common processes are involved in acquiring world knowledge, skilled social interaction, and language. Examples are not hard to find: Learning to decompose tasks into constituent routines and then to recombine the constituents into new procedures is, for example, a well-observed feature of the infant's sensorimotor learning (Bruner, 1973). In a formal sense, it is the same kind of process involved in learning to decompose and recompose the flow of language into its constituents. Or, indeed, certain rules of perceptual attention can operate as effectively in spotting diacritica in speech as they can for spotting distinctive sensory features in sensory learning. Segmenting action into goal-completion cycles may, as noted, predispose to spotting aspectual completives. Slobin's (1973) account of how the child learns to pick up stressed, initial, and terminal elements of words and phrases is based upon this assumption.

There is a diachronic side to this issue as well that, alas, must remain untestable. Language systems in their earliest development probably had to be based upon cognitive skills that were widely distributed and readily accessible to all members of the human group, in order to assure universal participation. If that were the case (the alternative being that the possession of language initially marked off a human elite that were then selected for their language ability), then the forms of language that came into being would be of a kind that would somehow be easy for human beings to learn. This would either mean that they were "natural' cognitive skills, or that they were peculiarly well-matched to the mode of social interaction into which human beings naturally entered. On *a priori* grounds, based on Julian Huxley's dictum of biological redundancy in all communication systems, I find it most plausible to accept both these propositions. There is one other good reason to give a central place to the operation of general cognitive capabilities in the acquisition of language. So much of human language operates deictically, by dint of using nonlinguistic context for making meaning clear, that it is difficult to imagine how a *special* gift for language could have emerged independently of other ways of processing information about the environment.

Shared Formats and Language Acquisition

I want to begin with the role of pragmatics in language generally and in language acquisition particularly. I think of pragmatics as entailing quite different processes from those involved in mastering a set of syntactic or semantic codes. Semantics and syntax are formulated to deal almost exclusively with the communication of information, and that, I suppose, is why one can refer to each as embodying a code of elements which "stand for" some knowledge in the "real world." Pragmatics is not restricted in that way. It is the study of how speech is used to accomplish such social ends as promising, humiliating, assuaging, warning, declaring, requesting. Its elements do not "stand for" anything: They *are* something. Even silence, though it cannot be specified syntactically or semantically, may speak volumes in the context in which it occurs. It is certainly not just like a grammatical deletion rule where patterned absence implies presence. In this perspective, language is a vehicle for doing things with and to others, many of which could not be conceived but for language. Pragmatics deals, then, with the extension of social interaction by the use of speech. It is a *commitment* to social interaction by the use of speech.

In this view, pragmatics necessarily relates to discourse and, at the same time, is always context dependent, that is, dependent upon a *shared* context. Discourse presupposes a reciprocal commitment between speakers. It is a complex commitment that includes at least three elements: (1) a shared set of conventions for establishing speaker intent and listener uptake, including procedural conventions like those proposed by Grice (1975) in his celebrated discussion of Conversational Principles; (2) a shared basis for exploiting the deictic possibilities of spatial, temporal, and interpersonal context, subject to "shifting" in Jakobson's classic sense (1971–79); and (3) a conventional means for jointly establishing and retrieving presuppositions. These three elements—announcement of intention, regulation of deixis, and control of presupposition—give discourse its future, present, and past orientations.

A great many acts of discourse will be found to be ways of "tuning" these forms of reciprocal commitment. Indeed, some linguistic theorists have even proposed that the grammatical categories of language exist, *inter alia*, to assure such tuning and calibration as well as to assure reference and meaning. Benveniste (1971) raised the question of the function served by personal pronouns, a universal feature of all known languages. Why are they needed, he asked, when in fact we could accomplish the same semantic ends more reliably by using nominals to specify people or objects rather than having to employ tricky, shifter pronominals. His answer, of course, was that shifters like "I" and "you" serve as economical ways of sharing and calibrating the perspectives of two speakers through reciprocal role shift.

I think it will be apparent from the foregoing that pragmatics of discourse cannot be based upon ordinary grammatical categories alone. For grammer is traditionally based upon the concept of the sentence and on "sentence parts." Yet the performance, deictic, and presuppositional rules of discourse depend for their power upon the privileges of occurrence of expressions in discourse, not just in individual sentences. You will perhaps recall that the object of the

Prague School was to derive sentence grammar constitutively from discourse such that, for example, topic and subject were said to be the "given" in discourse and comment or predicate the "new."

There is another sense in which interaction motivates grammatical rules. One of the major tasks in interacting with another is the regulation of joint attention. Fillmore (1977) proposes that the function of sentence grammars is to establish a *perspective* on a *scene* that the sentence depicts or represents. Perspective setting demands forefronting and backgrounding for the direction of attention, and there are many grammatical devices for accomplishing these ends, such as subject placement, passivization, clefting, etc.

We will see in a moment that early interaction abounds in procedures for regulating attentional perspective on scenes in the form of vocatives, demonstratives, pointing gestures, intonation contours, etc., employed by both adult and child. It also abounds in role shifting and in the other forms of discourse tuning to which I have referred. This brings me to the central issue.

All of this leads to the hypothesis that in order for the young child to be clued into the language, he must first enter into social relationships of a kind that function in the manner consonant with the uses of language in discourse—relating to intention sharing, to deictic specification, and to the establishment of presupposition. Such a social relationship I shall call a *format*. The format is a rule-bound microcosm in which the adult and child *do* things to and with each other. In its most general sense, it is the instrument of patterned human interaction. Since formats pattern communicative inter- action between infant and caretaker before lexico-grammatical speechs begins, they are crucial vehicles in the passage from communication to language. Let us consider their nature in more detail.

A format entails formally a contingent interaction between at least two acting parties, contingent in the sense that the responses of each member can be shown to be dependent upon a prior response of the other. Each member of the minimal pair has a goal and a set of means for its attainment such that two conditions are met: first, that a participant's successive responses are instrumental to that goal, and second, that there is a discernible stop order in the sequence indicating that the terminal goal has been reached. The goals of the two participants need not be the same; all that is required is that the conditions of intraindividual and interindividual response contingency be fulfilled. Formats, defined formally in this sense, represent a simple instance of a "plot" or "scenario."

Formats, however, grow and can become as varied and complex as necessary. Their growth is effected in several ways. They may in time incorporate new means or strategies for the attainment of goals, including symbolic or linguistic ones. They may move toward coordination of the goals of the two partners not only to agreement, but also to a division of labor and a division of initiative. And they may become conventionalized or canonical in a fashion that permits others within a symbolic community (e.g., a "speech community") to enter the format in a provisional way in order to learn its special rules.

Formats are also modular in the sense of being amenable as subroutines for incorporation in larger-scale, longer-term routines. A greeting format, for example, can be incorporated in a larger-scale routine involving other forms of joint action. In this sense, any given format may have a hierarchical structure, the parts being interpretable in terms of their placement in a larger structure. The creation of higher-order formats by incorporation of subroutine formats is one of the principal sources of presupposition. What is incorporated becomes implicit or presupposed.

Formats, save when highly conventionalized, cannot be identified independently of the perceptions of the participants. In this sense, they have the property of contexts generally in being the result of joint definition by the participants. The communal definition of formats is one of the major ways in which a community controls the interaction of its members. Once a format is conventionalized and "socialized," it comes to be seen as having objective status. Eventually, formats provide the basis for speech acts and can be reconstituted as needed by linguistic means alone.

One special property of formats involving an infant and an adult (though it may be a property of formats in general) is that they are asymmetrical with respect to the "consciousness" of the members, with one "knowing what's up," and the other knowing not or knowing less. Consciousness in this sense is not intended to imply psychological heavy weather. I hope I can make that clearer later. I intend it in the sense used by Vygotsky (1962) when he discussed how the adult helps the child achieve realization of the Zone of Proximal Development. The adult serves as model, scaffold, and monitor until the child can take over on his own. A good illustration of this is provided in a study by Kaye and Charney (1980) in which the adult takes over the function of keeping turns in discourse alternation until the child develops the procedures necessary to do so on his own.

Let us now return to the three rubrics with which I introduced the idea of discourse: intentions, deixis, and presupposition. With respect to the goal-oriented aspect of formats, early formats usually involve joint, overt activity with a clear-cut, ritualized, successive structure (e.g., games like Hide-and-Seek, Give-and-Take, Peek-a-Boo, etc.) As my colleagues and I (Bruner & Sherwood, 1976; Ratner & Bruner, 1978) have tried to show, signaling marks the successive steps toward the final goals of these games, with such aspectual completives as "All-Gone" and "Dere" among the first on the scene, much like the young Brazilians reported by Campos (1979). Once children learn to respond to these action formats, they soon learn to call them up and to expect uptake. The signaling becomes increasingly conventionalized and consensual (with the mother imitating the child more often than in the reverse direction) and the child increasingly takes over initiative. (Bruner, 1978). As the signaling becomes more adept, it begins to pace the game rather than being merely an accompaniment to it (Bruner, 1978).

Before the second year is far advanced, the child-mother pair are well launched not only into games but also into procedures for realizing basic linguistic functions like indicating and requesting. Consider the case of requesting reported by Bruner, Ratner, and Roy (1982). There is a long preliminary period in which Richard, one of the children they observed, first mastered ways of requesting nearby visible objects by pointing and then by intonation on an appropriate nominal; then invisible objects by indicating direction or canonical locus of objects; then on requesting assistance in carrying out actions: "invitations" and offers. This is particularly difficult, for it requires his analyzing the structure of a task and signaling *that* he wants assistance, on *what* object, but also what *kind* of assistance it is. He has learned nominals, verbs, vocatives, demonstratives—all in aid of his requests. At 20 months old, Richard adopted a "successive guidance" strategy for managing complex requests for assistance in action. He starts the round of exchanges with a requestive vocative or with an intonationally marked nominal or verb. When his mother signals uptake but incomprehension of what *kind* of help he is requesting, he follows by introducing a second element, usually a locative, to indicate the place where the objects is or the locus of the desired action. This may be followed by a verb indicating the action requested. And so it continues step by step until he succeeds in getting the message across in successive steps.

By the time Richard is 22 months, however, his mother will no longer tolerate being dealt with in this robotic way and insists that he fulfill one of the felicity conditions on requestiong—full disclosure of intention in advance. "No, Richard, tell me what you want *first*," she demands. Richard responds with one of his first three-word sentences, strung together with slight pauses but including "Mummy" as Agent, the required Action, and the sought-after Object, the whole marked with what is to be the requestive intonation contour of such utterances on later occasions. All of which is not to say that there was anything in the prior interaction per se that could have given Richard any clues about how to linearize such a sentence. There is no "natural order" in action that tells you the order of corresponding elements in a sentence— though I was once tempted to believe something like that about Subject-Verb-Object orders (Bruner, 1975). It is the familiarity and structure of the request formats that frees Richard and guides him in finding the linguistic procedures required. The adult helps hold the child's goal invariant against distraction, reduces the degrees of freedom in the choices he has to make lexically and grammatically by coordinating her own utterances with established action segments, and generally serves as linguistic scaffold. Above all, she helps him link his intentions to linguistic means for their attainment.

In the limited space available, I would like to touch very lightly on the second feature of formats: their role in providing a base for context sensitivity and deixis. It was Grace DeLaguna (1927) who noted in her remarkable book of more than half a century ago that you could not know what a child meant without knowing what he or she was doing while speaking. The key to going beyond this primitive deictic indexicality depends upon waht C. S. Peirce (1931–59) called the transformation of "sign vehicles." (It is to Michael Silverstein (1981) that I am particularly grateful for pointing out the relevance of Peirce's proposal for developmental linguistics.)

Peirce proposed that initial language is indexical and necessarily deictic, dependent upon a contiguity or "pointing" relation between sign and significate. With the development of a sign system, a second feature is added: Language can then operate intralinguistically in the sense that signs can point to or be related to other signs. The context to which reference is made may still be concrete and specific, but it is linguistic. As the child gains further insight into the language as a codified system of representation, he comes to operate not on concrete events, whether directly in experience or represented in words, but upon possible combinations derived from operations on the language itself. This last accomplishment Peirce refers to as the metapragmatic level, and at this point the child is able to turn around on his language, correct it as needed, quote it, amplify what was meant, even define it. A good example of the transition from intralinguistic to metapragmatic speech is provided in Maya Hickman's (1982) paper on children reporting what they had seen and heard in an animated cartoon. This last stage of the child's development, however, takes place later than the ages I want to consider and need not concern us.

Let me illustrate the manner in which, thanks to the presupposition-conserving structure of a continuing and growing format, the child and mother switch from indexical to intralinguistic procedures. Consider how the mother and child come to signal "given" and "new" in their interaction when Richard is between 18 and 22 months. In the growth of labeling (cf. Ninio & Bruner, 1978), Richard's mother sets up a routine for book reading in which she employs four invariant discourse markers: an initial attentional vocative in the form "Oh look, Richard"; followed, when his attention is gained, by the query "What's that, Richard?" with stress and rising intonation peaking at the second word; followed, if Richard should reply by any vocalization even in the form of a babble string initially, by "Yes, that's an X"; and terminated by a reinforcing remark like "That's very good."

At this point when Richard can reliably produce the correct label or some phonologically constant form that his mother can imitate herself, her intonation contour changes. For items of this "known-to-be-known" class, she still uses her second discourse marker ("What's that, Richard?"), but now with a falling intonation on the second word. It is as if she is signaling that she knows that he knows, and the shift often produces "knowing smiles" between the two. Then, shortly after, she introduces an extended routine where, after the presuppositionally marked request for a label, she asks a second question calling for an answer in the form of a predicate of action or of state related to the child's just-provided label—for example, "What's the X doing?"—with stress and rising intonation on the terminal word. The same sorting of given and new can be observed in the development of request, when Richard's mother responds to his wave toward a canonical locus, where he thinks an object may be, with "Something in the ice box? What do you want in the ice box?" At each opportunity the mother is cannily adding nominals or even anaphoric pronominals to the indexical procedures the child is using, and then using these an intralinguistically presupposed in later discourse.

In short, formats in discourse provide the necessary microcosms in which the child can signal intentions, operate indexically and then intralinguistically, and develop presuppositions, all within the interactions that have properties that are easily mapped onto the functions and forms of language. At the start, formating is under the control of the adult. Increasingly formats become symmetrical and the child can initiate them as readily as the adult. All cultures do not, of course, format early discourse in the same way—as we know form the pioneering work of Schieffelin (1979) on the Kaluli of Papuan New Guinea who, unlike us, "show" more than they interact. But the hypothesis I am putting forth is that all cultures have ways of formating interaction and discourse so as to highlight those features of the world and of social interaction that map most readily onto linguistic categories and grammatical rules. It is this feature of early interaction that I have referred to as the Language Acquisition Support System, or LASS, without which an acquisition device, LAD, could not make much progress.

Some Conclusions

Let me return to Marilyn Shatz's (1982) discussion of the ways in which social interaction might aid the child in developing insights into syntax—and it is important to note that it is syntax with which she is exclusively and (I think) properly concerned. She presents four views that can be briefly characterized as follows: (1) Syntax is derived directly from prior social knowledge; (2) syntax is derived from prior semantic representations that achieve deep structure by being transformed by social interactions; (3) syntax is not derived from social interaction but merely faciliated by the routinization of social interaction which frees necessary processing capacity; and, as already mentioned, (4) syntax and the complexities of rule-bound social interaction depend upon the same types of cognitive processes at any given stage of development, and consequently children about the learning of the two different systems in a common way.

Shatz's analysis is useful; I can even sail happily under the flag of her last two rubrics. Yet I find her classification system constricting for its failure to give a full enough role to the adult and for its incomplete analysis of the nature of the formats in which the child's interactive learning and syntactic acquisition occur. In effect, she treats the child as if he were flying solo, in the best tradition of both theories of learning and of information processing. But the solo model of social learning, however useful it may be in goading us to look for internal structures and processes, is just not good enough.

What I mean by this assertion requires me to revert briefly to Vygotsky's (1962) conception of the Zone of Proximal Development, mentioned earlier in passing. Vygotsky comments on the child's progress from arithmetic to algebra in mathematical learning in a way that is relevant to our discussion. It is not possible, he notes, for the child to move to the "higher ground" of algebra unless he has grasped enough of concrete arithmetic operations to appreciate hints that relate to the more categorical status of these operations—that any number can be treated as an unknown, x; that while a blind Venetian and a Venetian blind cannot be substituted for each other, three twos can substitute for two threes; and so on. In teaching language, unlike in teaching algebra, the tutor is by the nature of the medium bound to be implicit or tacit in the lessons given. The progress that results is much more like that described by Braine in the movement from rote nonproductive utterances, in formulaic pivot grammar, to a more productive use of the same constituents once the child has had an opportunity to master and then to extend the forms. By means of scaffolded use, the child learns what a form can do.

Vygotsky offers the hypothesis that mastery of a lower form has as its terminal state an increase in consciousness (or if you prefer, metacognition). He rather picturesquely characterizes this step across the Zone of Proximal Development as a "loan of consciousness" by the adult to the child until the time when the child can manage on his own. It is done not only by arranging the world suitably, but by providing "hints" and "props." Now, to the degree to which adult and child can stay within an informative but undemanding format, the hinting and the propping will be assimilable. And it is for this reason that I have made so much of the role of formats as essential aids to assisted learning.

Finally, to revert to the argument of writers like Peirce (1931–59), Benveniste (1971), and Jakobson (1971–79) about the 'intersubjectivity" of linguistic forms. Peirce commented particularly on the duality of symbolic forms in natural language. They serve both to *represent* concepts and to *communicate* them, he says. This creates complexities, since one's own perspective differs from the perspective of an interlocutor. It was Benveniste who noted the resort to shifters as universal means of dealing with problems of perspective. The credit goes to Jakobson, finally, for exploring the interconnections of pronominal shifters in such contrastive deictic pairs as *this* and *that, here* and *there, to* and *from*, and even verb forms like *come* and *go*.

The message that I read into the writings of these towering linguists is that it would be impossible to learn a language without knowing in advance or learning concurrently the perspectival complexities involved in using the same set of symbols for representation and communication. That is why I am so reluctant to consider language acquisition to be either the virtuoso cracking of a linguistic code, or the spinoff of ordinary cognitive development, or the gradual takeover of adult speech by the child through some impossible inductive *tour de force*. It is, rather, a subtle process by which adults artificially arrange the world so that the child can succeed culturally by doing what comes naturally, and with others similarly inclined.

Acknowledgment. Permission to reproduce some sections from my book "Child's talk: Learning to use language" by the publisher, W. W. Norton & Co., is gratefully acknowledged. Copyright © 1983 by Jerome Bruner.

References

Benveniste, E. (1971). *Problems in general linguistics*. Coral Gables, FL: University of Miami Press.

Bruner, J. S. (1973). Organization of early skilled action. *Child Development, 44*, 1–1.

Bruner, J. S. (1975). The ontogenesis of speech acts. *Journal of Child Language, 2*, 1–19.

Bruner, J. S. (1978). Learning how to do things with words. In J. S. Bruner & A. Garton (Eds.), *Human growth and development: Wolfson lectures, 1976*. Oxford: Oxford University Press.

Bruner, J. S., & Sherwood, V. (1976). Early rule structure: The case of "peekaboo." In R. Harre (Ed.), *Life sentences: Aspects of the social role of language*. New York & London: Wiley.

Bruner, J. S., Ratner, N., & Roy, C. (1982). The beginnings of request. In K. Nelson (Ed.), *Children's language* (Vol. 3).

Campos, F. (1979). *The emergence of causal relations and the linguistic development of Brazilian children*. Unpublished doctoral thesis, University of Campinas, Brazil.

Clark, H. H., & Clark, E. V. (1977). *Psychology and language: An introduction to psycholinguistics*. New York: Harcourt Brace Jovanovich.

DeLaguna, G. (1927). *Speech: Its function and development*. New Haven, CT: Yale University Press.

Fillmore, C. J. (1977). The case for case reopened. In P. Cole & J. M. Sadock (Eds.), *Syntax and semantics: Vol. 8. Grammatical relations*. New York: Academic Press.

Grice, H. P. (1975). Logic and conversation. In. P. Cole & J. L. Morgan (Eds.), *Syntax and semantics: Vol. 3. Speech acts*. New York: Academic Press.

Hickman, M. E. (1982). The implication of discourse skills in Vygotsky's developmental theory. In J. Wertsch (Ed.), *Culture, communication, and cognition: Vygotskian perspectives*. New York: Academic Press.

Jakobson, R. (1971–79). *Selected writings*. The Hauge: Mouton.

Kaye, K., & Charney, R. (1980). How mothers maintain "dialogue" with two-year-olds. In D. Olson (Ed.), *The social foundations of language and thought*. New York: W. W. Norton.

Ninio, A., & Bruner, J. S. (1978). The achievement and antecedents of labelling. *Journal of Child Language, 5*, 1–15.

Peirce, C. S. (1931–59). *Collected papers*. Cambridge, MA: Harvard University Press.

Ratner, N., & Bruner, J. S. (1978). Games, social exchange, and the acquisition of language. *Journal of Child Language, 5*, 391–401.

Schieffelin, B. (1979). How Kaluli children learn what to say, what to do, and how to feel. Unpublished doctoral dissertation, Columbia University, New York.

Shatz, M. (1982). Relations between cognition and language acquisition. In W. Deutsch (Ed.), *The child's construction of language*. New York & London: Academic Press.

Silverstein, M. (1981). *Aspects of function in culture and language*. Paper presented at SSRC Seminar on Culture and Mind, New York.

Slobin, D. (1973). Cognitive prerequisites for the development of grammar. In C. A. Furguson & D. Slobin (Eds.), *Studies of child language development*. New York: Holt, Rinehart & Winston.

Snow, C., & Ferguson, C. A. (Eds.). (1977). *Talking to children: Language input and acquisition*. New York & London: Academic Press.

Vygotsky, L. (1962). *Thought and language*. Cambridge, MA: MIT Press.

Chapter 3
Situational Variations Within Social Speech Registers

Harry Levin and Catherine Snow

The Nature of Speech Registers

Register has been defined (Ferguson, 1964; Hudson, 1980) as speech which is set off from other speech by its function as well as its form. For example, baby talk (BT), the most widely studied register, qualifies as a register because it is characterized both by a particular function—addressing infants and young children—and by a set of formal characteristics (high pitch, exaggerated intonation contours, special lexical items, frequent use of diminutives, grammatical simplicity, etc.) not present in normal conversation between adults. Similarly, foreigner talk (FT; see the papers in Clyne, 1981) has both functional and formal properties that set it off from other speech. The use of the formal properties of some particular register with an inappropriate function (e.g., using a BT utterance to address an adult), usually constitutes a novel, socially negotiated meaning such as humor or insult.

Some confusion in the literature on registers has arisen because of the failure to take function as the primary definer of a particular register. In our view, a register is defined by function, and formal properties are a dependent variable, the register-specific characteristics that then require to be identified and described. Thus, it is nonsense to ask questions like "Do people use baby talk to animals?" By definition, people use animal talk to animals; BT is for addressing babies. It is not, however, nonsense, and has in fact turned out to be quite informative (see Hirsh-Pasek & Treiman, 1982; Levin & Hunter, 1982) to examine the degree to which the formal characteristics of animal talk resemble the formal characteristics of BT. Similarity on formal characteristics would suggest some dimensions on which animals and babies are seen as similar. The notion that registers must be seen as multidimensional was introduced by Brown (1977), who suggested clarification and affection as the major dimensions motivating the formal characteristics of BT. The implication, not explicitly drawn before now, is that the form of BT itself will vary depending on the dimension being emphasized, that is, the task being accomplished. Furthermore, Brown's list of the dimensions of BT was certainly not exhaustive; capturing and maintaining attention, eliciting responses, maintaining contact, and reinforcing status differences, as well as clarifying for communicative effectiveness and expressing affection, are tasks accomplished via BT, all of which probably affect the formal characteristics of the BT.

Situational Variations in the Baby-Talk Register

The fact that the formal characteristics of a register vary depending on the situation and the immediate task of the speaker is confirmed by causal observation. For example, we have heard a nurse use FT to a foreign patient when she saw that the listener did not understand and drop it for those parts of the conversation that he obviously could follow. The nurse later pointed out to us that she was aware of what she was doing and deliberately adopted a simplified form of speech only when she had some cues that she was not getting across. Since she was speaking to a well-educated foreigner who understood most of her speech, she felt it was demeaning to maintain an FT register with him consistently.

There are a variety of ethnographic reports of variability in register use in a single setting. In hierarchically organized groups such as businesses or the military, registers, especially components such as forms of address, reflect the status differences between speakers. However, when the topic of conversation shifts from military matters to a social event, for example, the status difference is submerged and the register reflects what Brown and Gilman (1960) have called solidarity. Social speech registers, then, have usually been defined by the contextual circumstances eliciting the register and the language appropriate for such contexts. However, the tasks facing the speaker and the listener, which to a large extent determine the formal characteristics of the register, must play an important part in defining the social linguistic phenomena. With all other factors constant, the variations in function can create variations within registers. From this reasoning and from causal observation it seems that registers are not consistent phenomena but are variable and have to be discussed in terms of variable rules. Such situational register variations are the subject of this chapter.

We studied the speech of mothers to 21 children aged 4 to 9 under various circumstances. The parents had elected for their children to have minor surgery. We were able, therefore, to record the mother's speech to the child at home a week prior to the hospital visit, to observe most of them in the hospital during a preoperative period, and to observe all of them during the period immediately after surgery. Finally, a week later we were again able to record the mother and her child at home.

The mother's speech at home was collected in the context of an instructional game, during which the mother was trying to teach and direct the child. During the preoperative period the mother was trying to soothe and allay the anxieties of the child and to pass time. After the operation she was dealing with a child showing many signs of illness. And, finally, at home the child was again in a normal setting. In essence, then, we were able to investigate variations in the BT register as a function of four quite distinct interaction situations.

The Speakers

We studied the 21 children aged 4 to 9 and their mothers who were contacted for participation in the study via their otolaryngologist after determination that the children would undergo elective surgery for treatment of recurrent ear infections. Fifteen of the children underwent myringotomies with tubes (insertion of small, hollow tubes through the ear drums, to allow for drainage), an outpatient procedure that requires a total stay of about three hours in an ambulatory surgery facility. The other six children underwent tonsillectomies or adenoidectomies in addition to myringotomies, and were treated as inpatients. They stayed in the hospital 24 to 36 hours.

Table 3-1 presents information about the age, sex, and hospitalization status of the children. Although we attempted to include equal numbers of

Table 3-1. Description of Subjects

S	Sex	Age	Hospitalization (A-ambulatory, I-inpatient)
1	M	5.2	A
2	M	7.1	A
3	M	4.1	A
4	M	7.3	A
5	F	5.4	A
6	F	4.9	A
7	F	9.4	A
8	F	6.5	A
9	M	8.1	A
10	M	6.9	A
11	F	4.2	A
12	M	5.1	A
13	M	6.1	A
14	M	4.1	A
15	M	5.0	I
16	M	4.6	I
17	M	6.0	A
18	M	4.0	I
19	M	5.5	I
20	M	6.0	I
21	F	9.10	I

boys and girls in two age groups, the sex distribution in the patient population made this impossible. No criteria for inclusion in the subject population were established except for parental consent and residence within 70 miles of Boston. None of the children had seriously delayed language, although several of them had suffered intermittent hearing decrements during ear infections. Their families ranged from working class through professional middle class.

The Data: The Four Situations

Home Visit I: The Playing-at-Home Situation. Since the surgeries were elective and scheduled in advance, an experimenter could visit the mother and child at home approximately a week before hospitalization. The mother and child first played a construction game, called the Geoboard, which involves making patterns by connecting rubber bands of various colors to pegs on a board. The mothers received cards showing schematics of the patterns to be formed using several colors. Each mother was asked to instruct her child about how to make the patterns and use the right colors. She could give the child as much help as she wanted without showing him the pattern or actually doing it for him. The patterns varied in difficulty; the mother was given patterns appropriate for the child's age.

The second home activity required the mother to read a book to the child describing a child's accident and visit to an emergency room. The third activity involved the experimenter and the child in a role-playing situation having to do with hospitals and illness. (This procedure was designed to see how much the child had learned about hospital speech and is reported elsewhere, in (Snow, Shonkoff, Lee, and Levin, in preparation.) The total home visit, as well as the conversations in all of the other settings, were tape-recorded.

The Preoperative Hospital Situation. The outpatients' experience in the hospital typically started with a wait of 45 to 90 minutes in a small, private room. During this time, the children's parents (fathers were present during many of the hospitalizations) helped them to undress, then stayed with them until it was time for the surgery.

The Postoperative Hospital Situation. The surgical procedure took 10 to 20 minutes, after which the child was taken to a group-recovery room. The parents were allowed to be with the child as soon as he or she woke up, though the child had to stay in bed for one hour before dressing and leaving for home. We recorded the interaction during the presurgery wait, and the speech heard around the child's bed in the recovery room. The experimenter placed the tape recorder appropriately, then left the child alone with the parents in the waiting room and in the recovery room except for brief checks of the tape. Before surgery the children were all healthy and without pain, though frequently they were somewhat anxious and always hungry from not having had breakfast prior to anaesthesia. After surgery they all experienced considerable discomfort for 15 to 45 minutes, including nausea, headaches, and earaches, as well as impatience at having to stay in bed.

The six inpatients were admitted to the hospital late in the evening and were scheduled for early-morning surgery. We were, thus, unable to record any preoperative sessions for them. After surgery they were brought to their semi-private rooms from a recovery room as soon as they woke up. The parents stayed with them, urging them to drink frequently for several hours after surgery. Usually, the children were allowed to go home in the late afternoon or evening. We placed a tape recorder near the child's bed and recorded all the speech that he or she heard during the postsurgery period. In addition to parents, there were usually several visits from nurses and aides. The children suffered the same complaints as the myringotomy patients, with sore throats as well.

Home Visit II: The Postoperative Play Situation. The procedures for the second home visit, which occurred about a week after the child left the hospital, were exactly the same as those during the first home visit.

Data Analysis

All of the recordings made at home and in the hospital were transcribed verbatim. A large number of variables were coded from either the transcript or tapes or a combination of the two. The following variables were selected for consideration in this chapter:

1. Total number of utterances. The total number of utterances during the Geoboard Game session in each of the home visits as well as the number of utterances during the preoperative and postoperative periods were counted. An utterance was defined as a complete thought separated from surrounding utterances by pauses. Two coders working with six randomly chosen cases agreed on 83% of their utterance divisions. Since only five minutes of the Geoboard Game was transcribed for analysis, and since the length of the pre- and postoperative sessions was variable (ranging from 30 minutes preoperatively to two hours postoperatively), the data on number of utterances (see Table 3-2) are presented only for background information.
2. Percent of utterances that were nurturant. Nurturant utterances were defined both by what the mother said and by intonational qualities of the utterance as being nurturant and soothing to the child. Examples of nurturant utterances are:
   Mother to son, postoperative:
   a. I love you, Tommy. Just relax.
   What's the matter?

Table 3-2. Number, Nature, and Rate (words/sec.) of Utterances by Mothers to Child in Various Settings (n=21)

	Geoboard I	Pre-Op[a]	Post-Op	Geoboard II	Significant Differences		
					Geoboard vs. Pre-Op	Geoboard vs. Post-Op	Pre-Op vs. Post-Op
No. of utterances	65.29	213.27	269.62	67.13	—	—	—
% Regular	86.83	94.25	71.59	86.22	.05	.002	.0005
% Nurturant	1.73	2.48	18.26	1.83	ns	.0005	.001
% Supportive	11.43	3.55	10.15	9.95	.01	ns	.01
Rate, regular utterances	2.91	4.11	3.83	3.05	.02	.05	ns
Rate, nurturant utterances[b]	2.50	4.58	3.17	4.54	.01[c]	ns	.02
Rate, supportive utterances[b]	3.09	3.67	3.33	3.11	ns	ns	ns

[a] n=15
[b] n may be less than 15 or 21, if some mothers failed to produce certain utterance types in a given setting
[c] different from Geoboard I only

Don't worry about a thing. Nobody's going to give you a shot.
Mother to daughter, postoperative:
b. You're a brave little girl. They didn't hurt you.
They made you all better.
3. Percent of utterances that were supportive. Supportive utterances differed from nurturant ones in that they were either soothing and reinforcing in content or in intonational quality but not both. Examples of supportive utterances are:
Mother to son, preoperative:
a. I bet she never saw such funny feet.
Father to son, postoperative:
b. That wasn't any big deal, was it?
4. Percent of regular utterances; that is, all utterances that were coded neither as nurturant or supportive.
5. Rate of speech. Each utterance was timed in seconds, from which the total amount of time for regular, supportive, and nurturant utterances in each session was calculated. The total number of words for each time of utterance was counted and the three rate measures are given in words per second.

Two coders scoring five cases independently agreed on 93% of the classifications of utterances as nurturant, supportive, or regular during the Geoboard task. They agreed on 81% of the assignments of utterances to these three categories during the pre and postoperative sessions.

The Findings

In order to illustrate our thesis that speech registers are variable and that their variability must be understood both in terms of the structure of the register and the situational functions they serve, a small number of variables were compared across several situations. The situations analysed were: Geoboard Game at the first home visit, Geoboard Game at the second home visit, preoperative period in hospital, and postoperative period in hospital. We are first concerned with the total number of utterances from the mother to the child and the division of these utterances into three categories: regular, supportive, and nurturant. Finally, we will look at the rate of speech in the various settings.

As can be seen in Table 3-2, the Geoboard interaction during the first and second home visits did not differ on any of the variables. Therefore, we are able to simplify the exposition by treating only the comparisons between the first Geoboard interaction and the pre- and postoperative sessions.

Types of Utterances. The total number of utterances were categorized into three types: *nurturant* utterances, which were soothing and comforting both in content and in intonation; *supportive* utterances, which involved saying pleasant things to the child, which during the Geoboard period at home were instances of the mother reinforcing the child for his or her correct acts; and *regular* utterances, a residual category which included all the other kinds of talk that occurred between the mother and the child. All totaled, these three categories of speech accounted for one hundred percent of the utterances. (A more elaborate analysis of the nature of nurturant utterances is presented in Levin, Snow, and Lee, 1984).

Regular utterances were by far the most frequent both at home and in the hospital. The highest occurrence of nurturant utterances was, as predicted, in the postoperative period. Even here, however, only 18.26% of the total number of utterances were nurturant. This is an important point which will be taken up later. However, it is our strongest evidence that register rules are variable; that is, even under a condition where the task of the parents and the function of the language are to be nurturant, not all the language falls into that category. Mothers during the postoperative session are not totally nurturant; in fact, their most common utterances are regular, everyday kinds of talk to their children.

There were significantly more nurturant utterances during the postoperative condition than during both the Geoboard and the preoperative periods. In turn, mothers uttered more nurturant items to their children at home than they did during the preoperative period. The amount of nurturance in the preoperative period differs very little from the proportion of nurturant utterances during the home visits. In other words, the most dramatic consequence of the child's illness was the increase in nurturant talk from the mother to the child, but regular talk appropriate to many settings and for many functions was still dominant in the mothers' speech to their children.

The use of supportive utterances presents an interesting, more complicated picture. About 11% of the utterances during the Geoboard Game session were supportive. This represents the mothers' reinforcing the child as part of his or her learning during that instructional setting. Some reinforcements during the Geoboard session which were scored as supportive utterances are:

a. *Mother to son*:
   That's a good boy.
   Okay, that's right.
b. *Mother to daughter*:
   That's a girl.
   Very good!

Mothers were found to be less supportive at home than during the postoperative period.

The proportion of utterances that were categorized as regular are, of course, related to the incidence of nurturant and supportive talk. The highest incidence of regular utterances was during the preoperative condition (94.2%), and the lowest was during the postoperative period (71.6%). The second, of course, follows from the fact that the supportive and nurturant utterances were high during the postoperative period. In terms of the functions of preoperative talk, the mothers tried to make the children comfortable and to make the waiting time as free from anxiety as possible. Hence they spoke about many things, maintaining the usual kinds of conversation between mothers and children, and thus increasing the proportion of regular utterances.

Speech Rate. The rate of speech for regular utterances averaged approximately 3.5 words per second across the three settings. The most rapid rate was during the preoperative period; the slowest rate was during the Geoboard Game session, in the home. The rate of speech for both pre- and postoperative periods was similar. The mothers talked more slowly during the Geoboard session because the utterances were short and directed to the exchange of specific information. The mother gave the child information, the child performed, and the mother evaluated the performance. During the preoperative period, as we have suggested, mothers were trying to be as "normal" as possible. During the postoperative period the mothers had more to say to the children in terms of asking how they were, whether they wanted to change their position, whether they wanted to have the nurse called, telling them they were getting better, and so on. The mothers expected and received little conversation from their children. They essentially carried on monologs. In fact, none of the rates for regular utterances differed significantly from setting to setting. The rate of nurturant utterances was again fastest during the preoperative period, and the only significant differences among the various periods of nurturant talk was between the pre- and postsessions—the former being more rapid.

Supportive utterances again were spoken at the rate of 3½ words per minute, but the speed of such speech did not vary significantly between the various situations.

These findings present a coherent picture about variations in register-related speech as a function of the interaction situation. The speech between the mother and the child gathered in the home derived from an instructional game in which the kinds of things the mother said were limited to instructions about the game and positive feedback or expressions of annoyance at the child. The speech in the preoperative session seems to reflect a mother trying to entertain and distract the child by conversing about a variety of subjects. Consequently, most of the utterances were regular ones rather than nurturant and supportive. Mothers spoke most rapidly during this session.

The most dramatic setting in which we observed the mothers was during the postoperative periods when the children were sleepy, dazed, whiney, uncomfortable, and often in pain. It was obvious that the mothers wanted to soothe the children, to make them feel better, and to allay their fears. There was little conversation. The incidence of nurturant utterances was higher in this session than in any of the others, as was also the incidence of supportive statements. In fact, about 29% of the utterances were nurturant or supportive during the times that the child was obviously ill. The rate of speech tended to be somewhat faster for regular utterances in pre- and postoperative settings.

There is a tendency for the rate at which nurturant utterances were spoken to be slower in the postoperative than in the preoperative condition.

Some General Considerations

Social speech registers are sometimes thought of as similar to dialects, and the same misconceptions occur about registers as about dialects (Hudson, 1980). Registers are defined by a number of dimensions—speaker, listener, their relationship, task or purpose, setting, etc.—yet each of these dimensions is complex and may influence the formal characteristics of a register in complex ways. In the present study, mothers talked to their children at home and in the hospital during periods when the children were awaiting surgery or immediately following surgery. We expected the postoperative interaction to be dominated by a *sick room* register, where nurturant and supportive language would prevail. In fact each of these settings and tasks involved different aspects of the same dimensions, so that the form of the talk differed both across and within settings. For example, the home talk could be labeled mainly instructional, and though most of the mothers' utterances were "regular," they still were more supportive then than during the preoperative condition. The supportive utterances took the form of reinforcements for the child's performance. Most of the speech items in the preoperative setting were "regular," a finding made understandable by the mother's desire to distract the child from the upcoming surgery.

We expected the sick room register to be most obvious during the postoperative period, and in fact there were more nurturant and supportive items under this condition, though "regular" items still dominated.

These findings do not gainsay our belief in the value of the concept of "social speech register." A combination of circumstances and some incidence of the speech forms indicative of the register permit us to usefully label the situational context and the speech as one or another type of register. However, one should not expect to find the speech in a register to be homogeneous. Speech will vary as the tasks within the register vary, since the dimensions of "task," or "purpose," are not simple ones. Just as situational features influence the interpretation that hearers place on language features (cf. Gallois & Callan, this volume, Chapter 9), speakers can adapt the formal characteristics even of such highly specific registers as baby talk, to suit the requirements of a particular situation.

It is indeed remarkable that registers, themselves highly specialized adaptations of that elusive abstraction "normal" speech, can be so sensitive to the functions of situations such as, for example, the pre- and postoperative encounters studied here. No doubt many other features of speech (paralinguistic characteristics, for example) would show situational variability similar to the pattern found in our data. Our findings are also consistent with the notion that communication between children and their caretakers is based on shared interaction formats that not only facilitate language acquisition (see Bruner, this volume, Chapter 2), but continue to play a subtle role in influencing exchanges throughout childhood. The situational influences on the baby-talk register found here are thus entirely consistent with the accumulating evidence for the role that situations play in regulating discourse throughout our lives (cf. van Dijk, and Hoppe-Graff, Hermann, Winterhoff-Spurk, & Mangold, this volume, Chapters 4 and 5).

Acknowledgments. We are indebted to the Spencer Foundation for their support of this research. We wish to thank Jan Vorster for useful comments on the chapter and a number of people who helped with the research: Dr. Marshall Strome, Fredi Shonkoff, Kathy Lee, Kathryn Immler, Judy Kim, and Patricia Phillips.

References

Brown, R., & Gilman, A. (1960). The pronouns of power and solidarity. In T. A. Sebeok (Ed.), *Style in language* (pp. 253–276). New York: Wiley.

Brown, R. (1977). Introduction. In C. E. Snow & C. A. Ferguson (Eds.), *Talking to children*. Cambridge: Cambridge University Press.

Clyne, M. G. (Ed.) (1981). Foreigner talk. *International Journal of the Sociology of Language*, Serial No. 28.

Ferguson, C. A. (1964). Baby talk in six languages. *American Anthropologist, 66*, 103–114.

Hirsh-Pasek, K., & Treiman, R. (1982). Doggerel: Motherese in a new context. *Journal of Child Language, 9*, 229–237.

Hudson, R. A. (1980). *Sociolinguistics*. Cambridge: Cambridge University Press.

Levin, H., & Hunter, W. A. (1982). Children's use of a social speech register: Age and sex differences. *Journal of Language and Social Psychology, 1*, 63–72.

Levin, H., Snow, C., & Lee, K. (1984). Nurturant talk to children. *Journal of Language and Speech, 27*, 147–162.

Part II

Psychological Factors in Situated Language Use

Chapter 4
Cognitive Situation Models in Discourse Production: The Expression of Ethnic Situations in Prejudiced Discourse

Teun A. van Dijk

Introduction

The impressive advances in psychology and artificial intelligence of the past decade in the field of discourse processing have, among many other findings, resulted in the important recognition that understanding discourse not only presupposes knowledge of the language, but also knowledge of the world. The understanding and cognitive representation of social situations in particular are a crucial component of the processes of discourse production and comprehension. This volume bears witness to the growing importance attached to this assumption in several disciplines. There seems to be an emerging consensus among many researchers that the construction of *models* in memory, linking situation representations to discourse processing, promises to be the most fruitful approach to this issue. Yet we still know very little about the nature and the uses of such memory models. In this chapter, we shall show how cognitive models of social situations are related to the production of discourse, and we shall illustrate the practical usefulness of this approach by analyzing a discourse domain of great social importance: everyday talk about minority groups.

Establishing an explicit relationship between social situations, cognition, and discourse requires an interdisciplinary approach. Notions from cognitive and social psychology, microsociology, and discourse analysis are needed. In particular, the theoretical background of this chapter will include the following research areas: (1) *a cognitive theory of strategic information processing*, which emphasizes the strategic nature of discourse production and comprehension as a flexible, multiple-level, and on-line process (van Dijk & Kintsch, 1983); (2) *a sociocognitive theory of discourse*, which extends this strategic processing model toward an account of the role of beliefs and attitudes in discourse processing (van Dijk, 1982); (3) *social cognition and the theory of social situations*, which provides the general framework for our discussion about the cognitive dimension of such social situations (Argyle, Furnham, & Graham, 1981; Forgas, 1979, 1981; Furnham & Argyle, 1982); and finally, current research about (4) *ethnic stereotypes in cognition and conversation* (Hamilton, 1981a; Tajfel, 1981, 1982). In earlier work we have developed, against this background, a sociocognitive theory of the representation and the structure of ethnic prejudice and its strategic expression in everyday discourse (van Dijk, 1983b, 1984a). In the present chapter we want to further develop the assumption that (ethnic) situation models play a prominent role in the memory organization of ethnic beliefs and opinions, as well as in their expression in conversation. We thus hope to be able to answer the question of how people perceive, understand, and memorize ethnic encounters, and how such information is "reproduced" in talk.

Our empirical data will be drawn from a large set of nondirected interviews with (white) Dutch people from several neighborhoods in Amsterdam. The topic of talk in these interviews was groups of people considered "foreigners" in the Netherlands, specifically, immigrant workers from Mediterranean countries (mostly Turkey and Morocco) and people from the former Dutch colony of Surinam (adjacent to Guyana). These groups form a prominent issue of thought and talk among the dominant majority, and are victims to rapidly expanding prejudice and discrimination. Although there are several sources for this ethnic prejudice, such as the subtly negative portrayal of minorities in the media (van Dijk, 1983a), many stereotypes seem to be communicated through informal everyday conversation. This study, thus, tries to probe deeper into the sociocognitive mechanisms that underlie the perception, the representation, and the attitudes about such groups, and the ways that these become strategically expressed in talk and thus shared throughout society.

Situation Models in Memory

Recent developments in psycholinguistics and in cognitive theories of discourse processing have proposed that semantic *models* in memory play an important role in understanding (Johnson-Laird, 1983; van Dijk, in press; van Dijk & Kintsch, 1983). This assumption has been influenced by the notion of a "model" in formal linguistics and logic, which constitutes the basis of interpretation rules. Such formal models are, so to speak, representations of fragments of the world with respect to which expressions are meaningful, or may be assigned a truth value. The psychological correlate of this notion are models in episodic memory (therefore also called "episodic models"). They function as partial, subjective, and relevant cognitive mappings of the real world, and hence also of social situations. We therefore also call such models "situation models." Instead of "real" world fragments or situations, the cognitive models provide the referential basis for the interpretation of discourse. Their localization in episodic memory suggests that models are integrated structures of previous experiences of individuals. They represent the personal knowledge and beliefs of people about concrete events and situations. This means, also, that models are the experiential basis for more general and abstract "frames" or "scripts" in (semantic) memory, as they have been discussed in much recent work since Schank and Abelson's (1977) influential book. Our notion of a model is close to what Schank (1982) now calls a "script," but in order to avoid confusion, we will use the notion of script only in its more abstract, general, and decontextualized sense. Subjective situation models not only feature knowledge about concrete events, but also beliefs and opinions (evaluative beliefs). Finally, models may have an analogical nature, that is, embody spatial or other figural properties of events and situations.

In earlier theories of discourse understanding (e.g., Kintsch & van Dijk, 1978), it was assumed that the main aim of comprehension is the gradual construction of a *textual* representation in episodic memory. We now assume that *in addition* to such a representation, people also construct a model of what the text "is about," that is, of some situation. In fact, the model becomes the major aim of the understanding process, and the textual representation is mostly only a means toward that end. In reality, reproduction of texts often means the retrieval and reproduction of model fragments, especially if specific semantic representations of a text are no longer retrievable. In general, then, information acquisition and use involve the updating and other transformations of episodic models.

A distinction is made between *particular* and *general* models. Particular models represent unique information about one specific situation, for instance the one "now" being processed. General models may combine information from several particular models about the "same" or the same "kind" of situation. Particular models may contain the "new" information with which general models are updated. Thus, Schank's (1982) process of "reminding" may involve the retrieval of a previous particular model, *or* the retrieval of a general model about a situation that is "recognized."

General models that appear to be socially relevant may be transformed to *frames* or *scripts* in semantic ("social") memory, for example by further abstraction, generalization, and decontextualization. Hence, we now have a gradual transition from personal, particular models, via more general models, to socially shared general frames or scripts.

We may also have models about future situations. Planning is the construction of such models from previous model fragments, together with general information about action structures, our abilities, and our motivations and goals.

Some Characteristics of Situation Models

Once we know what models are used for, we need to attend to the question of their structural representation: What do they look like? Answers to that question must satisfy some general requirements. First, they should allow fast, effective, and relevant representation and retrieval of information about (social) situations. Second, if models are to become the basis of frames and scripts, they should have patterns that are similar to those of scripts. Third, operations such as updating, or other transformations, must be easy to apply to models.

The structural setup of models that we propose is a *categorial* one. The skeleton of a model, then, is a schema consisting of a number of fixed categories. Such a schema will be strategically effective in our continuing task of understanding social situations. From such situations we tend to process specific "kinds" of information, and these "kinds of information" will be stored in the respective categories of the schema (see Argyle et al., 1981; Forgas, 1979; and Furnham and Argyle, 1982, for surveys about similar and other proposals for the structure of social situations). Forgas (1979) proposes that social situations are interpreted and memorized especially in terms of their affective dimensions: "pleasant," "formal," or "dangerous." Such an approach is not inconsistent with a more structural conception of models. Scalar, affective dimensions can be represented conceptually as part of models—in a Modifier category, for example, attached to each category. This may be the case for the "situation as a whole," that is, for the highest node, but also for lower-level categories (e.g., actor or event).

It follows that we distinguish between *global* and *local* levels of representation, or between *macro-* and *microstructures* (van Dijk, 1980a). Such a hierarchical organization allows fast and effective search, as well as relevant uses, which satisfies the requirements we have formulated above.

Our categorial approach is similar to the componential analysis proposed by Argyle et al. (1981). They "analyze" situations in terms of participants, goals, rules, environmental props, and actions. But, since representations of unique situations in particular models are episodic, we locate rules in semantic (social) memory, even though social participants may know and use rules when participating in a social situation. Other research focuses on specific elements of situations; Barker (1968), for instance, pays specific attention to behavior types and settings. Our concern, however, is to specify which *cognitive* categories are involved in the understanding and representation of, or the participation in, social situations. Evidence for such a cognitive representation may be drawn from various sources, ranging from direct observations, personal accounts, and interviewing, to experimentally controlled judgmental tasks (such as sorting and rating). Besides these psychological approaches, there is also evidence from the microsociological analysis of situations, such as the account of strategies of interaction by Goffman (1959, 1967).

Linguistic Evidence

There is also linguistic evidence about the hypothetical structures of models in memory. Language users produce sentences and discourse in order to describe situations. It is therefore plausible that grammatical and discourse structures may indicate some features of models. This will also allow listeners to reconstruct effectively the contents and the organization of an "intended" model. Thus, functional grammar (Dik, 1978) assumes that sentences have semantic representations featuring a category of a central predicate (denoting an action, event, process, or state) and a number of participants that may serve in various "roles," such as Agent, Patient, Object, or Instrument. These semantic roles may be indicated by cases or word order in sentential syntax. Thus, Agents tend to be expressed as subjects, and often in early (topical) positions in the sentence.

Similar observations may be made for the organization of discourse. Thus, Labov (1972) has shown that stories may exhibit conventional categories such as Setting, Complication, Resolution, Evaluation, and Coda. Some of these categories correspond to the structural features of models of situations in memory. Indeed, stories *are* (partial, relevant) expressions of such models, although they will specifically select "interesting" experiences and not models of any situation we have witnessed. In general, then, there are not only cognitive constraints on sentences and discourse, but also pragmatic, contextual, communicative, or interactional ones.

In artificial-intelligence research about stories, as well as in so-called "story grammar" approaches in psychology, various cognitive correlates have been suggested for story structures and their understanding (Bruce, 1980; Wilensky, 1978; and the papers collected in van Dijk, 1980b). Essentially, stories in this work tend to be analyzed in terms of the action structures they denote: plans, goals, and their participants.

From these various sources of evidence, we may now conclude that models (1) are hierarchical, categorial structures of propositions, forming a strategically effective "schema," and (2) that the categories involve, Setting (Time, Location, Environment, Conditions), Participants in various roles, and Events or Actions, each with a possible Modifier category, specifying a subjective evaluation.

Strategic Uses of Models

Structural representations are only half of the answer to the question about the nature of situation models. We also need to specify the operations, and in particular the *strategies*, that apply to such model structures. For instance, high-level macro-organization of models allows level-dependent search. Sometimes only the most important information of a model is necessary, for instance when we summarize a situation (or a story about such a situation). The different categories, then, allow us to selectively retrieve models by specific Time, Location, or Participant cues. In addition, recent work on mood and memory (e.g., Bower, 1980) has shown that we may even selectively retrieve experiences by emotion cues: We can better recall "pleasant" events, for example, when we are in a "pleasant" mood.

Current attribution theory (e.g., Jaspars, Fincham, & Hewstone, 1983), following the earlier ideas of Heider (1958), also implies some suggestions about the strategic uses of models. Thus, people may view and memorize situations either from an observer or an actor "point of view," or they may explain actions by attributing them to "internal"—motivational or personality—characteristics of the actor, or by attributing them to situational or environmental forces. Such naive analyses of action by participants is possible only when they make such differences also in their models of the situation. This also means that people not only use model schemata, but also more general action, event, and person "theories" in the understanding of situations (cf. Hastie et al., 1980). Depending on the kind of task involved (understanding an explanation, for example), people may attend to different features of models, such as the internal organization of the component categories (Setting, Participants, or Action).

Situation Models in Discourse Production

Whereas much of our earlier work on discourse processing has focused on comprehension (van Dijk & Kintsch, 1983), we shall here deal with discourse *production*. We do so against the background of the framework sketched above. That is, we view production essentially as a process originating in situation models. Depending on a number of constraints, language users, so to speak, "read off" relevant propositions from their situation models, and thus construct the semantic representations, or "text base," that underlie a discourse. We ignore surface structure formation, such as processes of lexicalization and syntactic formulation (Butterworth, 1980).

What are the major components of this theory of discourse production?

The Context Model

Of course, discourse production does not take place in a vacuum, but is an integral part of a communicative context. For speakers to be able to fit what they say into this context, they must also have a memory representation of that context, that is a *context model*. This model contains information about the speech participants and their goals, and about the type of social situation involved (e.g., breakfast, a doctor's visit, or a parliamentary debate). The context model controls style but also content, and hence *what* information may or must be retrieved from the situation model. Some topics are forbidden in some situations. Hence, context models monitor the strategic searches through episodic memory (what models are relevant?) as well as within models (what information about the situation should be mentioned?).

The Control System

This contextual information will at least partly be stored in an overall *Control System*. This system regulates the flow of information between short-term memory and long-term memory. It specifies what kind of models and scripts must be activated and which of their fragments must actually be retrieved for production. CS will also feature the actual *topic(s)* being talked about, and these macropropositions may act as retrieval cues in the search for relevant situation models, which—as we have seen before—are also dominated by macropropositions. In addition, CS contains the kind of *speech act* and communicative goals which must be accomplished by the utterance of a discourse in a given context (e.g., assertion, threat, or accusation), both at the local level of individual speech acts, or at the global level of "macro-speech acts" that control a longer stretch of discourse (van Dijk, 1977, 1980a, 1981).

Finally, the Control System features information about the *type of text* to be produced. Depending on context and communicative goals, we may want to produce a story or a police report about a situation, a news story, or a scientific report. Obviously, text type will control the style and the overall organization, but also the possible contents of a discourse, and hence the information to be drawn from the model about a situation. A story about a theft may focus on my personal predicament and evaluations, whereas a police report may focus on the identity (appearance) of the thief or on particulars of the stolen goods. In other words, search, activation, use, and semantic (re)construction of model information are all strategically monitored by the overall control of the Control System.

Semantic Production

The semantic production of discourse takes place under the constraints formulated above and involves the construction of a semantic representation for a discourse, that is, of a "text base." The information included in such a text base is mostly drawn from situation models, although in addition, more general knowledge, as well as information about the context, may be included (as in metacommunicative statements, which specify fragments of the context model). Text-base production is a strategic process. It takes place on-line, with continuous input from activated and retrieved situation models, but under top-down control from Control System information, such as actual or general topics of a discourse. Given a context and text type dependent topic (e.g., after a question of a previous speaker), the actual speaker will use the topic as a search cue to look for relevant models that are subsumed under such a topic. Activation may be partial, because only part of a model may be relevant. In a conversation about holiday experiences, for instance, the topic "I was in Spain last year" may activate only specific models or model fragments (e.g., "It was nice at the beach"), whereas in the context of a business talk or a job interview, one would be more likely to address his or her professional experiences in Spain. Hence, a contextually relevant (sub)topic may be chosen or constructed, and that will act as the topic of discourse, which is the macroproposition that guides semantic production.

Another important feature of the semantic production process is that the semantic text base need not be as complete as the model. In principle, each proposition that can be inferred by the hearer from other (model or script) information can be "deleted." The text base will therefore include only the information that is necessary and *relevant* in the actual context (van Dijk, 1979), although, of course, spontaneous talk may include apparently "superfluous" (repeated, inferrable) information. There are, however, strategic boundaries to this form of "overcompleteness." In a story about a restaurant, for instance, it would be strange in most cases if the speaker would express the presupposed knowledge that there was a waiter/waitress working there. Designation by definite description is enough, given model and script knowledge (Schank & Abelson, 1977).

Macroproduction

Thematical macropropositions, we suggested, may be "read off" the top of situation models, but we also assumed that specific text and context constraints can modify such topics. That is, topics may actually need to be *constructed*. Indeed, in telling a story about a theft to our friends, we may focus on different aspects of the situation than what was given in a report to the police about "the same events." The same will hold for the police report production itself. These constraints may also influence the (1) hierarchical organization of topics (some information may be "upgraded" in relevance during production), and (2) the linear ordering—sometimes thematic "causes" may be expressed later than they figure in a model, for example, in explanations. Thus, in crime stories the identity of a murderer may only be revealed at the end, and similar suspense-enhancing production strategies exist in everyday stories as well.

In much the same way, macropropositions must fill *schematic categories*, for example, of a narrative or an argument. This means that text type may determine which topical information must come "first," as with Setting information in a story.

Microproduction

The production of the actual sequence of (micro)propositions of a text base takes place under the overall control of topical (macro)propositions. This process is also on-line, generally speaking, although some local reordering is possible. A first principle (and problem) is linearization (Levelt, 1982): Which information should come first? We assume that the model may guide the strategic moves in local semantic production, in that first propositions in the model will become first propositions in the text base. This is a case of "normal ordering." Yet transformations may be called for under various—pragmatic, cognitive, rhetorical, communicative—constraints (mentioning B before A may be more effective, relevant, elegant, subtle, polite, etc.). Next, propositions in a sequence must be linearly coherent (van Dijk, 1977). This means that they should denote related "facts" as represented in the model, such as relations of condition/cause and consequence. Besides this conditional coherence, however, "functional" coherence may also be established. This is the case if two subsequent propositions A and B are related by "generalization," "contrast," "example," "repetition," and so on. Finally, the now locally and globally coherent sequence of propositions may be partially reordered due to local differences in relevance, presupposition, topic/comment, or focusing (foreground/background) operations. The actual expression in clauses, complex sentences, or sentence sequences is a function of these local semantic constraints (van Dijk, 1981). Also, the surface syntax (word order, cases, etc.) and intonation, which we don't analyze here, will further signal these operations (Givón, 1979). This means, indirectly, that surface structures also depend on the strategies that transform model information into a semantic text base.

The Expression of Ethnic Prejudice

To illustrate the theoretical assumptions made in the previous sections, we shall analyze in somewhat more detail a specific type of social situation and a specific type of discourse: ethnic encounters and everyday talk about ethnic minorities. This analysis takes place within the framework of an ongoing, interdisciplinary project at the University of Amsterdam. Research in this project has two major aims: to develop an explicit cognitive theory of ethnic attitudes (and of prejudice in particular), and to empirically analyze the ways that people talk about ethnic groups and may thus express such prejudice in everyday conversation. Unlike the prevailing experimental approaches to ethnic stereotypes, we obtain our data from informal interviews with (white) majority members. In this final section we want to account for some properties of these data in terms of the cognitive notion of a situation model. If situations in general are perceived, understood, and represented as episodic models, we may assume that this is also the case for the kind of situations we here call "ethnic encounters." People will routinely engage in talk about such encounters. And by analyzing, for instance, their stories about their experiences with ethnic minority members, we at the same time may get more insight into the representation of social situations in general, and into the—possibly prejudiced—representation of ethnic encounters in particular.

Our discussion in this section will focus on these cognitive representations and the strategies operating in them. Less attention will be paid to the discourse characteristics of prejudiced talk, which have been reported elsewhere (van Dijk, 1983b, 1984a). Discourse about minorities is influenced not only by underlying cognitive attitudes, but also by communicative and interactional strategies. We have found, for instance, that talk about minorities is highly strategic: On the one hand people want to express possibly negative experiences or evaluations, but on the other hand social norms force them to make a good impression, and not appear as racists. These sometimes conflicting strategies of self-expression and positive self-presentation (face-keeping) can be witnessed in many semantic moves, stylistic choices, rhetorical devices, and conversational elements (such as pauses, repairs, corrections, or false starts). Part of the properties of talk on the other hand may be interpreted as observable "signals" of ongoing cognitive strategies for the management of "delicate" beliefs and opinions.

Ethnic Attitudes

Ethnic prejudice is considered here to be a predominantly negative social attitude about ethnic minority groups and their members. Although this characterization has a cognitivistic flavor, it should be emphasized that such prejudices are not just personal or individual beliefs, but shared attitudes of a (dominant) social group, and embedded in historical, economic, or socio-cultural frameworks as they characterize our "north-western" societies. Although we are not concerned here with these social or societal constraints on ethnic attitudes, it should be borne in mind that the acquisition, the "uses" or the enactment of prejudice, and therefore also their cognitive organization and strategic management, are a function of group interactions within a social context. This means that we try to combine and further develop research results from both the American and the European paradigms in research about ethnic stereotypes and intergroup relations, as they are represented, for example, by the work of Hamilton et al. (Hamilton, 1981a), and Tajfel and his associates (cf. Tajfel, 1978, 1981, 1982), respectively. Earlier definitions and research about ethnic prejudice cannot be gone into here, but serve as historical background (Allport, 1954; Ehrlich, 1973; Katz, 1976; among many other publications). Although our own perspective on prejudice may be localized in the new area of "social cognition" (Forgas, 1981; Higgins, Herman, & Zanna, 1981), our overall impression of this line of research is that on the one hand it is not cognitive enough, and on the other hand it is not social enough—a well-known predicament of social psychology, which also extends into research about ethnic prejudice.

If we take ethnic prejudice as a specific kind of social attitude, we need a sound theory of attitudes as a starting point. Disregarding for a moment the vast social psychological literature about attitudes of the past fifty years or so, we essentially view attitudes as complex cognitive frameworks of socially relevant beliefs and opinions (Abelson, 1976; van Dijk, 1982). Just like frames or scripts, they have a schematic organization, and are located in semantic (or rather, "social") memory. Opinions are taken to be evaluative beliefs, and an attitude basically consists of a hierarchical configuration of general opinions. Particular or personal opinions characterize episodic memory structures, such as situation models. Indeed, both our theory and our data suggest that opinions expressed in talk about ethnic minorities may find their origin either in general attitude schemata or in episodic situation models. Obviously, much of the information that is absent in situation models (due, for instance, to a lack of personal experiences with ethnic minority group members) may be filled in by instantiation from the general, socially shared attitudes. This is precisely what happens, and we here witness one of the *strategies* that define ethnic prejudice. In other words, prejudice should not only be explained in terms of the representations (schematic structures, categories, and contents) of attitudes and situation models, but also by the dynamic processes operating in the actual use of such information in concrete processes of talk and interaction in the social context.

Ethnic attitudes are organized by a number of fundamental categories, defining the *attitude schema*. Such a schema will be used in the acquisition or transformation of new attitudes. The categories involve the origin or appearance of ethnic groups or group members, their socioeconomic position, their sociocultural characteristics, and their attributed personal properties. These categories are not arbitrary, but derive from social interaction and perception among groups, and represent those central information "organizers" that are relevant for a dominant group. Crucially, ethnic prejudice is represented in "negative" attitudes. This means that negative opinions dominate the higher levels of an attitude. Obviously, ethnic attitudes are not only inferred from other attitudes or from meta-attitude schemata, but also from concrete experiences, that is, from the subjective representation of such experiences in ethnic situation models, on which we shall focus in the remainder of this chapter.

Ethnic Situation Models

Episodic models of ethnic situations embody the subjective experiences of social members in interethnic encounters. They represent both the understanding and the evaluation of such encounters. We use the term "interpretation" to denote the integrated process of subjective understanding and evaluation. New situations will be interpreted as a function of both general situation models, construed on the basis of previous experiences, as well as under the influence of general, stereotypical attitudes. For prejudiced social members, the overall evaluation of such new, particular situations typically will be negative, due to the prevailing negative content of the general models and attitudes. And if the new ethnic situation is also negatively represented in episodic memory, it will confirm previous knowledge, beliefs, and opinions. There is substantial experimental evidence for this kind of "biased" social perception (see Hamilton, 1981a, for surveys). Acts of ethnic minority members are "seen" as more negative (Duncan, 1976), and people also tend to have better memory for negative acts of minority members. In general, majority members establish "illusory correlations" when interpreting ethnic social situations (Hamilton, 1979, 1981b; Hamilton & Rose, 1980). Our own data bear witness and specify details about such processes. For instance, negative properties of one aspect of the social situation, such as the neighborhood or poor housing, will be transferred to a prominent minority group in that situation. Of course, this is only one strategy of prejudiced information processing (intuitively known also as "scapegoating"), and in order to get an explicit picture, the full structures and cognitive operations involved must be made explicit. Situation models are crucial in such an account, and not (only) stereotypical schemata (attitudes). If people use information about a concrete event for talk or further action, they will draw upon their models of such an event. The presence of, for instance, negative opinions as macropropositions in the hierarchy of a situation model, then, explains why recall of negative aspects of a situation may be better, or why negative concepts are more easily "available."

The strategies involved in ethnic model building by prejudiced social members are geared toward such a negative organization of situation models in memory. The strategy of "transfer" has been mentioned as an example above: a negative evaluation of the setting, the environment, events, or actions in a situation may be transferred to minority participants in the situation. Similarly, top-down and bottom-up strategies may "spread" overall negative situations downward to specific participants, or specific negative dimensions assigned to an action property may be "pushed up" to characterize the participant from an ethnic group. "Missing actors," as in representations of criminal events, may be inserted (with minority participants), given the instantiations of the ethnic attitude.

Storytelling About Ethnic Groups

Majority group members regularly engage in storytelling about minorities and ethnic encounters. This also was the case in our informal interview data. In a selected 50 interviews (from a total of about 130 interviews), we found 133 stories about "foreigners." These stories are interesting for our discussion, because we define a story simply as a discourse expression of a situation model, that is, of a situation model featuring events and actions of the storyteller that for any reason are "interesting" for the listener (see Ehlich, 1980; Labov, 1972; Polanyi, 1985; Quasthoff, 1980, for various discourse characteristics of such everyday stories). Hence, stories about minorities may reveal properties of ethnic situation models in memory. Other elements of stories are, of course, geared toward the accomplishment of social goals, such as effective performance, interesting the listener, self-presentation, or persuasion (see van Dijk, 1983b and 1984, for detail).

Basically, stories are composed of a Setting and an Episode. This Episode usually consists of some kind of Complication and a Resolution. In addition, a (mostly) discontinuous Evaluation will accompany the description of events and actions, featuring the personal evaluations of the storyteller concerning the events or participants. Stories about minorities, however, seem to have a rather remarkable feature. As shown in Table 4-1, the more or less obligatory

Table 4-1. Narrative Categories and Their Frequencies in Stories About Minorities

Inter-views	N story-tellers	N stories	Occa-sioning	Sum-mary	Setting	Orien-tation	Compli-cation
Group I	20	50	22 (44%)	6 (12%)	50 (100%)	21 (42%)	50 (100%)
Group II	30	83	22 (27%)	9 (11%)	81 (98%)	45 (54%)	81 (98%)
Total	50	133	44 (33%)	15 (11.3%)	131 (98.5%)	66 (49.6%)	131 (98.5%)

Inter-views	Reso-lution	Evalu-ation	Expli-cation	Conclu-sion	Stories/teller	N of cate-gories/story
Group I	24 (48%)	33 (66%)	13 (26%)	17 (34%)	2½	4.7
Group II	48 (58%)	49 (59%)	20 (24%)	27 (32%)	2¾	4.6
Total	72 (54.1%)	82 (61.6%)	33 (24.8%)	44 (33.0%)	2⅔	4.7

Note: Stories in interviews of Group II were explicitly elicited.

category of the Resolution is absent in nearly half of the stories. This means that in the model of situations told about, people have stored some (mostly negative) event or action by minority members, but not "what they have done about it." That is, people see ethnic situations as a narratable kind of event—not in order to account for their own positive actions (there are few "hero stories"), but rather to complain about the actions of the outgroup. Resolution actions mostly are about efforts to deal with the "predicament," such as protests or complaints, but they often fail. Institutional agents, such as the government or the police, are usually represented as ineffective: "They don't/can't do anything about that." The resulting "picture," that is, the situation model, is clear: Minority members are represented—across situations—as threats to our norms, values, economic interests, or personal safety and well-being. The ingroup members are represented as victims. Indeed, storytellers will strategically make sure that the correct interpretation (hence the desired model) is conveyed to the listener, by emphasizing that they themselves cannot possibly be blamed for the negative events or actions of others. The Evaluation and Conclusion categories will guarantee not only that the events are portrayed as they see them, but also that they are evaluated according to shared and accepted norms ("We are not used to that kind of thing" or "we don't do such things"). The macro-topics in stories about minorities, then, can be summarized as aggression (crime, fights, violence), everday harassment (smells, noise, dirt), and strange habits (clothing, cooking, living, family structure, and behavior). Such stories are told especially in neighborhoods where everyday contacts with minority members take place. In other neighborhoods people will predominantly give more general opinions. Thus, stories can be differentiated according to their model-based or their attitude-based nature.

From these few observations we may conclude first that ethnic situation models are organized by high-level negative (macro-)opinions. Second, these evaluations will focus on the ethnic minority participants. Third, due to the attitude, a selected number of relevant topics are chosen: aggression, harassment, and cultural differences. Fourth, evaluations pertain to the general "difference" or "threat" that minorities are perceived to represent for the ingroups's norms, values, habits, or beliefs. Fifth, ingroup members tend to be represented as victims.

This kind of model may become standardized. It is not only reproduced in stereotypical stories, but also in reports in the media about prejudices and "experiences" of ingroup members. This generalization of very specific models in turn may "confirm" the ethnic attitude, and will monitor the interpretation of new situations.

Some of these features of ethnic situation models may be observed in two sample stories from our data (see Appendix). Both are about a central feature of ethnic situation models. In the first story, black neighbors (from Surinam) are represented as violent and as deviant in other respects (as regarding noise). There is no successful Resolution in this story, and while the second story has a Resolution episode (help is supplied by the storyteller and her husband for a black neighbor's wife), it also conveys negative reactions on the part of the neighbor and the lack of help from the authorities. Notice that both stories feature the elements of social situations discussed above: *Time* (weekend, New Year's Eve), *Location* (house of storyteller), *Circumstances* (routine activities of storyteller), special ("complicating") *Events*, and *Participants* and their local or overall evaluations as *Modifiers*.

Apart from the specific contents of ethnic situation models (negative actions and evaluations of minority members), there is also a specific structural dimension that characterizes such models: the opposition of WE-group and THEY-group members. This organization reflects the intergroup conflict as experienced by WE-group members, and at the same time represents the different *perspective* on ethnic situations. Style, pronouns, rhetorical devices, and story structures express this group opposition and perspective, as is evident in the first story: WE had to get up early, while THEY could throw parties late at night. An example of a situation model embodying this kind of "biased" information is given in Figure 4-1.

Stories also suggest how ethnic situation models are accessed. Often, a story is told as "evidence" after a general, negative statement is made about minorities. Apparently, the general statement serves as a topical search cue for relevant situation models. The topic of the story itself, then, may be expressed in an initial Summary, which also may contain an overall Evaluation. This suggests that an evaluative category is present high in the ethnic situation model, as is also suggested by Forgas (1979) for situation interpretations and memory in general. Next, model actualization in the story follows the

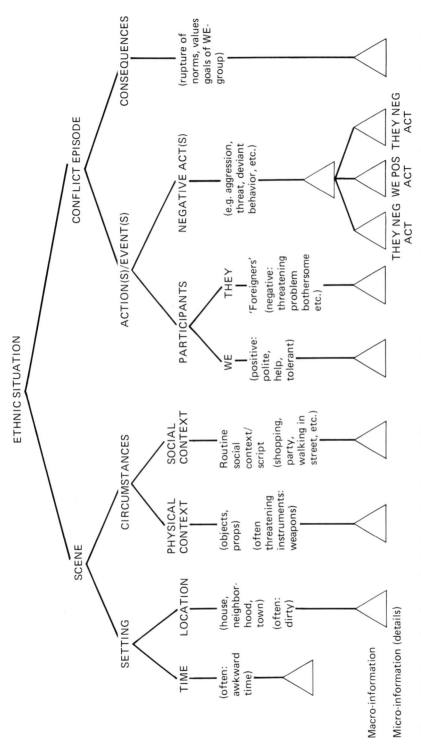

Figure 4-1. Example of a typical ethnic situation model in memory. Each category dominates sequences of macropropositions that dominate sequences of (detailed) micropropositions. At each node, modifiers may also dominate evaluative propositions (personal opinions). The situational model is organized both by the model schema and its categories, by hierarchical macro-micro ordering of propositions, and by local (temporal, conditional) ordering at each propositional level.

principles outlined before: from top to bottom and from left to right, although special-effort reorderings are possible. In other words, model expression in narrative is an interplay between model structures and strategies, and between narrative and conversational constraints.

Conclusions

In this chapter we have first argued that social situations are represented in episodic memory as models. These models are construed as the result of understanding and evaluating events in social situations. They act as the personal, experiential basis for the formation of frames, scripts, or attitudes. Models embody the knowledge and beliefs of language users, which underlie their understanding and production of discourse. They are the "starting point" for the production of discourse, and thus provide the information that may be used (or must remain implicit) in the generation of the semantic text base of a discourse. Strategies are used for the search, retrieval, and selection of information from situation models. Evidence from various sources has been considered about the structural organization of situation models. This structure is hierarchical and categorical, and features such elements as Setting, Circumstances, Participants, and Event or Action. The process of model formation and use is monitored by the Control System, which among other "central" information contains macropropositions (topics), and a Context Model, representing the major dimensions of the communicative context.

Second, we have applied this theoretical framework to an account of ethnic prejudice and its expression in discourse. Thus, we are able to link ethnic encounters, via subjective (and biased) representations in models, to general ethnic attitudes. Evidence from natural storytelling about minorities was used to speculate about the specific nature of "ethnic situation models" and the strategies for their use in intergroup (WE vs. THEY) encounters or the intragroup diffusion of prejudice through everyday conversation.

Appendix

(1) (D2) (About Surinamese Neighbors)

Well, look when we have to get up Monday morning at seven to go to work, and they are still having parties Sunday morning at five, then that is not exactly nice, you see, and that was not just once, and not twice, that happened all the time, and when one went upstairs to ask politely, if they could be somewhat more quiet, one could get a knife in one's back ... that is, my husband, I wouldn't go upstairs for all the gold in the world ... I was sitting with my children in the middle of the night in the living room, because we couldn't sleep, and *my* husband works and my neighbors did not work, so they could have parties ...

(2) (D4) (About Surinamese Neighbors)

That Surinamese women who lives downstairs, she was nice and he too in a way, but well, look to have yourself beaten up ... It was New Year's Eve and they had a party and I don't know what happened but she wanted to do something he didn't like, changing a record or something like that, and then a bottle of gin was thrown at her head, one of those stone bottles, she had quite a gash in her forehead, and then we came home in the middle of the night and then she showed it to my husband and says I am not allowed to go to the police, and I am not allowed to go the hospital, nothing, otherwise he beats me up again, and so in the morning my husband took her to the police station, and he said they should come back in the afternoon, he couldn't make even a report, so that she could file a complaint, and in the hospital it was too late to put stitches in her head, so now she has this dent in her head. Well, such small things ...

References

Abelson, R. P. (1976). Script processing in attitude formation and decision making. In J. S. Carroll & J. W. Payne (Eds.), *Cognition and social behavior* (pp. 33–46). Hillsdale, NJ: Erlbaum.

Allport, G. W. (1954). *The nature of prejudice*. Reading, MA: Addison-Wesley.

Argyle, M., Furnham, A., & Graham, J. A. (1981). *Social situations*. London: Cambridge University Press.

Barker, R. G. (1968). *Ecological psychology*. Standford, CA: Stanford University Press.

Bower, G. H. (1980). Mood and memory. *American Psychologist, 36*, 129–148.

Bruce, B. C. (1980). Plans and social actions. In R. J. Spiro et al. (Eds.), *Theoretical issues in reading comprehension* (pp. 367–384). Hillsdale, NJ: Erlbaum.

Butterworth, B. (Ed.). (1980). *Language production*. London: Academic Press.

van Dijk, T. A. (1977). *Text and context*. London: Longman.

van Dijk, T. A. (1979). Relevance assignment in discourse comprehension. *Discourse Processes, 2*, 113–126.

van Dijk, T. A. (1980a). *Macrostructures*. Hillsdale, NJ: Erlbaum.

van Dijk, T. A. (Ed.). (1980b). Story comprehension. *Poetics, 9*, nrs. 1/3 (special issue).

van Dijk, T. A. (1981). *Studies in the pragmatics of discourse*. The Hague: Mouton.

van Dijk, T. A. (1982). Opinions and attitudes in discourse comprehension. In W. Kintsch & J. F. LeNy (Eds.), *Language and comprehension* (pp. 35–51). Amsterdam: North Holland.

van Dijk, T. A. (1983a). *Minderheden in de media* (Minorities in the media). Amsterdam: Socialistische Uitgeverij Amsterdam.

van Dijk, T. A. (1983b). Cognitive and conversational strategies in the expression of ethnic prejudice. *Text, 3*, 375–404.

van Dijk, T. A. (1984). *Prejudice in discourse*. Amsterdam: Benjamins.

van Dijk, T. A. (in press). Episodic models in discourse processing. In R. Horowitz & S. J. Samuels (Eds.), *Comprehending oral and written language*. New York: Academic Press.

van Dijk, T. A., & Kintsch, W. (1983). *Strategies of discourse comprehension.* New York: Academic Press.

Dik, S. C. (1978). *Functional grammar.* Amsterdam: North Holland.

Duncan, B. L. (1976). Differential social perception and attribution of intergroup violence: Testing the lower limits of stereotyping of blacks. *Journal of Personality and Social Psychology, 34,* 590–598.

Ehlich, K. (Ed.). (1980). *Erzählen im Alltag.* Frankfurt: Suhrkamp.

Ehrlich, H. J. (1973). *The social psychology of prejudice.* New York: Wiley.

Forgas, J. P. (1979). *Social episodes.* London: Academic Press.

Forgas, J. P. (Ed.). (1981). *Social cognition.* London: Academic Press.

Furnham, A., & Argyle, M. (Eds.). (1982). *The psychology of social situations.* London: Pergamon Press.

Givón, T. (Ed.). (1979). *Discourse and syntax.* New York: Academic Press.

Goffman, E. (1959). *The presentation of self in everyday life.* Garden City, NY: Doubleday.

Goffman, E. (1967). *Interaction ritual.* Garden City, NY: Doubleday.

Hamilton, D. (1979). A cognitive-attributional analysis of stereotyping. In L. Berkowitz (Ed.), *Advances in experimental social psychology* (Vol. 12, pp. 53–84). New York: Academic Press.

Hamilton, D. (Ed.). (1981a). *Cognitive processes in stereotyping and intergroup behavior.* Hillsdale, NJ: Erlbaum.

Hamilton, D. (1981b). Illusory correlation as a basis for stereotyping (pp. 115–144). In D. Hamilton (Ed.), *Cognitive processes in stereotyping and intergroup behavior.* Hillsdale, NJ: Erlbaum.

Hamilton, D., & Rose, T. L. (1980). Illusory correlation and the maintenance of stereotypic beliefs. *Journal of Personality and Social Psychology, 39,* 832–845.

Hastie, R. et al. (Eds.). (1980). *Person memory: The cognitive basis of social perception.* Hillsdale, NJ: Erlbaum.

Heider, F. (1958). *The psychology of interpersonal relations.* New York: Wiley.

Higgins, E. T., Herman, C. P., & Zanna, M. P. (Eds.). (1981). *Social cognition: The Ontario symposium* (Vol. 1). Hillsdale, NJ: Erlbaum.

Jaspars, J., Fincham, F. D., & Hewstone, M. (Eds.). (1983). *Attribution theory: Conceptual, developmental and social dimensions.* London: Academic Press.

Johnson-Laird, P. N. (1983). *Mental models.* London: Cambridge University Press.

Katz, P. A. (Ed.). (1976). *Towards the elimination of racism.* New York: Pergamon.

Kintsch, W., & van Dijk, T. A. (1978). Towards a model of text comprehension and production. *Psychological Review, 85,* 363–394.

Labov, W. (1972). The transformation of experience in narrative syntax. In W. Labov, *Language in the inner city* (pp. 354–396). Philadelphia: University of Pennsylvania Press.

Levelt, W. J. M. (1982). Linearization in describing spatial networks. In S. Peters & E. Saarinen (Eds.), *Processes, beliefs and questions.* Dordrecht: Reidel.

Polanyi, L. (1985). *The American story.* Norwood, NJ: Ablex.

Quasthoff, U. (1980). *Erzählen in Gesprächen.* Tübingen: Narr.

Schank, R. C. (1982). *Dynamic memory.* London: Cambridge University Press.

Schank, R. C., & Abelson, R. P. (1977). *Scripts, plans, goals and understanding.* Hillsdale, NJ: Erlbaum.

Tajfel, H. (Ed.). (1978). *Differentiation between social groups.* London: Academic Press.

Tajfel, H. (1981). *Human groups and social categories.* London: Cambridge University Press.

Tajfel, H. (Ed.). (1982). *Social identity and intergroup relations*. London: Academic Press.

Wilensky, R. (1978). Understanding goal-based stories. New Haven, CT: Dept. of Computer Science, Yale University.

Chapter 5
Speech and Situation: A General Model for the Process of Speech Production

Siegfried Hoppe-Graff, Theo Herrmann,
Peter Winterhoff-Spurk, and Roland Mangold

For a long time research on speech production[1] was the stepchild of the psychology of language. In the last few years the situation has changed. As a result of growing interest in the subject we now find general models (e.g., Chafe, 1977a; Herrmann, 1983; Schlesinger, 1977; Zammuner, 1981) as well as theoretical and empirical work on specific aspects of the production process (e.g., on the linearization problem: Ehrich & Koster, 1983; Levelt, 1981, 1982a, 1982b; Ullmer-Ehrich, 1979, 1982; on principles of sentence production: Osgood, 1980; Rosenberg, 1977; on discourse coherence: Hobbs, 1979; Marslen-Wilson, Levy, & Tyler, 1982; McCutchen & Perfetti, 1982). In this chapter we briefly describe a general approach to speech production, which is the result of theoretical and empirical work done by the "Research Group on Language and Cognition" in Mannheim, West Germany. A more detailed theoretical account of our model is given by Herrmann (1983); some of the empirical studies are presented in our research reports Nos. 10, 20, 23, 27, and 28.

We begin with the statement of the basic presuppositions and assumptions of the speech-production model. Its focus is on *situational* influences on production; therefore, the next section is on this topic. We then compare our framework with Schlesinger's (1977) production model. The last sections concern empirical tests. We have already applied the model to the production of object names, the variation in level of speech, and the production of requests and discourse production. We shall illustrate the content of the model and the logic of the empirical studies for one specific domain: the production of requests.

---

[1]We prefer to use the term "*speech* production" instead of "*language* production." This preference indicates that our interest is in what the speaker does—speech—not in the results of this activity as studies by linguists—language.

The General Model

A model is not only made up of assumptions, but is also *based* on premises that are not part of the model itself. One such "presupposition" of our production model is the premise of the *goal-directedness* of verbal utterances. That is, we assume that in a certain situation the speaker has an intention, or pursues a goal. He or she believes that the attainment of the goal demands the generation of a verbal utterance (and not a nonverbal action). For example, he or she has to tell, to request, to inform, or to ask for something. This means that we can explain each utterance by referring to specific goals that people try to pursue in a given situations. In this respect, verbal actions are not fundamentally different from nonverbal actions.

When does a speaker reach his or her goal? There are two criteria: (1) The utterance has to be understood by the hearer, and (2) it has to be comprehended in the same way as the speaker intended it. That is, the utterance has to be understood correctly and interpreted as intended by the speaker. If the hearer understands *what* the speaker meant, the utterance has fulfilled its *informative* function. If he or she comprehends *how* it was meant and reacts as anticipated by the speaker, it has fulfilled its *instrumental* function. In our view it is a basic demand upon production models to take into consideration these two communicative functions of speech.

In our general model, speech production is conceptualized as the transformation of nonverbal cognitive content into verbal utterances. This transformation can be decomposed into a multistage sequence of planning and execution processes. Figure 5-1 shows what we consider to be the central part of the production procedure.

Speech production in a certain situation "begins" with the execution of the *situation-interpreting program*. The application of the program leads to the construction of a cognitive representation of the situation. In addition to the specification of the situational parameters important for determining the utterance (e.g., features of the communicative context such as social distance between speaker and hearer), the interpretation of the situation also leads to the activation of declarative knowledge: If the situation is understood as a request situation, the knowledge required is of requests; if it is perceived as a narrative situation, then the knowledge required is of narratives, and so on. We designate this knowledge as the *propositional base* (PB) of the utterance.

It must be noted that we use the term "proposition(al)" differently from philosophers of language, especially speech-act theorists (Austin, 1962; Searle, 1969). For speech-act theorists the term refers to the *meaning* of an utterance, while we are not concerned with the meaning of a sentence or a text. In our model PB is the nonverbal cognitive prerequisite for any utterance.

PB embodies what the speaker *intends* in his or her utterance, that is, *what he wants to express*. PB also embodies what the hearer must have reconstructed from the utterance if he or she comprehends the speaker's intention.

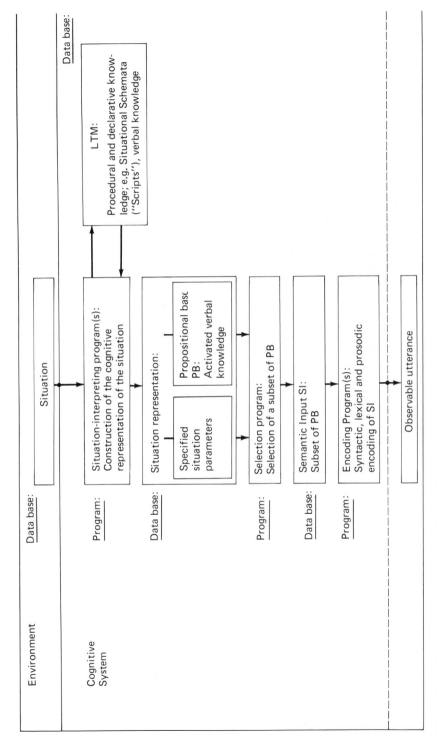

Figure 5-1. The general speech production model.

Using an expression from computer jargon we can refer to PB as the *data base* for the production processes. This data base is by nature *not verbal* but *cognitive*: It is part of our (conceptual) knowledge structures (see also Rommetveit, 1968; Selz, 1922, p. 369 ff.; Schlesinger, 1977). Therefore, utterances in different languages may have the same propositional base PB.

If a speaker tells about certain events, the hearer must be able to reconstruct the events from what is said; otherwise he or she will not understand the narration. If the speaker requests an action A it must be possible for the hearer to infer from the utterance that the speaker requested something from him or her, that the speaker wants A, that the speaker presupposes that the hearer is able to do A, and so on. In case of a request, the propositional base PB is the activated "request knowledge," and the hearer has to reconstruct this knowledge if he or she is to understand the utterance as a request.

PB is identical to what the speaker *means* and what he or she wants the hearer to comprehend. But this is not identical to what he or she *says* to the hearer: *What is meant is always "more" than what is said.* The cognitive content that directly underlies the speaker's verbal expression is called the *semantic input* (SI). SI is not the same as the utterance itself, because SI is a cognitive and not a verbal structure. The transformation of SI into the observable verbal expression takes place at the next stage of the production process (see Figure 5-1), the stage of encoding (phonetic, prosodic, syntactic, and lexical). The control structure guiding this encoding process is the encoding program.

What kinds of transformations intervene "between" PB and SI? Though this question is at the center of our interest, there is no conclusive answer at the moment. From the fact that SI is only a part (subset) of PB, it follows that one transformation has to be a *selection process*. This selection, we assume, operates by way of a selection program (see Figure 5-1). Another kind of transformation that necessarily takes place in most speech events is the linearization process, about which we will have more to say later.

A basic characteristic of speech is its strict temporal order, or "left-to-right structure" (Levelt, 1982a, p. 199). However, many domains of our world knowledge have no strict linear order per se, and can be expressed in a variety of orders. If such knowledge domains are activated as propositional base PB in the production process, the speaker has to choose the order for expressing those parts of PB that he or she selects as semantic input SI. Take, for example, a speaker who is asked to describe the layout of an apartment (a task studied by Linde and Labov, 1975). He or she is confronted with the task of mapping a two-dimensional structure, the layout, on a linear order of clauses. Till now we have restricted our model to the selection problem; for research on the linearization problem, see, for example, Ehrich and Koster (1983), Levelt (1981, 1982a); and Ullmer-Ehrich, (1979, 1982).

We may conclude that one kind of transformation that necessarily takes place "between" PB and SI is the selection of some components of PB. We call this principle the *"Pars-pro-toto principle."* What the speaker says is only part of what he or she means. He or she verbalizes pars pro toto. The implications for the hearer's comprehension process are considerable. To comprehend what the speaker means, the hearer has to (1) decode the semantic input SI from the speaker's utterance, and then (2) reconstruct on the basis of this utterance—totum ex parte—the propositional base PB. If the hearer only decodes SI, he or she understands what the speaker *says*, but *not* what the speaker *means*.

Obviously the hearer can reconstruct PB from what is said only when the following conditions are satisfied: (1) He or she can make use of knowledge structures that are sufficiently similar to the speaker's PB; (2) the speaker has selected SI in such a way that—using this input—the hearer can find that knowledge domain that corresponds to the speaker's PB.

It is not at all trivial to interpret the transformation from PB into SI as a pars-pro-toto selection of specific components from PB. Basically it would be possible to conceptualize SI as a *generalization* of PB or as an additional cognitive *construction* based on PB. Such transformation operations are, for example, part of Kintsch and van Dijk's (1978) theory of macro-operators (see also van Dijk, this volume, Chapter 4). In contrast, we assume that the transition from PB to SI can be viewed as the operation of deleting most parts from PB so that only a few (or even one) of its components remain in SI.

Within the framework of our speech-production model, we make use of the pars-pro-toto principle to predict which components of PB will be selected as SI. On a very *general* level we have already stated the selection criteria: The speaker selects a specific part of PB so as to make his utterance both informative and instrumental. But which part of PB will fulfil these criteria in the case of a concrete utterance depends on the *specific* features of the speech situation. It is the aim of our research on speech and situation to specify those situational aspects that determine the selection process; this will make it possible to predict the speaker's utterances with a certain degree of success.

Situational Influences

As a preliminary classification of situational factors determining speech production, we suggest the distinction between (1) contextual, (2) speaker-dependent, and (3) hearer-dependent influences.

If the speaker's task is to name an object in the context of other objects, the naming will depend on this object context (Herrmann & Deutsch, 1976; Olson, 1970). The object context is a situational condition that is independent from the hearer's and speaker's (communicative) actions. The above example demonstrates *contextual influences*. The fact that the speaker's actual utterance often depends on what he or she has said before exemplifies the category of *speaker-dependent influences*. Finally, *hearer-dependent influences* determine the utterance when, for example, the speaker accommodates his or her answer to the hearer's questions.

We assume that the speaker's utterance may be determined not only by each of these factors but also by interactions between the speaker and hearer. An example of such an interaction is the following case: The speaker's utterance at time t_i depends on the previous utterances by the hearer at t_{i-1} and the speaker at t_{i-2}. Research by Foppa and Käsermann (1981) demonstrates that an explanation of some of a child's utterances is possible by taking into consideration his or her previous discourse and the hearer's previous expressions of missed comprehension.

Our general proposition that speech production is (co)determined by situational factors should be valid at all stages of the production process. That is, features of the communicative situation influence which "domain of knowledge" (or PB) the speaker wants to communicate to the hearer, which part of knowledge he or she selects pars pro toto, and how the semantic input SI is encoded. Furthermore, we propose that these influences take place via feeding different programs (see Figure 5-1) with information about the situational parameters. Most of our empirical research has concentrated on depicting the relevant situational variables to fill in the selection program (see in more detail Herrmann, 1983, and below, where we describe the parameters determining the selection of requests).

Comparing the Model with Schlesinger's Approach

Of all the other general models of speech production (Chafe, 1977a, 1977b; Schlesinger, 1977, 1979; Zammuner, 1981), Schlesinger's is the most prominent and most elaborated psychological approach. At first glance it seems to be very similar to our own model. We have distinguished three stages, or levels of production: the activation of PB, the selection (and linearization) of SI, and the encoding of SI into the observable utterance. Schlesinger also divides speech production into three levels. The production process "begins" with the activated "cognitive structure" (level 1), which is then by "coagulation" transformed into "I-markers" (level 2). Finally, by the use of realization rules the I-markers are transformed into observable verbal utterances (level 3). We will now compare Schlesinger's with our own model in some important aspects. By showing the fundamental differences, we hope to make clearer the main features of our own approach (for a more complete comparison between Schlesinger's and our own model, see Herrmann, 1983, chap. 7).

1. Our own model has at its focus the *transformation of the propositional base PB into the semantic input SI* (level 1 → level 2 transformation), while Schlesinger's model concentrates on the verbal realization of the I-markers (level 2 → level 3 transformation).
2. *The selection of SI out of PB does not mean a change in the "code." Both PB and SI have the same representation mode—they are nonverbal cognitive structures.* It is because of this code identity that we can think of

SI and PB as a part-whole relation. In contrast, Schlesinger's cognitive structure and I-markers can not be related in a part-whole fashion. They are qualitatively different. The cognitive structure is nonverbal, whereas I-markers exist in a "proto-verbal" code. To emphasize: Schlesinger not only postulates a three-level approach but also three modes of representation—nonverbal, proto-verbal, and verbal—whereas we distinguish only between two modes, cognitive-conceptual and verbal.

3. *In our model differences between specific languages are restricted to differences in the encoding phase. Even individuals speaking different languages may have the same semantic input.* For Schlesinger these differences are already present in the coagulation of the I-markers.

4. *Situational variables (parameters) are at the center of our interest: Our model describes how situations determine the speaker's utterances,* whereas these aspects are irrelevant to Schlesinger's model building.

Applying the Model to the Production of Requests

By verbal requests we mean the following: An utterance is produced by the speaker with the intended effort of obligating the hearer to perform some act A. In addition, the following conditions must be fulfilled on the side of the speaker S: (1) *S has a primary goal E,* (2) *he or she assumes that the hearer H is basically willing and able to undertake action A, and (3)he or she assumes that he or she has the legitimation to oblige the hearer to do A.* These necessary conditions are implicatively associated with regard to one another as well as with the performance of request acts; therefore, we speak of a *partial structure of implication,* which is constituted by the framework of necessary conditions.

The verbal realization of requests need not be manifested in an *explicit* obligation for the hearer; rather, it may consist in verbalizing the conditions. In this regard we distinguish by way of definition three classes of requests:

1. *E-requests,* in which the speaker foregrounds his or her primary goal E.
2. *A-requests,* in which the speaker expresses his or her secondary goal (that the hearer should perform A), or inquires as to his or her interlocutor's willingness or ability to perform A.
3. *V-requests,* in which the speaker either directly requests the partner to perform A, or expresses his or her legitimation to make such a request of the hearer.

E-requests can be generally regarded as very indirect or as not at all explicit; they carry reference neither to the interlocutor and the desired act A, nor to the speaker's legitimation. V-requests, on the other hand, are very direct and unambiguous, while A-requests occupy the middle ground in this respect. (See also the somewhat different request classification schemes of Gibbs, and Blum-Kulka, Danet, and Gershon, this volume, Chapters 6 and 7).

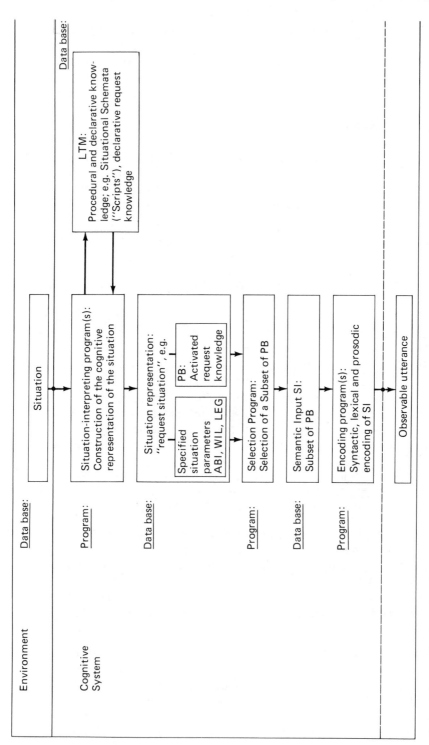

Figure 5-2. Application of the general model to the production of verbal requests.

Figure 5-2 shows schematically the application of our general model to the production of requests. The figure makes clear the psychological interpretation of the general request knowledge, represented as a structure of implications, held by the speaker. This framework serves the speaker as the propositional base (PB) from which he or she draws, pars pro toto, certain parts to use as the semantic input (SI) in his or her utterance, or, in other words, the knowledge structure that the speaker actualizes in planning a verbal request and producing an utterance.

The Situation Features Studied

Which parameters of the (cognitive) situation representation determine the choice of a specific request variant from PB? To answer this question empirically, we did the following pilot study. We constructed a questionnaire consisting of situation descriptions that were presented in combination with E-, A-, or V-requests (for example: Student S is working in the library . . . He says to another student sitting nearby, "Please do not disturb me, I want to read"). The subjects were asked to read the questionnaire carefully and reconstruct the processes that led Student S to the utterance of the request.

By this procedure we collected from 64 students from the University of Mannheim 378 reconstruction protocols. The content of the protocols was analyzed by several raters. In 238 cases the raters agreed that the subjects had interpreted and reconstructed the situation frames as request situations (coefficient for interrater agreement was .85). The content analytic evaluation of these protocols showed that the following situation parameters were mentioned: the hearer's ability to perform act A, his or her willingness to perform A, and the speaker's legitimation to request for A.

These results were confirmed by other similar empirical studies, and they were in agreement with our theoretical considerations (see Herrmann, 1983, Chapter 6). This led us to the general assumption that the following cognitively represented parameters of communicative situations exert a systematic influence on the selection of request forms E, A, or V:

1. *Hearer's ability* (*ABI*): The speaker can rate his or her interlocutor's ability to perform act A very highly (ABI+), or can rate it as low or limited (ABI*) in the situation.
2. *Hearer's willingness* (WIL): The speaker can rate his or her interlocutor's willingness as high (WIL+) or low (WIL*).
3. *Hearer's legitimation* (*LEG*): The speaker's legitimation has—in his or her own view—a strong deontic foundation (LEG+), or the legitimation can be present, but deontically weak (LEG*).

In some of our recent studies we were also interested in the question of how the assessment of values for the cognitive construction of the situational dimensions willingness (WIL), ability (ABI), and legitimation (LEG) takes place.

Recent schema-theoretical considerations (e.g., Rumelhart & Ortony, 1978; Schank & Abelson, 1977) suggest a fundamental distinction between the possible ways in which a situation may be represented, namely as *standard* or *nonstandard* situations. In standard situations, such as often-recurring routine situations, the actual input is interpreted and dealt with as if "following a script." The perception of situational characteristics leads to the activation of knowledge (scripts, schemata) specific to that class of situations and to the insertion of schema variables. The result is that the recognition of the situation and the consequent information processing depends almost exclusively on the activation and specification of what is already known. In uncommon or rarely occuring situations—nonstandard situations—the interpretation and mastering of the situation depends on the use of more general declarative and procedural knowledge (plans, heuristics, etc.) and on extensive application of information drawn from the context.

Referring back to our model (Figure 5-2), we see that there are very different paths by which the variables in the selection program can be determined: In standard situations the values for WIL, ABI, and LEG are defined in accordance with the experience of the speaker. He or she assumes with a fair amount of certainty that the partner is able and willing to perform act A, and that the speaker him- or herself is highly legitimized to make such a request. In nonstandard situations, however, the value assignment for the situational determinants ABI, WIL, and LEG can be established only through the active search for and use of information from the environment.

Standard and nonstandard situations should therefore lead to differential application of the request forms E, A, and V. We would expect that speakers in standard situations will use the very indirect E-requests, since the risk of a misunderstanding is slight, and a direct or impertinent request can be damaging and provocative. A-requests should be not so frequent here, and V-requests very highly unlikely. In nonstandard situations the selection of a request form should be governed by the assignment, which is determined by situational feedback, of values to ABI, WIL, and LEG. The danger looms again here of creating an undesired reaction in the hearer by an overly forceful request, in addition to the problem of real or pretended misunderstanding on the part of the hearer because the request is too indirect. The preferred request form in nonstandard situations therefore ought to be the A-request. E-requests

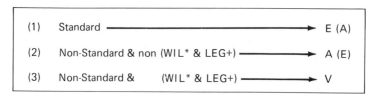

Figure 5-3. Hypotheses about the influence of the situation (standard vs. nonstandard) on the request forms.

should occur much less frequently, and then only when the risk of being misunderstood is not present. We should expect V-requests to occur only in the special case in which the search procedure leads to the assignment of values WIL* and LEG+. That is, the speaker regards him- or herself as highly legitimized and the willingness of his or her interlocutor appears low.

In Figure 5-3 our hypotheses about the relationship between standardization and request form are summarized.

The Experimental Paradigms

We have tested these hypotheses in a series of experiments. We used a variety of tasks and a wide range of specific situational scenarios in these studies in order to ensure the ecological validity of our findings. A few words describing each of our experimental scenarios below should give the reader the flavor of these various data-collection methods.

1. In the *detective experiment*, there were always two actors who played the roles of two detectives with certain orders. At some point in the play one of the detectives (the subject) had to ask his partner (stooge) for a pistol.
2. In the *film experiment*, the subject was informed that he should help in writing a script for a television film for children. Specific film episodes were then presented to him as comic drawings, and he was asked to complete the drawings by finding suitable utterances.
3. In the *distribution experiment*, the subject worked together with a partner (stooge) and gained a certain reward. By experimental manipulation this reward was always handed over to the partner, so the subject had to ask verbally for his share.
4. In the *scaling experiment*, the subject received some questionnaires with descriptions of situations and 12 request variants. He had to estimate the subjective probabilities of using the requests in each of the situations.
5. In the *questionnaire experiment*, the subject had to estimate the subjective probabilities not only of certain request variants, but also of specific situational parameters.
6. In the *monitor experiment*, the subject read rather general descriptions of situations presented in combination with specific request variants on a monitor. He was asked to evaluate (judge) how well the requests fitted the situation. If needed he could ask for further information about situation parameters by pressing a button.
7. In the *eye-movement experiment*, the subject saw drawings that presented certain situations in combination with specific request variants. He had to scan the scene and evaluate the fit of the request variant.
8. In the *bookstall experiment*, people's requests for newspapers in the bookstall of a railway station were recorded.

As this list shows, we used a wide range of data-collection procedures, ranging from naturalistic interactions to highly controlled experiments, to test the predictions derived from our theory. Figure 5-4 summarizes the experiments and their results (for a more detailed description, see Herrmann, 1983). The left side of Figure 5-4 shows the name of each experiment and the respective subject sample. The middle column shows the situational conditions applied in each experiment: standard or nonstandard. In the nonstandard condition it is further specified in accordance with our hypotheses whether the combination of WIL* and LEG+ is under consideration (see the hypotheses in Figure 5-3). The results are presented in such a way that the three request forms are ordered according to their empirically obtained frequency of occurrence. For example, in the first experiment, the detective experiment, V ~ A > E means that the forms V and A occur with about the same frequency, and that both are more frequent than the E-form when the condition is nonstandard and low willingness, but high legitimacy (WIL* & LEG+) applies. In the second row, A > E ⩾ V means that A-requests occurred more frequently than E-requests, and that V-requests were much less frequent than E-requests. Both results of the first experiment correspond with our expectations concerning the preferred request forms in different types of nonstandard situations. This is noted in the far right column, marked "Agreement With Hypothesis," by a "+".

When going through the chart in this manner, it can be seen in the far right column that in the final analysis, our three hypotheses about the relationship between standardization of the situation and request form bear out: E-requests are preferred in standard situations. If legitimation of the speaker is high and the (perceived) willingness of the partner low in nonstandard situations, then V-requests are preferred. Except for this special case, the "standard request" in nonstandard situations is the A-request.

Conclusions: The Present Status of the Model

To sum up, we interpret the results in Figure 5-4 as clear evidence for the model's value when applied to the explanation of the situation-specific variation of requests. However, in order to point out its most important advantage, we have to go beyond requests. We were also successful in applying this model to the domains of object naming and variation in level of speech (see in detail Herrmann, 1983, Chapters 4 and 5). This means that the model is a *heuristic theoretical framework integrating per se heterogeneous phenomena* in the study of speech production. One of the main features of our pars-pro-toto principle therefore is its integrative power.

In its present status the model can be classified as an "*interdependence*" or "*condition*" *model*. Given specific situational conditions, we can predict what the speaker will utter; in other words, the current focus is on the interdependencies between situation parameters and the speaker's utterances. Our final aim is the formulation of a *cognitive-process model*. This will require additional assumptions about the relative amount of time consumed at each

Name of the Experiment	N	Situational Conditions	Results	Agreement with Hypothesis
1. Detective Experiment	144	NONSTANDARD & (WIL* & LEG+)	$V \sim A > E$	+
		NONSTANDARD & non (WIL* & LEG+)	$A > E \gg V$	+
2. Film Experiment	222	NONSTANDARD & (WIL* & LEG+)	$V > A > E$	+
		NONSTANDARD & non (WIL* & LEG*)	$A \gg E > V$	+
3. Distribution Experiment	179	STANDARD	$E > A > V$	+
		NONSTANDARD & (WIL* & LEG+)	$E \gg V > A$	$(\overline{+})$
4. Scaling Experiment	577	Increasing Willingness	Increasing probability for A	(+)
		Decreasing legitimation	Decreasing probability for A	(+)
5. Questionnaire Experiment	63	STANDARD	$E > A \gg V$	+
		NONSTANDARD & non (WIL* & LEG+)	$A > E \gg V$	+
6. Monitor Experiment	61	STANDARD	$E > A \gg V$	+
		NONSTANDARD & non (WIL* & LEG+)	$A > E \gg V$	+
		NONSTANDARD & (WIL* & LEG+)	$A > V \sim E$	±
7. Eye movement Experiment	24	STANDARD	$E > A \gg V$	+
		NONSTANDARD & non (WIL* & LEG+)	$A > E \gg V$	+
8. Bookstall Experiment	601	STANDARD	$E \gg A > V$	+
		NONSTANDARD & non (WIL* & LEG+)	$A > E > V$	+

Figure 5-4. Summary of the results of our experiments concerning the selection of requests in standard and nonstandard situations.

stage of the production process, and about the sequentiality or simultaneousness of these various processing phases.

As the model stands now, speech production begins with the application of the situation-interpretation program. But an *overall*-process model should also include the formulation of the situation-specific goal, the decision for an utterance (as against other kinds of action) as a means of goal attainment, and a range of other relevant psychological and social variables (cf. Gibbs, and Blum-Kulka et al., this volume, Chapters 6 and 7).

In our continuing research project we are going to apply the model to other linguistic phenomena, such as the production of reports about personal experiences. From the first results we may conclude that the model will have to be elaborated in the following respects.

When the speaker utters a whole discourse (e.g., a report), in most cases he or she can choose between different ways of sequencing the utterance. This is obvious when the "object" of the utterance has no temporal sequence in itself, for instance in the case of descriptions of two-dimensional layouts (pictures, rooms, places, etc.; see Levelt, 1982a, 1982b; Ehrich & Koster, 1983). But even if there is such a temporal sequence, as in the case of reports about personal experiences, the speaker normally can choose between different options to sequence the utterance. The theoretical implication of this observation is the necessity to add a *linearization program* intervening between PB (propositional base) and SI (semantic input) to the model. The instance that "decides" about the application of the different programs—situation-interpretation program, linearization program, and so on—should be conceptualized as a kind of "general processor." The specification of the metaphorical use of "general processor"—to make it part of our theoretical assumptions—is one of the tasks of our future research. We believe that through the further elaboration and extension of our processing model in the light of accumulating empirical evidence, we shall be in an increasingly strong position to account for situational variations in speech production. In contrast to linguistic and ethnographic research strategies (cf. Blum-Kulka et al., this volume, Chapter 7), the present model has its roots in information-processing cognitive psychology. We prefer to see these alternative research strategies as complementary rather than contradictory, and consider their appearance side by side within the same volume as a promising development for the future integration of this important field of research.

References

Austin, J. L. (1962). *How to do things with words*. Oxford: Oxford University Press.

Chafe, W. G. (1977a). Creativitiy in verbalization and its implications for the nature of stored knowledge. In R. O. Freedle (Ed.), *Discourse production and comprehension* (pp. 41–55). Norwood, NJ: Ablex.

Chafe, W. G. (1977b). The recall and verbalization of past experience. In R. W. Cole (Ed.), *Current issues in linguistic theory* (pp. 215–246). Bloomington, IL: Indiana University Press.

Ehrich, V., & Koster, C. (1983). Discourse organization and sentence form: The structure of room description in Dutch. *Discourse Processes, 6*, 169–195.

Foppa, K., & Käsermann, M. L. (1981). Das kindliche Wissen über Sprache: Überlegungen zu einem ungelösten Problem. In R. Groner & K. Foppa (Eds.), *Kognitive Strukturen und ihre Entwicklung*. Bern, Switzerland: Huber.

Herrmann, Th. (1983). *Speech and situation*. New York: Springer-Verlag.

Herrmann, Th., & Deutsch, W. (1976). *Psychologie der Objektbenennung*. Bern, Switzerland: Huber.

Hobbs, J. R. (1979). Coherence and coreference. *Cognitive Science, 3*, 67–90.

Kintsch, W., & van Dijk, T. A. (1978). Toward a model of text comprehension and production. *Psychological Review, 85*, 363–394.

Levelt, W. J. M. (1981). The speaker's linearization problem. *Phil. Trans. Royal Society London, B 295*, 305–315.

Levelt, W. J. M. (1982a). Linearization in describing spatial networks. In S. Peters & E. Saarinen (Eds.), *Processes, beliefs, and questions* (pp. 199–220). Dordrecht: Reidel.

Levelt, W. J. M. (1982b). Cognitive styles in the use of spatial directions terms. In R. J. Jarvella & W. Klein (Eds.), *Speech, place, and action* (pp. 251–268). Chichester, England: Wiley.

Linde, Ch., & Labov, W. (1975). Spatial networks as a site for the study of language and thought. *Language, 51*, 924–939.

Marslen-Wilson, W., Levy, E., & Tyler, L. K. (1982). Producing interpretable discourse: The establishment and maintenance of reference. In R. J. Jarvella & W. Klein (Eds.), *Speech, place, and action* (pp. 339–379). Chichester, England: Wiley.

McCutchen, D., & Perfetti, Ch. (1982). Coherence and connectedness in the development of discourse production. *Text, 2*, 113–139.

Olson, D. R. (1970). Language and thought. *Psychological Review, 77*, 257–273.

Osgood, Ch. (1980). *Lectures on language performance*. New York: Springer-Verlag.

Rommetveit, R. (1968). *Words, meanings, and messages*. New York: Academic Press.

Rosenberg, S. (Ed.) (1977). *Sentence production: Development in research and theory*. Hillsdale, NJ: Erlbaum.

Rumelhart, D. E., & Ortony, A. (1978). The representation of knowledge in memory. In R. C. Anderson, R. J. Spiro, & W. E. Montague (Eds.), *Schooling and the acquisition of knowledge* (pp. 99–135). Hillsdale, NJ: Erlbaum.

Schank, R. C., & Abelson, R. P. (1977). *Scripts, plans, goals and understanding: An inquiry into human knowledge structures*. Hillsdale, NJ: Erlbaum.

Schlesinger, I. M. (1977). *Production and comprehension of utterances*. Hillsdale, NJ: Erlbaum.

Schlesinger, I. M. (1979). Cognitive and linguistic structures: The case of the instrumental. *Journal of Linguistics, 15*, 307–324.

Searle, J. R. (1969). *Speech acts*. Cambridge: Cambridge University Press.

Selz, O. (1922). *Zur Psychologie des produktiven Denkens und des Irrtums*. Bonn: Cohen.

Ullmer-Ehrich, V. (1979). Wohnraumbeschreibungen. *Zeitschrift für Literaturwissenschaft und Linguistik, 9*, 58–83.

Ullmer-Ehrich, V. (1982). The structure of living space descriptions. In R. J. Jarvella & W. Klein (Eds.), *Speech, place, and action* (pp. 219–249). Chichester, England: Wiley.

Zammuner, V. L. (1981). *Speech production: Strategies in discourse planning. A theoretical and empirical enquiry*. Hamburg: Buske.

Chapter 6
Situational Conventions and Requests

Raymond W. Gibbs, Jr.

The competent use of language lies in knowing how to use words to get listeners to make the right inferences about what is meant. Simply knowing the meanings of individual words, along with the rules for concatenating them into grammatical sentences, is not sufficient to ensure the proper understanding of speakers' messages. People need to know additional information about the social setting, the particular roles that speakers and hearers play in conversations, the interaction of speakers' and hearers' beliefs, and their presuppositions about each other's plans and goals in different discourse situations. This pragmatic information constitutes the shared or mutual knowledge that allows speakers and hearers to achieve successful communication.

Perhaps nowhere is the coordination between speaker and hearer more necessary than in the use of requests in conversation. Consider the following conversation recorded in a luncheonette (from Merritt, 1976).

A: Do you have coffee to go?

B: Cream and sugar? [starts to pour coffee]

A: Cream only.

B: Okay [putting cream in]

This exchange is quite typical of the many interactive episodes we engage in throughout a normal day. Both speaker and addressee make their contribution effortlessly, without much conscious reflection. Yet closer examination reveals that this episode is more than just a collection of isolated utterances. Speaker A begins with a question, which according to the rules of English grammar, requires a yes or no answer. But B's reply is also in the form of a question and seemingly takes no notice of A's question to him. The relationship between the first two utterances only becomes clear if we assume that B implicitly understands what A is looking for, namely a cup of coffee. Since there are no obvious linguistic clues, we must look beyond the surface content of A and B's actual language, and realize that A and B must share common knowledge that allows the interaction to take place in the way that it does. Both speakers depend on their shared knowledge of the particular social situation, and it is this knowledge that regulates what each says and how they comprehend each other. The question is: What is this knowledge and exactly how do people use it in making and understanding requests?

The focus of this chapter is on the situational conventions that influence how people make, understand, and remember requests. I will argue that people's knowledge of particular social situations results in certain requests being seen as conventional. These situational conventions enable speakers and hearers to coordinate what they know about each other's plans and goals, in order to facilitate communication. My starting point will be to show how social contexts constrain the ways in which people comprehend indirect requests. I will then go on to review a variety of empirical findings supporting the idea that the conventionality of an indirect request depends on the social context in which it is used. In the next section I will sketch a new proposal that specifies how the structure of social situations directly determines the surface forms used by speakers in making requests. I will then summarize and make some concluding remarks in the final part of the chapter.

Social Context and the Understanding of Requests

According to many linguists and philosophers (Bach & Harnish, 1979; Gordon & Lakoff, 1971; Searle, 1975), when speaker A says *Do you have coffee to go?* he is performing two acts, which can be labeled Meaning 1 and Meaning 2.

Meaning 1: "I ask you whether you sell coffee to go." [a question]

Meaning 2: "I request of you that if you do sell coffee to go, that you sell me some."

Meaning 1 is often called the direct or literal meaning of the utterance, and Meaning 2, the indirect or implied meaning. Searle (1975) argued that Meaning 2, A's request, is performed by means of Meaning 1, A's question. One possibility, then, is that understanding indirect requests, such as *Do you have coffee to go?*, requires a person to first analyze the direct or literal meaning of the utterance, before the indirect meaning can be derived. Some researchers (Clark & Lucy, 1975; Searle, 1975) have proposed a three-step process model for the interpretation of indirect requests. First, a listener computes the literal meaning of the utterance. Second, the listener decides if the literal meaning is defective given the context. And finally, if the literal meaning is inappropriate, the listener is led to seek the indirect meaning via a conversational postulate (Gordon & Lakoff, 1971), or by some other maxim of conversation (Grice, 1975; Searle, 1975). Generally, information about the social context is not evaluated until the literal meaning of an indirect request is determined.

Although this seems like a reasonable model of the comprehension process, there is good reason to doubt it as an accurate psychological theory. In Gibbs (1979) I questioned whether people must first process the literal meaning of an indirect request before deriving its nonliteral, conveyed interpretation. I argued that with appropriate social and linguistic context, people can comprehend a speaker's intended meaning in a sentence like *Can you pass the salt*? without first analyzing its literal interpretation. Two experiments were conducted to test this hypothesis. Subjects read stories, one line at a time on a CRT, ending in either indirect requests (such as *Must you open the window*?, meaning *Please leave the window closed*), literal uses of the same sentences that were considered to be literal questions in their contexts (such as *Must you open the window*?), and direct requests (such as *Do not open the window*). After each story subjects made a paraphrase judgment of that story's last line.

If people actually compute the literal meaning of an indirect request before deriving its nonliteral interpretation, then indirect requests should take longer to process than either literal uses of the same sentences or direct requests. The results of these studies, however, showed that indirect requests took *no* longer to read than either literal sentences or direct requests when these sentences were read in an appropriate context. Yet without any preceding context, subjects took *much* longer to read and make paraphrase judgments for indirect requests than they did for literal sentences. These results suggest that people do not analyze the literal meanings of indirect requests before deriving their indirect interpretations when these expressions are seen in appropriate situational contexts.

More recently I have shown that people do not process the literal interpretation of an indirect request at the same time they comprehend its conveyed meaning (Gibbs, 1982, 1983). In these studies, when subjects read conventional, nonliteral uses of expressions such as *Can't you be friendly*? (meaning *Please be friendly to others*), they were not subsequently faster in making sentence/nonsentence judgments for paraphrases of the literal meanings of these utterances than they were in making the same judgments for unrelated paraphrases. If subjects computed the literal interpretations of indirect requests, then there should be some facilitation for subjects' responses to literal paraphrase sentences. Since there was no facilitation here, it is doubtful that people computed the literal meanings of these expressions during the comprehension process. It appears, then, that if people read or hear indirect requests in normal social and linguistic situations, they can understand their interpretations without any analysis of these expressions' literal meanings.

Convention and Context in the Use of Requests

One factor that has been shown to play an important role in understanding indirect meaning is *convention*. For people to understand one another, they must coordinate their knowledge in such a way as to determine what each of them means. Lewis (1969) has proposed that language is used primarily as a set of conventions to solve these coordination problems in communicative settings. For instance, when a speakers want to refer to a four-legged animal that barks, they'll use *dog* because it is the convention in their linguistic community to call these animals this name. Speakers will comfortably use conventional words and phrases in many social situations because they can assume that hearers share this knowledge. The recurrence of many communicative situations has led to the evolution of a variety of conventional, linguistic routines to facilitate understanding. In making requests, for example, speakers often use sentence forms that are generally known and well-accepted, like *Can you tell me the time*? (see Morgan, 1978). Hearers easily understand these expressions as requests even though they are questions syntactically. The use of conventional indirect requests, then, may lead to a relatively "direct" interpretation of the intended request force in contrast to more involved inferential processes needed to comprehend nonconventional indirect requests. But what determines the conventionality of a particular indirect request? Are there standard syntactic forms for making conventional requests across all social situations, or does the conventionality of an indirect request depend on the specific social context in which it is used?

In Gibbs (1981a, Experiment 1) I attempted to examine the different types of requests used by people in public places. While there has been much analysis of indirect requests in linguistics, philosophy, and psychology, there have been no systematic investigations of the indirect requests that adults use whne making requests in the real world. I was interested in seeing if speakers use relatively few grammatical forms in making requests in all contexts or if the form of an indirect request depends on the particular social situation in which it is used. Furthermore, what sentence types do speakers and hearers view as being conventional forms for making requests?

Subjects were presented with a number of different real-world scenarios, each of which was set in a public place on a familiar university campus, and asked to state how they would make requests in the different contexts. For each one of the scenes subjects were told to imagine that they were the protagonist. Their task was to write five different sentences that they would say to get another person to comply with their wish. A pilot study showed that when subjects were asked to state their requests verbally, the results generated were quite similar to those produced when the subjects just wrote the requests down.

Here is an example of one of the 16 contexts used in this study (a complete list of the situations used is shown in Table 6-1):

> You are playing tennis at the Muir College tennis courts one afternoon with a friend. Unfortunately, you are just a beginner and are not very good. At one point during the game, you accidently hit the ball over the fence into the next court. You need the ball back and so you say to one of the people playing in the next court. . . .

Table 6-1. Social Contexts Used in Gibbs (1981a)*

1. Getting drop card stamped at the Psychology office.
2. Buying cigarettes at campus store.
3. Getting battery jump start from campus police.
4. Getting help at computer center.
5. Getting change for dollar at ice cream store.
6. Request to fix Xerox machine.
7. Ordering beer at pub.
8. Requesting student to shut door in classroom.
9. Buying stamps at post office.
10. Request to get tape recorder fixed.
11. Buying parking sticker.
12. Ordering hamburger at cafeteria.
13. Getting article off reserve at library.
14. Getting ball from next tennis court.
15. Finding exam grade from teacher.
16. Requesting the time from passerby.

Across the different contexts, subjects generated a total of 2,178 requests. An analysis of these revealed that subjects used 13 sentence forms in making the requests. Table 6-2 presents examples of requests along with the actual proportion generated for each category type. The 13 categories are given below, in order of their frequency.

1. *Want/desire.* The speaker asserts a particular want or desire from which the hearer can infer that he or she is to take some action to fulfill the speaker's wish.
2. *Ability.* The speaker asks a question about the bearer's ability to perform the desired action.

Table 6-2. Proportion of Requests Generated for Each Category*

Category	Sentences	Proportion
1. Want/Desire	I would like ...	.20
2. Ability	Can ...?	.16
3. State of the World	That's my tennis ball.	.12
4. Permission	May I ...?	.12
5. Direct Question	What time is it?	.12
6. Name Only	Hamburger.	.08
7. Possession	Do you have ...?	.06
8. Direct Request	Give me a hamburger.	.05
9. Imposition	Would you mind ...?	.03
10. Commitment	Will you ...?	.03
11. Unique	How about a hamburger?	.02
12. Embedded	I was wondering if you ...	.01
13. Obligation	Shouldn't you ...?	.001

*Tables from Gibbs, 1981a copyright © Academic Press. Reprinted with permission.

3. *State of the world*. The speaker states a fact about the world from which the hearer is to infer that some action is necessary.
4. *Permission*. The speaker asks that the hearer grant permission for the speaker to have his or her request fulfilled.
5. *Direct question*. The speaker asks a direct question of the hearer. The difference between this and other requests with an interrogative surface form is that the answer to the question completely complies with the request.
6. *Name only*. The speaker simply states the name of the object that he or she wants the hearer to perform some action on.
7. *Possession*. The speaker asks if the hearer has or knows about some desired action.
8. *Direct request*. The speaker states a direct, imperative request to the hearer.
9. *Imposition*. The speaker is offering the hearer the opportunity to perform the desired action.
10. *Commitment*. The speaker asks the hearer if he or she will commit him-or herself to performing the desired action.
11. *Unique*. Here, there is no generality of type. This category consists of only a few, unique items.
12. *Embedded*. The speaker embeds one category type for making the request within another.
13. *Obligation*. The speaker asks whether the hearer is under some obligation to perform the desired action.

The variety of sentence types generated suggests that speakers are not limited to a restricted number of ways for making indirect requests. Although each of the different sentence types can be viewed as conventional ways of making requests, this doesn't mean that each type is equally conventional for a particular situation. A good measure of a sentence's conventionality is how frequently it is used in a particular context. It would be misleading to say that some sentence types are always conventional if they are frequently used in some situations and hardly at all in others. It seems important, then, to consider requests as being conventional or nonconventional only with regard to specific social contexts.

Given this view of conventionality in language, the most interesting result in this experiment was the interaction between the frequency of a particular sentence type and the social context in which it was used. While certain sentence types tended to be more conventional across all contexts, closer examination reveals that many types are quite frequently used in some social situations and hardly at all in others. Requests of the Category 4 (Permission) type, for example, were used frequently in the context of buying stamps at the post office (26%), but rarely in the Psychology Department office where a student was trying to get his drop card stamped, and never in the situation of getting someone to fix a Xerox machine at the library. Similar results were found for other utterances in many other categories. Forty-two percent of all utterances used to request help in operating a key-punch machine were from Category 2, Ability. On the other hand, only 3% of all requests for beer made to the waitress in the campus pub were in this category. Similarly, 46% of the utterances generated to get someone to fix the Xerox machine simply indicated that the machine didn't work or that it needed to be fixed (Category 3, State of the World), but only 1% of the utterances generated in the context of buying cigarettes were of this type. Finally, sentences like *I would like ...* or *I need ...* (Category 1, Want/Desire), occurred 41% of the time in the context of getting a drop card stamped at the Psychology Department office and 35% of the time when ordering a hamburger, but only 1% of the time when requesting that someone throw back a tennis ball that accidentally went into their court. These results indicate that there is an interaction between the conventionality of an indirect request and the social context in which it is made.

Although these frequency data are useful, it is important to show that there are differences between conventional and nonconventional indirect requests for each situation. In a second study (Gibbs, 1981a, Experiment 2), a different group of subjects rated how likely they would be to use a particular indirect request in a specified social context. Subjects first read each scenario followed by ten different sentences that were requests appropriate to the particular context. Each of these requests was generated by subjects in the earlier experiment. The utterances selected came from as many different categories as possible, although not all of the categories were represented in each context. The subjects' task was then to rate on a scale of 1 to 6 each of the alternatives according to how likely they would be to use that sentence as a request in the given context (1 being very unlikely and 6 being highly likely). An example of a scenario, with its ten different sentences, is given below.

Campus Pub

After a hard day studying, you decide to go over to the pub to drink a few beers. You walk in and sit down at a table. A waitress comes up and you say to her ...

May I have a beer?
A beer, please.
I sure could use a beer.
Could I have a beer?
I would like to have a beer.
How about a beer?
Give me a beer.
I'm dying for a glass of beer.
Do you think you could get me a beer?
Let me have a beer.

The results showed that for each particular social context, people judged certain ways of making requests as being significantly more conventional than others. Thus, in the context of ordering beer at the campus pub, subjects rated a sentence from Category 1, Want/Desire, such as *I would like a beer*, as being more appropriate or conventional than a sentence from Category 4, Permission, like *Let me have a beer*. Similarly, the utterance *Could you tell me the time?* (Category 2, Ability) was viewed as being a more conventional way of requesting the time from a stranger than was *I need to know the time* (Category 1, Want/Desire).

Interestingly, there was not a significant effect of request type on subjects' conventionality ratings. There was, however, a good reason for this: Similar to the pattern of results for the first study, there was an interaction between the context in which a request was given, and its conventionality. That is, for a given request type there were significant differences in subjects' conventionality ratings for utterances in different social situations. This effect was present for 12 of the 13 request types. Thus, indirect requests rated as being conventional in one context were nonconventional in another situation. For instance, in Category 4, Permission, the utterance *Can I have a parking sticker?* had much lower conventionality rating (2.59) than *Can I have a beer?* (4.57). Similarly, for Category 2, Ability, the utterance *Could you tell me the time?* (5.04) was rated higher than *Could you fix my tape recorder?* (2.72), yet they have exactly the same surface form. Category 3, State of the World, has the nonconventional indirect request *That's my ball* (2.36, meaning "Throw me my ball"), as well as the higher-rated conventional utterance *My keypunch is broken* (4.21). Even direct requests (Category 8) differed in their conventionality according to the situation. Thus, *Give me a pack of Camels* (4.18) was rated as being considerably more conventional than *Throw me my ball* (1.93).

Processing and Remembering Indirect Requests

The different conventionality ratings for requests of similar type in different social situations indicates that the interaction between convention and context may be important in the interpretation of indirect requests. What does this suggest about how people process and remember indirect requests in conversation? In Gibbs (1981a, Experiment 3) I examined the speed with which people understood conventional and nonconventional indirect requests.

Subjects in this study read stories that contained dialogue, each one ending in either a conventional or nonconventional indirect request, as determined by the ratings in the previous experiment. Subjects read each story, one line at a time, on a CRT screen. Their task was simply to push a button as soon as they understood each line. The last line of each story was a target sentence, and after reading it subjects made a paraphrase judgment for that line.

My hypothesis was that nonconventional indirect requests should take longer to comprehend than conventional requests because, in order to be integrated into the conversational context, they involve a more complex inference process regarding the speaker's beliefs and intentions. Conventional indirect requests should be understood more quickly because it is easier for the hearer to assume the speaker's intended meaning.

The data showed that conventional targets, such as *I'll have a hamburger*, took less time (1777 msec.) to process than nonconventional targets, such as *How about a hamburger?* (2081 msec.). A similar finding was demonstrated for the paraphrase judgments. Subjects took significantly less time to make the paraphrase judgments for conventional indirect requests (1965 msec.) than they did for nonconventional indirect requests (2305 msec.). These results confirmed the hypothesis that subjects understand the meanings of conventional indirect requests more readily than those of nonconventional requests. Moreover, they suggest that understanding nonconventional indirect requests requires a more elaborate process of inference about speakers' intended meanings than is used for comprehending conventional indirect requests, where the meanings are easily assumed.

Examination of the individual item data provided additional support for the interaction between convention and context found in the earlier experiments. Specifically, indirect requests from Category 7, Possession, such as *Do you have . . . ?*, were used in some contexts as conventional utterances and in others as nonconventional requests. Mean reaction times for *Do you have . . . ?* types showed that subjects took 209 milliseconds more to understand *Do you have . . . ?* type sentences when they were seen as nonconventional (2120 msec.) than when they were viewed as conventional indirect requests (1911 msec.). This was so despite the fact that the conventional sentences were longer in average number of words (8.5) than the nonconventional sentences (6.0).

These data, once again, indicated that indirect requests are conventional only in light of a partciular social situation. Given some context, indirect requests lie on a continuum between highly conventional and nonconventional utterances. The more conventional the utterance, the easier it is to find an appropriate interpretation in the given situation. Comprehension of nonconventional indirect requests requires more inferences by the listeners, necessitating them to use their knowledge of the speaker and the conversational context.

In a final study (Gibbs, 1981b) I investigated the role of conventionality in surface memory for requests in conversation. It seemed possible that memory for conventional indirect requests would not be as distinctive as that for nonconventional indirect requests because conventional utterances do not require elaborative processing in order to be integrated into the conversation. To test this idea, subjects were shown a videotape (with an audio channel) that depicted people making requests in public places on the University of California's San Diego campus. Immediately afterwards, or 48 hours later, they were given a written, five-alternative-choice memory test for the specific requests made in the 16-minute film.

It was predicted that nonconventional indirect requests would be better recognized as having been heard in the videotape than would conventional indirect requests. Moreover, when subjects did not recognize the target sentences, they would have a tendency to remember nonconventional indirect requests as conventionally indirect. Thus, subjects may remember nonconventional utterances, such as *How about a hamburger?*, as having been stated in a conventionally indirect form, such as *I would like a hamburger*. This should be particularly so given that people have knowledge as to which sentence forms are conventional for a specific social context.

A second version of the experiment examined the role that social and linguistic context had on people's memory for requests. Subjects were simply presented with all of the requests used in the conversations, along with some additional filler sentences, in a list-learning paradigm. Subjects listened to the sentences with no supporting context and then were given the same recognition test used in the oral version of the study, either immediately after or 48 hours later.

My prediction here was that if the social context is removed, then both conventional and nonconventional indirect requests should be remembered equally well. Overall, then, there should be an interaction between the type of context (conversation vs. no context) and conventionality (conventional vs. nonconventional) in people's memory for requests.

The results of this study supported the main predictions. When subjects watched the videotape, they better recognized nonconventional indirect requests (76%) than they did conventional indirect requests (60%). This suggested that nonconventional indirect requests are remembered better because they are harder to integrate into the conversational context than conventional indirect requests. However, there was no difference in subjects' recognition of conventional (60%) and nonconventional indirect requests (60%) when they listened to the targets with no accompanying context. Moreover, the interaction between context and conventionality was indeed statistically reliable. This result is a strong demonstration of the importance of social context in memory for conversation. Specifically, the data suggested that nonconventional indirect requests were not intrinsically more memorable than conventional indirect requests. Rather, it was the conventionality of an indirect request *given some context* that determined how well it was remembered.

Subjects' false alarms to the other distractor sentences provided some interesting information about their reconstructive biases in remembering the target sentences. Subjects who watched the videotape had a strong tendency to remember nonconventional indirect requests as conventionally indirect. However, subjects did not often remember conventional indirect requests as having been stated in a nonconventional surface form. It appears, then, that when subjects were unable to remember the exact surface form of the target sentences, they guessed what the target might be given their knowledge of the social context and of the conventionalized sentence forms used to make requests in those situations.

What Makes Some Requests Conventional?

The results of these studies highlight the importance of situational conventions in making, understanding, and remembering requests in conversation. Speakers are not restricted to a limited number of sentence forms in making requests, but can use a variety of means appropriate for a specific social context. The particular sentence form used to make a request also has a marked effect on the speed with which people comprehend indirect requests, as well as on their ability to remember these expressions. The question remains: Exactly what is it about a social situation that makes some request forms appropriate or conventional?

Herb Clark and I (Clark & Gibbs, in preparation) have recently developed a theory of how people formulate requests for information that may provide an answer to this question. The central idea behind our proposal is that a speaker will attempt to specify in his or her utterance the greatest potential obstacle present for the addressee in complying with his or her request. For example, a person whom I will call A (for Ann) wants to get certain information that she lacks, and so she asks another person, whom I will call B (for Ben), for the information. This process has several parts. (1) A decides as best she can what information she wants. (2) She begins to formulate a plan for finding that information by determining a likely source—from a book, a look at an object, or another person. (3) Since her plan, in this case, is to get information from another person, she selects the person she wants to ask, Ben, by judging, among other things, who is most likely to know the information, who is most available, who is it socially possible for her to make a request of, and so on. (4) A then plans a social transaction with B in which she exchanges with B the information she wants for a certain return. And finally, A initiates the transaction, at each step, (5) formulating the wording of her utterances to conform to both her overall plan and to the momentary requirements of the transaction, and (6) utters each contribution. Many theories of requests for information take account only of A's lack of information (part 1) and some evaluation of B's information (part 3). We argue, however, that formulating questions depends on all six parts.

Formulating the right request, then, depends on designing a transaction that takes into account a good deal of different information. A must fit this transaction into B's apparent activities. In particular, A must find a way of inserting her plan for B's contribution (i.e., to respond to the request by providing the information) into what B is doing or planning to do at the moment. In some situations, like service encounters (see Merritt, 1976), B's primary activity may be as a filler of requests—as a drug-store clerk, for example. The expected transactions that arise in such situations are most easily planned for by a speaker. However, there are also detour transactions wherein A, in some way, interrupts B's activities, or projected plans, to impose her own goals. These situations are more difficult to plan for. But in each case, A finally designs her request as a turn in the transaction. To do this, she must first assess what reasons there may be for B not giving her the desired information. A will then formulate her utterance to deal with the greatest potential obstacle. By doing so, she thereby implicates that B will tell her what she wants to know.

Our proposal has a number of interesting consequences. First, it suggests that there is a hierarchy of request types that people can use in everyday speech depending on the transactional obstacles in each social situation. These range from higher-level, more general-purpose kinds of requests, like *Can you pass the salt?*, down to very specific cases, like *Do you happen to have the salt?* In my view, the high-level types of requests become conventional because they depend on conventional kinds of pretenses that speakers use in circumventing the addressee's obstacles. Second, the model asserts that producing and understanding indirect requests critically depends on how the speaker and hearer assess each other's goals and plans. An indirect request that adequately specifies an addressee's projected reasons for not complying with it may be *easier* to process than one that does not mention this information; indeed, the conventionality of an indirect request may well rest on how successfully it does this. Finally, this view has implications for a general theory of speech acts. Previous theories (Bach & Harnish, 1979; Gordon & Lakoff, 1971; Searle, 1975), although describing some of the ways in which requests for information can be accomplished, have been unable to specify why speakers choose one strategy over another. In contrast, our theory is able to specify actual utterance formulation at its surface level. We can now see exactly why speakers use a particular surface form in making a request.

Going back to the results of Gibbs (1981a), it becomes clear why certain sentence forms are conventional in some situations but not in others. The Clark and Gibbs (in preparation) theory suggests that the interaction between convention and context may be due to the different obstacles that speakers ascribe to their addressees' compliance in various conversational contexts. Thus, *Do you have the time?* may be conventional to use in requesting time of a passerby on the street because the greatest obstacle to the passerby in providing the information may be that he or she simply doesn't know what time it is and has no access to a timepiece. Since the speaker cannot rule out this most limiting case, he or she must design the request around it. However, saying *Do you know what time you close?* as a request to a store owner to find out what time the store closes is inappropriate because the owner presumably knows what time his or her business closes.

This theory suggests, then, that understanding and memory for indirect requests in conversation depends on how speakers take the addressees' goals and plans into account when formulating their utterances. What makes some indirect requests conventional is that people learn to associate specific obstacles for hearers with different situations. Speakers know what kind of sentence forms best fit these circumstances, and hearers utilize this surface information in determining speakers' intended meanings.

Summary and Conclusions

I have reviewed some psycholinguistic studies and outlined a new theory illustrating how people's knowledge of social situations affects the production, comprehension, and remembering of requests in conversation. I have shown that the conventionality of a request depends on the social context in which it is used. Speakers and hearers have very specific knowledge about most social situations and this information determines the exact surface forms of requests, which subsequently affects the processes of understanding and remembering requests. Specifically, speakers evaluate social situations to determine the greatest obstacle present for addressees in complying with requests. The knowledge people have about social situations allows them to easily determine the obstacles present. In many contexts, such as service encounters, evaluation of the situation is automatic, and requests in these cases can be most easily planned for and comprehended. This enables hearers to directly understand the meanings of many indirect requests without any analysis of the literal meanings of these expressions (cf. Gibbs, 1982). For other situations that are less routine, and less familiar, understanding a speaker's request will involve a more complex inference process in which the compositional structure of a sentence is examined in detail.

The situational conventions that affect the production and comprehension of requests can be viewed as a variety of *social schemas*. These cognitive representations are constantly used in determining the plans and goals of participants that underlie recovery of speakers' intentions (see Allen & Perrault, 1980; Clark, 1979). Understanding and responding to indirect requests, such as *Do you have coffee to go?*, can be accomplished via the social schemas that regulate a hearer's recognition of a speaker's goal in a particular conversational context. Although there are individual differences in how social situations are perceived, the routine nature of many interactive episodes facilitates coordination of what speakers and hearers know about each other and the context they are in. Speakers design their requests in light of the social situation and will assume that addresses will similarly use their knowledge of the context to figure out not only what is meant, but what they are supposed to do or say in return.

Acknowledgments. Preparation of this chapter was supported by a faculty research grant from the University of California, Santa Cruz. I wish to thank Gayle Gonzales and Rachel Mueller for their comments on an earlier draft of this chapter.

References

Allen, J., & Perrault, C. (1980). Analyzing intention in utterances. *Artificial Intelligence, 15*, 143–178.

Bach, K., & Harnish, S. (1979). *Linguistic communication and speech acts*. Cambridge, MA: M.I.T. Press.

Clark, H. (1979). Responding to indirect speech acts. *Cognitive Psychology, 11*, 430–477.

Clark, H., & Gibbs, R. (in preparation). On the process of formulating requests for information.

Clark, H., & Lucy, P. (1975). Understanding what is meant from what is said: A study in conversationally conveyed requests. *Journal of Verbal Learning and Verbal Behavior, 14*, 56–72.

Gibbs, R. (1979). Contextual effects in understanding indirect requests. *Discourse Processes, 2*, 1–10.

Gibbs, R. (1981a). Your wish is my command: Convention and context in interpreting indirect requests. *Journal of Verbal Learning and Verbal Behavior, 20*, 431–444.

Gibbs, R. (1981b). Memory for requests in conversation. *Journal of Verbal Learning and Verbal Behavior, 20*, 530–540.

Gibbs, R. (1982). A critical examination of the contribution of literal meaning to understanding nonliteral discourse. *Text, 2*, 9–27.

Gibbs, R. (1983). Do people always process the literal meanings of indirect requests? *Journal of Experimental Psychology: Learning, Memory, and Cognition, 9*, 524–533.

Gordon, D., & Lakoff, G. (1971). Conversational postulates. *Papers from the Seventh Regional Meeting, Chicago Linguistic Society*, 63–84.

Grice, H. P. (1975). Logic and conversation. In P. Cole & J. Morgan (Eds.), *Syntax and semantics: Speech acts (Vol. 3)*. New York: Academic Press.

Lewis, D. (1969). *Convention*. Cambridge, MA: Harvard University Press.

Merritt, M. (1976). On questions following questions in service encounters. *Language in Society, 4*, 315–357.

Morgan, J. (1978). Two types of convention in indirect speech acts. In P. Cole (Ed.), *Syntax and semantics 9: Pragmatics*. New York: Academic Press.

Searle, J. (1975). Indirect speech acts. In P. Cole & J. Morgan (Eds.), *Syntax and semantics: Vol. 3. Speech acts*. New York: Academic Press.

Part III

Social and Cultural Aspects of Language and Social Situations

Chapter 7
The Language of Requesting in Israeli Society

Shoshana Blum-Kulka, Brenda Danet, and Rimona Gherson

Consider the following exchanges:

1. *Girl, 3, to her mother, in the street*: Isn't it true that when you feel hot you want a drink? So I feel hot.
2. *Girl, 11, to her mother, at the girl's birthday party*: Mommy, fold it!
3. *Young man to young woman on the bus*: Hi. I have got a problem. I haven't got any money but I do have tokens. Would you be willing to exchange? You see, normally I don't pay on buses because ...
4. *Customer to clerk at post office*: Give me one stamp.

The little girl in 1 uses an elaborate indirect approach to ask her mother for a drink. The girl in 2 simply commands her mother to do as she wishes. The young man in 3 seems hesitant to make his request, while the customer in 4 does not use even the minimal marker of politeness ("please").

Why would children vary their strategies in making demands on their parents? Why would strangers find it appropriate to be direct on one occasion but not on another? Are there links connecting the child in 2 and the customer in 4 which explain the bluntness of both? And similarly, is there a common factor behind the indirectness of 1 and 3? Our investigation of situational variations in the language of requesting in Israeli society is motivated by these and similar types of questions. We have chosen to focus on the speech act of requesting here, because it offers the student of language and society extremely rich data about the ways in which the characteristics of everyday social situations influence the production and comprehension of discourse.

The Background to Studying Requests

Theoretical work on requests has shown, on the one hand, the complexity of the relationship between form, meaning, and pragmatic preconditions in realizing this act (Gordon & Lakoff, 1975; Searle, 1979), and on the other hand, the high social stakes involved for both speaker and hearer in the choice of the specific way in which the request is made. Requests are pre-event acts; they express the speaker's expectation toward some prospective action, verbal or nonverbal, on the part of the hearer. Thus, as pointed out by Brown and Levinson (1978), requests by definition are "face threatening." By making a request the speaker impinges on the hearer's claim for freedom of action and freedom from imposition. As far as we know, all languages provide their speakers with a wide range of alternative request strategies. The variety of ways to make requests is probably motivated by the need to minimize the imposition involved in the act itself. In choosing a strategy located at some point on the continuum of directness (from "Close the window" to "It's cold in here" in getting a window closed, for example), the speaker reveals his or her appraisal of the social situation, and the degree to which the situation calls for minimization of the imposition involved (see also Gibbs, and Hoppe-Graff, this volume, Chapters 6 and 5).

Despite the richness of the subject for sociolinguistics, there have been surprisingly few studies that have actually attempted to empirically document the use of requests in any particular society. Except for Susan Ervin-Tripp's work on directives in American English (Ervin-Tripp, 1976), most of what's been done in this area tends to focus on a variety of specific issues rather than on the empirical documentation of requesting behavior in any particular society. In the philosophical and linguistic approach to the study of requests, (Fraser, 1981; Gordon & Lakoff, 1975; Morgan, 1978; Searle, 1979), the focus has been on analyzing the complex relationships between form, meaning, and context as manifested in conventional indirect request strategies (such as "Could you do it?" in English) which seem to have parallels in most languages studied. Another approach, adopted by linguists and sociologists (Brown & Levinson, 1978; Lakoff, 1974; Leech, 1977), has been to study requests in the context of politeness phenomena. In this tradition, the main interest has been in trying to understand the links between requesting variation and politeness in a way that would make it possible to specify the rules that govern the choice of strategies in context. Thus, Brown and Levinson's notions of positive and negative politeness, and Leech's notion of "tact," for example, can be viewed as explanatory models for the phenomenon of indirectness in discourse.

Another line of research in this area has pursued the investigation of various speech acts (including requests) from a cross-cultural perspective. The cross-cultural approach to the investigation of speech acts is closely linked to issues in intercultural communication: To what extent can breakdowns in communication between speakers of different languages be explained by cross-cultural differences in interactional styles? Are cultural stereotypes of the "direct," or even "blunt," Israeli or the "standoffish" British anchored in actual patterns of language use in these two cultures? At least for requests and apologies, actual use of speech-act patterns under the same social constraints seems to be in line with cultural stereotypes. It has been shown that speakers of Hebrew chose to make directives in direct ways in cases where American, British English, and

Australian English speakers preferred indirect ones (Blum-Kulka, 1982, 1983; Blum-Kulka & Olshtain, 1984). Similar results were obtained in cross-linguistic speech-act studies of German and British English for requests and complaints, in this case the German speakers proving to be more direct than the British (House & Kasper, 1981). Yet the full range of direct and indirect strategies for various acts seems to be equally available to members of these respective cultures. What is, then, the degree of variation in actual use in any given culture? And if such variation is indeed shown to exist, what are the social and situational parameters that account for it? We have approached the study of requesting behavior in Israeli society with this emic point of view.

Our mapping of the repertoire of requesting strategies, or of speech-act patterns generally in Hebrew, is based on a number of assumptions: first, that although there might be a relatively large number of utterances with a request potential, there are but a small number of identifiable distinct request strategy types; second, that taken together, these strategies form a continuum of directness; and third, that the main cutting points along this continuum are shared across languages, though the strategies by which they are realized can be language specific. The search for the social parameters that account for variation in use is again based on a number of assumptions: first, that the variation, if observed, is indeed exploited in actual use, and second, that it is possible to detect the social rationale by which it is motivated.

Requesting as Strategic Interaction

The most comprehensive model of a universal social rationale for variation in request strategies has been developed by Brown and Levinson (1978). Brown and Levinson claim that the social rationale of variation in verbal strategies (for one act) is based on "face wants," which require "face work." When people interact they are concerned to present an image which has two aspects. The positive aspect of the speaker's face is his or her "want" to be approved of, to be seen as a supportive, contributing member of society. At the same time, though, a person wants to preserve some private space within which he or she has the right to feel one shouldn't be imposed upon. This aspect of face is negative face. Social interaction in Brown and Levinson's view consists of persons balancing their own positive and negative face wants against those of their interlocutors. Some verbal acts, like directives, intrinsically threaten the interactant's face, while others, like apologies, constitute a threat to the speaker.

Thus, actual choice of strategy is determined by the way in which the speaker assesses the degree of threat involved. The greater the threat is judged to be, the more face work will be needed in the form of higher levels of indirectness or other markers of politeness. The actual weight of the face threat depends on three major social parameters: relative social distance between speaker and hearer, relative power of speaker vis-a-vis the hearer, and the degree of imposition involved in performing the act.[1] Brown and Levinson admit that relative power, relative distance, and degree of imposition need not be the only relevant factors that affect assessment of threat to face, yet they claim that these three factors "subsume all others that have a principal effect on such assessment" (Brown & Levinson, 1978, p. 85). It is against this background that we have selected the potential explanatory variables of sex, age, relative power, relative social distance, request goal, setting, and medium to investigate situational variability in requesting behavior in one partciular society. Our study of the language of requesting in Israeli society was designed to answer the following three questions:

1. What is the range of variation in the use of requesting strategies?
2. What are the relevant aspects of the social situation that affect the choice of strategy in this society?
3. What is the relative weight of the explanatory variables in accounting for variation in use? In particular, are relative distance, relative power, and degree of imposition indeed the principal factors that subsume all others in explaining variation?

Design of the Research

The data were obtained using an ethnographic approach. Instances of requesting behavior were drawn from three sources: (1) spontaneously occurring requests in "live" face-to-face interaction anywhere they occurred (on the bus, in students' dorms, on campus, etc.; 116 tokens); (2) requests identified in transcripts of previously tape-recorded natural conversations (in the home, at the health clinic, at large dinner parties, etc.; 216 tokens); and (3) requests in written correspondence (official government letters, memos between secretaries and students on campus, etc.; 146 tokens). Altogether we obtained 478 request tokens uttered by 149 speakers in Hebrew.

Each request was coded on a number of different dimensions, of which seven will be discussed in this chapter. The first six presented below are predictor variables, and the seventh is our classification of request strategy types on a scale of directness, that is, the dependent variable. An additional dimension relates to internal modifications within these strategy types (downgraders and upgraders).

Setting

We use this term in Brown and Fraser's (1979) sense, as referring to the physical setting in which the interaction takes place. We did not expect the

---

[1]It should be noted, though, that in observing a particular direct or indirect pattern we can only hypothesize about the particular cluster of social parameters that motivated the actual choice. In other words, the relative weight given to any one of the social parameters is not apparent from the form itself.

physical setting per se to have a determining power over choice of requesting strategy. But settings are associated with the types of activities that take place in them, and with variation in the types of social relations: sending children on errands in the home, asking the secretary to type a letter at work and so on. In the light of these considerations, we hypothesized there would be more use of indirect strategies in public settings than in private ones.

Medium

We expected that directness in request strategies would vary with the type of medium or channel used. Because writing is the creation of typically decontextualized texts, less can be taken for granted in written communication than in face-to-face interaction. When paralinguistic and nonverbal cues are absent, readers must rely more heavily on the meanings derivable from words alone. Especially if the written communication is between strangers, it is likely that requests will be formulated in a fairly explicit, direct manner. Thus, though the transition from oral to written language can be expected to be marked by a register shift in the direction of a more elaborate style, in terms of choice of strategy this shift would be expressed by a rise in the level of directness. Visual cues are also missing in telephone conversations, though aspects of communication such as intonation and pitch can help to convey speakers' intentions; thus, we would expect requests made over the telephone to be intermediate in degree of directness, between face-to-face requests and written ones.

Sex and Age

Instead of recording the actual ages of the partners, we coded the relative ages of the two, on the assumption that the critical factor was their *relative* ages. We classed each speaker and listener as a child, a teenager, or an adult; speakers ten years of age or less were classed as children, those between 11 and 20 were grouped in the intermediate category, and those over 20 were considered adults. In the analysis to be presented below, we will deal with pairs of interlocutors—for example, a child addressing an adult, or a teenager addressing a child. Following the same principle, we will examine variation in request strategies by pairs of same-sex and opposite-sex speakers. We expected that indirection would be most frequent when relatively younger speakers addressed older ones, and that there would be greater use of direct request strategies both between peers and when older speakers addressed younger ones.

The view of Lakoff (1975) that women hedge and qualify their utterances because they lack the confidence to stand by them can be extended to include expectations about the use of indirection. We hypothesized, then, that women would use less direct strategies than men, especially when addressing a request to a male listener.

Social Parameters (Power and Familiarity)

By power we mean the power of the speaker over the hearer in a given role relationship. Thus, power would be considered high when a driver is speaking to a passenger, but equal if the exchange is taking place between two drivers. Social distance, or degree of familiarity between interlocutors, was assessed on the basis of social network membership: It was considered to be high for members of a nuclear family, medium for friends and relatives, and low for strangers. Following the reasoning of Brown and Levinson (1978) on face-saving acts, as well as the rich literature on norms of address (e.g., Brown & Ford, 1964; Brown & Gilman, 1960; Lambert & Tucker, 1976), we expected that persons of high relative power and well acquainted with their interlocutors would use direct strategies, while those of low power and only somewhat familiar with their interlocutors, or not familiar with them at all, would choose indirect ones.

Request Goal

The notion of "goal" relates to the relationship between the speaker's intention and the hearer's compliance as it can be inferred from the type of activity required from the hearer. We distinguished between the following:

1. *Requests for action*: Cases where compliance requires action on the part of the hearer, such as a request to open the window.
2. *Requests for goods*: Cases where compliance demands handing over material goods (which might be small or large, handed over temporarily or forever), such as a request for a loan.
3. *Requests for information*: Requests for information differ from other types of request goals in that they are aimed solely at *verbal goods*.
4. *Requests for permission*: Requests for permission are speaker- rather than hearer-oriented on two accounts: If granted, a request for permission activates the speaker and not the hearer, and it constitutes a threat to the requestor's rather than to the requestee's face. It should also be noted that the verbalization of a request for permission, such as a child asking for permission to go to a party, constitutes in itself an admission of asymmetric power relationships. Requests for permission are therefore especially likely to be indirect.

The degree of imposition involved in the request might vary by type of goal, but can also cut across goals. Thus, requests for permission seem to be lower in imposition than requests for action, but with requests for goods, the degree of imposition might depend on the real or symbolic value of the goods requested. In light of the above, except for requests for permission, we did not formulate hypotheses on the effect of the type of goal on the request's level of directness.

Strategy Type

The various request tokens were classified along nine mutually exclusive categories of strategy types, which together form a scale of directness. Thus, the dependent variable in this study was defined as the request's level of directness on this scale. The analyses that follow take into account either all nine categories of the scale (Tables 7.1 and 7.4), or classify requests into three major categories: direct, conventional, and indirect (Tables 7.2 and 7.3).

There have been several prior attempts in different languages to set up classifications of request strategies that, cross-culturally, might form a potentially valid scale of indirectness (Herrmann, 1983; Herrmann, Winter-hoff-Spurk, & Mangold, 1983; Hoppe-Graff et al., this volume, Chapter 5; Searle, 1975). On theoretical grounds, there seem to be three major levels of directness universally manifest in requesting strategies: (1) The *most direct, explicit* level is realized by requests syntactically marked as such, such as imperatives, or by other verbal means that name the act as a request, such as performatives (Austin, 1962) and "hedged performatives" (Fraser, 1975). (2) The *conventionally indirect* level includes requests that realize the act by reference to contextual preconditions necessary for its performance, as conventionalized in a given language. These strategies are commonly referred to in the speech act literature, since Searle (1975), as "indirect speech acts"; examples would be "Could you do it?" or "Would you do it?", meant as a request. (3) *Nonconventional indirect* includes the open-ended group of indirect strategies (hints) that realize the act by either partial reference to an object or element needed for the implementation of the act ("Why is the window open?"), or by reliance on contextual clues.

On the basis of observed variation of request patterns in Hebrew and other languages such as English, German, and Danish[2] (cf. Blum-Kulka & Olshtain, 1984), these three levels were further subdivided in our scheme into nine distinct "strategy types," which together form a scale of directness. The distribution of request strategy types is presented in Table 7-1.

Downgraders and Upgraders

Request tokens were further analyzed for the presence of linguistic elements that serve to mitigate, soften, or "downgrade" the act, or those that serve the opposite function, that is, "upgrading" aggravating elements. Both kinds of modifications have been widely discussed in speech act literature (e.g., Blum-Kulka & Olshtain, 1984; Edmonson, 1981; House & Kasper, 1981; Labov & Fanshel, 1977; Lakoff, 1973).

---

[2]The schema for request classification presented has been shown to capture variation in requests in English, German, Danish, and Hebrew in a cross-cultural study of speech-act patterns (see Blum-Kulka & Olshtain, 1984).

Results

Variation in Use

As observed for other languages (e.g., Ervin-Tripp (1976) for American English; Brown and Levinson (1978) for English, Tzeltal, and Tamil), speakers of Hebrew also manifest a need to vary the verbal patterns used for requests. Table 7-1 shows that all nine strategy types were exploited in actual use. This finding yields further support to the potential universality of requesting behavior. The distribution of strategy types along the directness continuum also shows a trend that is probably culture specific: In our Hebrew data, more than half of the strategies fall into the "direct" category (50.7 percent), with a mean of 6.5 on the scale of directness, where 9 is the most direct strategy type. These results seem to indicate a relatively high overall level of directness in Israeli society.[3] The second largest group was the middle conventionally indirect strategy, with 35 percent of the tokens, and the least frequent were the fully indirect types, with only 12 percent of the total.[4]

The Use of Downgraders and Upgraders

The data showed 94 cases of downgraders and 118 cases of upgraders. The distribution of downgraders by strategy type is as follows: 63.8 percent are used with direct strategies, 28.7 percent with conventional ones, and 7 percent with the indirect model. For upgraders, 66.6 percent are used with direct strategies, 22.9 percent with conventional ones, and 10.4 percent with the indirect mode. Thus, both types of internal modifications are found primarily within the group of direct strategies.[5]

---

[3]We do not know of comparable results, based on naturally occurring requests, in other languages. In a cross-cultural study of requests, using the same discourse completion test for elicitation in various languages, we have found significant differences in the overall level of directness for different languages across the *same* situations (unpublished results from the CCSARP project; for description of the study see Blum-Kulka and Olshtain, 1984).

[4]We had no way of collecting hints that were meant as requests but were not interpreted as such. Hence, full indirectness might be underrepresented in our data.

[5]Certain types of modifications were typically used with direct strategies, like tags, that served for mitigation (Tvakši meaba, tov?/Ask Daddy, Okay?"), while others, like 'ulay' (perhaps), were used for aggravating direct strategies as well as for mitigating other strategy types. Thus, 'ulay' in 'ulay tafsik?' ("Perhaps you'll stop?") aggravates the request, while in 'ulay at yexola la azor li' ("Perhaps you could help me") mitigates it.

Table 7-1. Distribution of Request Strategy Types in Hebrew

	n	%		%	n	
						Indirect
1. Mild Hint						
(It's cold in here.)	6	1.3				
2. Strong Hint			Indirect	13.2	(63)	
(The door is open.)	42	8.8				
3. Preparatory						
(Would you mind closing						
the door?)	15	3.1				
4. Conventionally Indirect						
(Could you close the door?)	66	13.8				
5. Question Directives			Conv.			
(Will you close the door?)	64	13.8	Indirect	35.2	(168)	
6. Scope Stating						
(I want you to close the door.)	38	8				
7. Locution Derivable						
(You should close the door.)	20	4.2				
8. Performatives						
(I'm requesting you to close			Direct	50.7	(242)	
the door.)	21	4.4				
9. Mood Derivable						
(Close the door.)	205	43				
Mean: 6.48						
SD: 2.58						Direct

Analysis by Predicor Variables

The role of predictor variables in explaining variation in requests was analysed using two types of statistical analysis: first, by cross-tabulation of each predictor variable with the three levels of directness, and second, by performing a stepwise multiple regression analysis that took into account all the variables. The results of the first analysis are presented in Tables 7-2 and 7-3, and the results of the second analysis are shown in Table 7-4.

The results can be summarized as follows:

1. The variables found to be significantly associated with choice on the directness continuum were age, power, social distance, request goal, setting, and medium.
2. The variables that best accounted for variation in requesting strategies (on the scale of directness) were the three types of request goals, the age of the hearer, and the relative power of the speaker.

In the following section, we shall first consider each of the predictor variables in turn, in an attempt to probe the unique contribution of each to the choice of request strategy. Then we shall discuss the findings of the regression

Table 7-2. The Connection Between Various Situational Conditions (Speaker and Hearer, Sex, Age, Power, Relationship, Social Distance, Goals, and Message Medium) and the Choice of Indirect, Conventional, or Direct Requests

Independent variables	Situational condition	Request type used (%)			Total	
		Direct	Conventional	Indirect	%	Number
1. Sex of Partners $x^2 = 6.98$ df = 6 p < .32	Female to female	45.4	38.8	15.8	100.0	(196)
	Female to male	47.4	43.8	8.8	100.0	(57)
	Male to female	45.1	41.8	13.1	100.0	(122)
	Male to male	60.0	20.0	20.0	100.0	(30)
2. Age of Partners $x^2 = 83.94$ df = 12 p < .000	Adult to adult	31.2	53.2	15.6	100.0	(186)
	Adult to teenager	80.0	20.0	—	100.0	(25)
	Adult to child	85.2	3.7	11.1	100.0	(54)
	Teenager to teenager	75.0	20.0	5.0	100.0	(40)
	Teenager to adult	39.7	41.3	19.0	100.0	(63)
	Child to adult	35.9	43.6	20.5	100.0	(39)
3. Power Relationship (Total Sample) $x^2 = 58.62$ df = 4 p < .000	S of higher status	82.8	9.0	8.2	100.0	(122)
	S and H equal	51.5	38.1	10.3	99.9	(97)
	H of higher status	36.4	40.0	23.6	100.0	(110)

				Total	N
4. Power Relationship (Adults Only) $x^2 = 10.39$ df = 4 p < .03					
S of higher status	71.4	28.6	0.0	100.0	(14)
S and H equal	35.2	51.9	13.0	100.1	(54)
H of higher status	29.6	44.4	25.9	99.9	(27)
5. Social Distance of Familiarity $x^2 = 11.53$ df = 4 p < .02					
High (family)	62.5	25.0	12.5	100.0	(56)
Medium (friends, non-nuclear kin)	59.0	27.6	13.4	100.0	(134)
Low (strangers)	45.6	41.3	13.1	100.0	(283)
6. Request Goal $x^2 = 158.34$ df = 6 p < .00					
Action	68.6	21.0	10.4	100.0	(328)
Goods	32.7	56.4	10.9	100.0	(55)
Information	1.7	84.5	13.8	100.0	(58)
Permission	5.7	51.4	42.9	100.0	(35)
7. Communication Medium[a]					
Face to face	57.1	27.6	15.3	100.0	(325)
Phone	14.3	73.6	12.1	100.0	(92)
Written	71.4	26.5	2.0	99.9	(98)

[a] 37 tokens of requests in writing were added to the data for this analysis, bringing the total to 515. The added written data were drawn from letters to the editor, made available to us by Chaim Eyal.

analysis, in an attempt to assess the relative importance of the various predictors in shaping choice of request strategy.

Discussion: Situational Variations in Requesting

The Role of Sex Differences

Sex was found to be the only predictor variable not significantly associated with choice of strategy (Table 7-2). The pattern of distribution is similar irrespective of the sexual composition of the dyad. Thus, contrary to the Lakoff (1975) hypothesis, in Israel at least, women were not less direct than men. It is only in the last group (between males) that the results show a slight increase in use of direct strategies (to 60 percent). This increase in the proportion of direct strategies in the male-male group might reflect a tendency on the part of men to express solidarity with other men through directness. No parallel distinction is detectable in the speech of women. These findings should not be interpreted to mean that there are no sex-associated speech differences in Israeli society, only that we have not found clear ones in the area of requests. It also might be the case that sex-linked differences in Israel are more a matter of expectations (i.e., stereotypes) than of actual use.

A study of the perception of powerful and powerless speech styles in an Israeli courtroom setting revealed sharp differences in what is considered desirable speech in men and women. The more powerful, and less hedged the speech style of a male speaker, the more favorably he was evaluated by both male and female listeners; in contrast, a female speaker speaking in the most powerful style was "punished" for this behavior. The highest marks went to the woman speaking in only a moderately powerful style. This effect was even stronger among female listeners than among males. If these findings are at all applicable to the study of requests, they suggest that a woman, other things being equal, will be "punished" for using a direct strategy, while a man will be evaluated favorably (see Danet & Troutzer, 1983).

The Role of Relative Age

Unlike sex, the age of the hearer relative to the speaker was found to be significantly associated with choice of request strategy. As Table 7-3 indicates, the trend is for *more* directness when the speaker is *older* than the hearer and for *less* directness in the reverse situation, or if the two are of approximately the same age.

The most striking effect of age difference appears in communication between adults and children. When adults address children, 85.2 percent of the strategies are direct. In contrast, when children address adults, only 35.9 percent of their patterns are direct.

The directness in speech to children might stem from the task-oriented nature of many of these exchanges, as exemplified in the series of directives uttered by one mother at her daughter's birthday party, in 5a and b:

5. (Mother to daughter and other children at a birthday party)
   a. to daughter: tilbši et ze (put it on)/tami, tefani makom (Make room for them.)
   b. to other children: laševet (sit down)/et hanyarot ani mevakešet lasim bapax (I'm asking you to put the litter in the litter box.)

In communication with small children, an additional factor might be the tendency of caretakers (Snow, 1979, in press) to adjust the linguistic input to the child's level of comprehension, hence the use of direct forms, which are also the most explicit and syntactically simple ones. It also might be the case that these differences simply reflect asymmetric power relations. This last suggestion is consistent with results for all unequal age groups.

Since indirectness requires the use of grammatically more complex forms than do direct strategies, it is hard to explain its presence in the speech of young children unless we attribute it to their awareness of asymetric power relations. As illustrated by the example given at the beginning of this chapter, a child of three is well aware of the fact that adults are in control of resources, and might resort to indirectness in making a request, especially if it is judged to be an unusual one. Children's use of indirect forms in our study is also in line with two types of findings from previous research: first, that children master early (by four) the full complexity of the linguistic system of requests (McTear, undated; Ervin-Tripp & Gordon, in press), and second, that by four they are selectively deferential to unfamiliar or older people (Ervin-Tripp, O'Connor, & Rosenberg, 1982).

Social Dimensions: Power and Distance

As expected, both relative power (P) and relative social distance (D) were found to be significantly associated with choice of request strategy type. In the total sample (Table 7-3), the trend is for an increase in directness with an increase in power. In downward speech (i.e., requests made by people endowed with power in a given role), 82.8 percent of the tokens were direct, showing directness to be the norm. In contrast, in upward speech, from persons in a powerless position, the proportion of *indirect strategies* is larger than that of the direct ones (36.4 percent direct; 63.6 percent conventional and indirect). We have asked ourselves whether this finding can be attributed to power differences associated with age, and hence also analyzed the distributions for the adult population only. This analysis revealed the same trend, with asymmetry in power being clearly associated with directness levels (Table 7-3).

Such requests by people in a position of power in our data come from directives given by nurses to patients, teachers to students, and drivers to passengers, as illustrated in 6, 7, 8, and 9:

Table 7-3. Distribution of Request Strategies by Power and Social Distance

Request type	Speaker more powerful than hearer (+ power)		Hearer more powerful than speaker (- power)		Speaker and hearer of equal power	
	High social distance (+ SD, strangers)	Low social distance (− SD, family)	High social distance (+ SD, strangers)	Low social distance (− SD, family)	High social distance (+ SD, strangers)	Low social distance (− SD, family)
% Indirect[a] Requests	16.7	18.6	65.6	60.0	73.0	39.6
% Direct Requests	83.3	81.2	34.5	40.0	26.9	60.2
Number	(n = 48)	(n = 48)	(n = 58)	(n = 50)	(n = 26)	(n = 68)

[a]Indirect includes both conventionally indirect and off-record indirect strategies.

6. (Nurse to patients: health clinic)
   Raq rega bevakaša, lo lhikanes iti, ani çrixa la'asot bdika
   (Just a moment, *don't come in*; I have to do a test.)
7. (Nurse to patient: health clinic)
   bseder, tašir et ze, telex vetaxzor yoter meuxar
   (Okay, *leave it here, go,* and come back later.)
8. (University teacher to students: film workshop)
   xevre, lo lehadlik velxabot miyad panasim, atem sorfim otam
   (Hey, don't turn the lights off and on immediately; you're burning them.)
9. (Bus driver to passengers: on the bus)
   xevre, ani avakeš lehorid raglayim mehamošavim
   (Hey, you guys, I'm requesting you to get your feet off the seats!)

When the request is made upward in rank or power, the speaker has to face the possibility not only of noncompliance, but also of being rebuked for making the request at all (of stepping outside his or her rights). Social conventions that call for a show of deference upward in unequal encounters can thus be seen both as an acknowledgment of status and as a self-protective measure. Even when the requester is within his or her rights, as the student asking for an overdue grade in 10, the inequality in power necessitates indirectness:

10. (Student to lecturer: on campus)
    li yes bxinat bayit eçlex kvar harbe zman
    (You've had my take-home exam for quite awhile.)

In speech between *equals* in power, requests are more likely to constitute a threat to both speaker and hearer. The proportionally high level of *conventional requests* (51.5 percent) between equals seems to reflect the need for threat minimization for both parties involved. The exchange in 11 exemplifies a case where "face work" is mainly self-oriented:

11. (Student to student: on campus)
    a. tagidi, ex ha'anglit šelax?
       (Say, how is your English?)
    b. bseder, lama?
       (Okay, why?)
    a. yeš kama d'varim bamamar, xašavti..yeš lax zman?
       (There are a few things in this article. I wondered [pause] would you have time?)

The dimension of social distance was found to be associated with choice of request strategy type in the same direction as depicted for American English (Ervin Tripp, 1976): The trend is for *more directness with an increase in familiarity*. In the total sample, 62.5 percent of requests between familiar speakers fall into this category. Typical examples of requests between familiar adults are exchanges around the dinner table, as in 12:

12. (Wife to husband, at dinner)
    Naftali, ten li kçat leben gam
    (Naftali, get me some yoghurt too.)

But how do relative power and distance interact with each other? Does the relative power of speaker and hearer make the same difference regardless of whether the two know each other or not? Similarly, does social distance affect the choice of strategy the same way in different constellations of power?

To answer these questions, we cross-tabulated the distribution of direct and indirect (conventionally indirect and "off record" strategies) by the two variables. Because of the small number of cases for the purposes of this three-way classification, we have collapsed the data in two ways (see Table 7-3). The following trends emerge:

1. In situations where the speaker is in power (+ P), he or she is *equally likely* to choose a direct strategy *regardless* of whether he or she is acquainted with his or her interlocutor. Thus, it seems that being endowed with power in a given role licenses the use of bald, on-record, direct strategies.
2. In upward speech, from a powerless speaker to a powerful one, the trend is reversed. The speaker is equally likely to choose an *indirect* strategy regardless of social distance. Thus, in upward speech, *indirectness* is preferred over *directness*.

Scollon and Scollon (1983) depict asymmetrical power situations as being by definition associated with social distance (+ D) and predict that in such situations the powerful person's first preference will be to be direct and that of the powerless to be indirect. Since asymmetric power relations can occur with no social distance (for example, parents and children) as well as with great social distance (in a monarchy, for instance), we think that the role of power in asymmetric situations should be considered relative to varying degrees of social distance. By adding this dimension to the analysis, we have found that at least in the society studied, the role of power overrides that of variation in social distance in asymmetrical situations.

3. Shifts in social distance seem to affect choice of strategy in situations of equal power. In equal encounters between strangers (when power is constant), the speakers' first preference is to be *indirect*, while between family and friends, the first preference is to be *direct*. It should be noted, though, that due to the small number of cases for the "strangers" (+ D) situation (n = 28), this finding needs further confirmation.[6] These findings are in line with Scollon and Scollon's (1983) proposal about the effect of social distance in symmetric power situations.

---

[6]Results meanwhile obtained within the CCSARP project (see Blum-Kulka & Olshtain, 1984) indicate that in phrasing a request to a stranger the trend in Hebrew, as well as German, Canadian French, and Australian English is toward *indirectness*.

The trends depicted by these results, if confirmed by further research, would *show social distance to affect choice of requesting strategies only in situations of equal power.*

Type of Request Goal

The aim of the request was found to be significantly associated with choice of strategy: The distribution patterns show requests for action as the most direct (68.6), and requests for permission as the most indirect (Table 7-4).

Requests for action, where compliance requires some activity on the part of the hearer, constitute the largest group in our sample (328 out of 478 tokens). The high level of directness in this group is partly explicable by the types of social motivations for directness suggested in the literature for other languages (Brown & Levinson, 1978; Ervin-Tripp, 1976; Herrmann, 1983).

One such motivation is the need for *efficiency*. In cases where quick compliance is essential for goal achievement, there is a need to formulate the request in the most explicit and shortest way possible, by the use of imperatives or elliptical forms. Communication between passengers and drivers on a crowded bus is one example of such a situation:

13. (Passenger to driver: on the bus)
    Passenger A: ptax et hadelet, nehag
                  (Open the door, driver.) (No response.)
    Passenger B: nehag, delet axorit
                  (Driver, rear door.)
                  (Compliance.)

Achieving fast results is also essential in warnings like 14:

14. (Woman to man: at a party)
    tizaher šeze lo yišaver
    (Careful that it won't break!)

The notion of "metaphorical urgency" (Brown & Levinson, 1978), when one speaks *as if* maximum efficiency were very important explains 15:

15. (Between roommates: student dorm)
    boi laxeder ani sonet et hamitbax haze, ze kaze margiz
    (Come to the room! I hate this kitchen; it's so upsetting!)
    (Referring to the mess.)

Requests for goods are formulated less directly than requests for action. Most of the former fall into the category of conventional indirectness (56.4 percent). Tokens in our sample mainly concerned free goods (Goffman, 1967) or goods of small value, as in 16, 17, and 18.

16. (Student to student: university cafeteria)
    efšar lehištameš baze ulay?
    (Would it be possible to use this perhaps? [referring to the salt shaker])

17. (Student to lecturer: in lecture hall)
    slixa, efšar lakaxat moxek exad?
    (Excuse me, would it be possible to take one eraser?)
18. (Student to librarian: on campus)
    ani yexola rega lekabel et?
    (Can I have a pen for a moment?)

In cases where the request is quite unusual, in that it concerns handing over goods not normally considered "free," indirectness might be further modified by using a mitigating element such as the use of a Yiddishized expression in 19:

19. (Man to woman: university cafeteria)
    ani uxal *lešnorer* mimex sigariya?
    (Can I beg a cigarette from you?)

On the other hand, bids for goods in service encounters, where compliance is normative, are typically direct:

20. (Customer to clerk: post office)
    tni li bevakaša asimon
    (Give me a token, please.)

Requests for information were mostly formulated by conventional indirect strategies. This finding is not surprising, considering the fact that such requests are normally composed of two parts: (1) a genuine question concerning an unknown fact, and (2) a request to be told the unknown fact. The verbal phrasing of such requests must necessarily include the former but might omit the latter, since it is implied by the initial question alone.
   Consider 21 and 22:

21. (Stranger on the street: Boston)[7]
    Could you tell me how to get to the bus station?
22. (Student to lecturer: on campus)
    at yodaat efo xayim ulay?
    (You know where Chaim is perhaps?)

In 21, the request for information is expressed by "Could you tell me?"; in 22 the request to tell is implied, and must conventionally be followed by an affirmative answer. Different degrees of politeness in information questions would thus be expressed by variations on how the information is requested, such as "Would you mind terribly telling me?" versus "Can you tell me?"

Requests for permission are the most indirect (94.3 percent conventional and off record). This indirectness might be related to power differences, since one is more apt to seek permission from a person of higher power than from a person of lower power.

---

[7]This sentence was spoken in English and hence is not part of the analyzed data.

Routine requests for permission tend to be verbalized in our data by conventional indirect forms, such as 23, while nonroutine ones are more elaborate, as in 24:

23. (Student to student: university cafeteria)
    efšar lakaxat kise?
    (Would it be possible to take a chair?)
24. (Patient to cleaning lady: health clinic)
    yafria lax im ani elex lakaxat mispar?
    (Would it bother you if I go to take a number?)

Setting

We distinguished between two major types of settings: public and private. As expected, requests in public were found to be less direct than requests in private, probably because setting is linked to degree of familiarity. Type of setting was associated significantly with level of directness.[8]

Medium

As noted earlier, we have distinguished between three types of channels: written communication, communication by phone, and face-to-face communication. The results indicated that channel is indeed significantly associated with level of directness. The trend was for written requests to be the most direct, and requests on the phone to be the least direct (Table 7-2).

A closer look at our written data from formal correspondence reveals that the shift in register from oral to written style is expressed by a transition from the use of imperatives or elliptical forms to the use of formally marked performatives, as in 25 and 26:

25. (Official notice for Applied Linguistics Conference)
    xavre ha'aguda mitbakšim lišloax et kol hahaçaot leharçaot betakçirim beivrit vebeanglit
    (Members of the association are *requested* to send suggestions for papers in the form of abstracts in Hebrew and English.)
26. (Librarian to members of the Faculty of Social Sciences and Humanities)
    morim hamunyanim bahadraxa kvuçatit lexitoteham mitbakšim lifnot elenu likviat moed veyeanu beraçon
    (Teachers interested in group tours for their classes *are requested* to *contact* us for setting a date and will be willingly helped.)

---

[8]The distributions, for adults only, were as follows: in the public setting, 13.9 percent indirect, 52.1 percent conventional, and 33.9 percent direct; in private setting, 12 percent indirect, 17.9 percent conventional, and 70.1 percent direct (n=282) (x^2 = 39.54935, 2 df, p < 0.000).

Indirectness in written requests appeared in memos from students to teaching assistants (27) or between peers (28):

27. (Student to teaching assistant: memo)
    leçaari neelaçti lehagiš targil ze beixur ... ode lax im tuxli livdok oto
    (Unfortunately, I had to hand in my paper late. *I would be grateful if you could correct it.*)
28. (Research assistant to research assistant: memo)
    at yexola letalfen elai 1 430-291? todah
    (Could you call me at 430-291? Thanks.)

The conversations by phone in our data mostly concerned requests for information between strangers in response to an ad.[9] The high proportion of conventional indirectness can thus be attributed to aim of request and social distance factors rather than to the specific medium.

The level of directness in face-to-face interaction among adults (59.1 percent) is similar to the level of directness in the total sample (50.1 percent), and since it might be linked to any or all of the social variables analyzed so far (power, distance, and goal), it will not be elaborated here any further.

Multivariate Analysis

To assess the relative importance of the various predictor variables, we performed a stepwise regression analysis of the data on request strategies. We used ten variables as predictors, selected on the basis of the results of the cross-tabulation (Table 7-2). Since the variable we have called "goal" of the request is a nominal one, we have entered the four categories of the original variable as separate, dummy variables. Age was entered for speaker or hearer as adult, teenager, or child.

The ten predictor variables accounted for 25.8 percent of variance in choice of request strategies (see Table 7-4). This level is reached with only five of the variables: action as request goal, age of hearer, relative power, and goods and information as types of request goal.

The most interesting finding in Table 7-4 relates to the variables that *are not shown* as explaining variance (had an increase of less than 0.5). Thus, neither permission as type of goal, sex, nor even social distance were shown as having strong explanatory value.

From among the three factors postulated by Brown and Levinson (1978) as

---

[9]The add concerned "Search for a home" for a puppy, and was placed in the local paper of Beer Sheba. All incoming calls were recorded and transcribed. Interested adults and children called to inquire further details and arrange a visit. The level of indirectness found in these requests might partly be due to topics discussed. For example, inquiries about whether the puppy is "house clean" tended to be phrased in the most indirect terms, possibly because there is no equivalent term in Hebrew, but probably also because of the touchiness of the subject.

Table 7-4. Stepwise Regression Analysis of the Predictors of Directness

Predictor Variables in the Equation:
I. Personal variables: 1. Sex of speaker. 2. Sex of hearer.
                            3. Age of speaker. 4. Age of hearer.
II. Contextual variables: 5. Status. 6. Familiarity.
III. Request goal variables: 7. Action. 8. Goods. 9. Information. 10. Permission.

Variable[a]	Multiple R	R^2	R^2 Change	Simple R
Action	0.43850	0.19224	0.19224	0.43845
Age of hearer	0.48134	0.23169	0.03944	−0.30813
Status	0.49282	0.24287	0.01118	0.30748
Goods	0.50302	0.25303	0.01016	−0.12370
Information	0.50863	0.25870	0.00567	−0.26369

[a]Only variables contributing at least 0.005 to the variance are included.

the principal ones accounting for variation in use, two were considered in our study: power and solidarity. When divorced from other factors, such as request goal, both power and social distance are shown to effect choice of strategy. But when all other variables are taken into account, the role of relative power in accounting for variation is relatively very low, and social distance between interlocutors does not seem to play any role at all. Our data suggest that as far as Israeli society is concerned, these two factors do not play as important a role as might be expected. In our view, these findings are in line with the general ethos of directness in Israeli society and, furthermore, they provide a clue to the social motivation behind this directness.

The Nature of the Ethos of Directness in Israeli Society: A Case of Solidarity Politeness?

Viewed in light of the research questions we set out to answer at the beginning of the chapter, the overall results of the study show the following trends:

Degree of Variation

The findings indicate that Modern Hebrew shares with other languages a rich repertoire of requesting strategies which is fully exploited in actual use. Yet, if viewed from a cross-cultural perspective, the general level of directness in Israeli society is probably relatively very high. One possible explanation for this high level of directness is an idealogical-historical one: The early settlers of Palestine were guided by an ideology of egalitarianism, which frowned on all manifestations of possible discrimination between people, including a show of deference in speech. Thus, A. D. Gordon, whose thinking had a major impact on the shaping of Israeli culture, preached the cult of "simplicity" in all areas of life and argued vehemently for the abolition of all forms of "politeness," which to him were neither simple nor natural (Gordon, 1943, p. 234). Looking back on those days, a kibbutz member in an interview that took place in the late Seventies sums up the egalitarian spirit in interaction with the following words: "We were a generation of revolutionaries; we wanted to liberate ourselves from all the norms and values of bourgeois middle class. Manners were one thing we scorned." And she adds by way of explanation, "It is as if we have stretched the sense of equality to an absurd degree" (Lieblich, 1981, p. 38). It is against this background that one should consider the directness of present-day Israeli society; though two generations removed in time and increased many times by diverse immigrant groups, the basic notion of simplicity in interaction is still highly valued.[10]

Social Parameters That Affect Variation

Our results also show, however, that directness is not a norm that prevails in all social interaction. Variability seems minimized where sex differences are concerned, but not for age or power differences, nor for degrees of social distance, different types of request goals, private or public interaction, or channel of communication. Each of these can be seen as one dimension in the multidimensional framework that speakers seem to rely on in choosing a specific request strategy to fit a social situation.

It should be kept in mind that most of the distributions do not show a sharply linear relationship between a social situation variable and the level of directness. Thus, though there is relatively more directness under the condition of minimal social distance than with great social distance (Table 7-2), indirectness also appears under both conditions, as well as under the "medium" condition. In actual use any given social situation is assessed by the speaker in terms of these and probably other dimensions. The decision for choice of strategy is likely to be made on the basis of a complex interaction between all or part of these social parameters, as well as personal preferences.

The Role of Solidarity Politeness in Israeli Society

The results of the regression analysis showed that when all variables are considered together, the most important predictors of request choice are the

---

[10]Katriel (1982) examined a way of speaking known in colloquial Israeli Hebrew as "dugriyut," i.e., "straight," "assertive," or "direct" talk. Israeli informats in open-ended and semistructured interviews characterized "dugriyut" as a way of speaking that involves "sincerity," "truthfulness," and "openness." The informants claimed that despite the threat to face involved in dugri speech, it still served the listener's best interests and was a sign of true respect. Katriel traces this overriding concern with truthfulness of the message about "self" to the social milieu of the culture's formative years, and concludes that the "dugri" way of speaking still occupies a privileged position in Israeli culture, especially in the subculture of the Israeli born.

types of request goal, the relative power of the speaker, and the age of the hearer, while neither sex nor relative social distance have a strong predictive value.

One possible interpretation of this finding is that *in Israeli society relative distance is never assessed as very great.* In Brown and Levinson's terms, such a culture qualifies as a "positive politeness" oriented one—namely, a society in which "the general level of the weightiness of the face threatening act tends to remain low; impositions are thought of as small, social distance as no inseparable boundary to easy-going interaction, and relative power as never very great" (Brown & Levinson, 1978, p. 250).

Findings from two other studies, in which language was not an issue, provide independent confirmation of our interpretation. First, Hofstede (1979) studied workers' perceptions of, and preferences for, psychological distance between themselves and their supervisors in the same multinational corporation in 40 countries. Remarkably, Israel came out next to last: She was outdone by only one country in the low degree of psychological distance workers experienced between themselves and their supervisors (Hofstede, 1979). Thus, even when formal roles within organizations are likely to foster feelings of distance between persons in this society, these feelings are overridden by superordinate feelings of national solidarity.

A second type of research pertinent to our interpretation focussed on the extremely widespread use of personal connections by the public to arrange things in Israeli public bureaucracy (Danet, in press; Danet & Hartman, 1972). The use of "protekzia," as it is called, is not necessarily a universally rejected type of behavior. The fact that bureaucrats might feel obligated to put personal considerations above public norms of behavior in their interaction with the public can be construed as further evidence for the high value placed on solidarity in this culture.

Positive politeness, or, to use Scollon and Scollon's (1983) term, *solidarity politeness*, is expressed by verbal strategies that emphasize in-group membership and the assertion or assumption of reciprocity. The notion of "politeness" is associated in the western world usually with "negative" or "deference" strategies: the show of deference expressed by the effort not to be heard as imposing on the hearer, by not assuming cooperation, and by leaving the hearer elegant options for noncompliance. Deviating from Brown and Levinson's model, Scollon and Scollon regard bald, on-record, direct strategies to form a part of solidarity politeness systems. Our findings corroborate this view. A closer examination of the use of direct strategies in our data shows that often such strategies are embedded in a conversational context that stresses common ground and shared assumptions of cooperation, as in 29:

29. (Passenger and driver: intercity bus)
    Passenger: Turn the light on, please.
       Driver: What?
    Passenger: Turn the light on, please.

Driver: It disturbs me.
Passenger: I wanted to read.
Driver: I can't drive like this.
Passenger: Turn it on just for fifteen minutes. I'm in the middle of a thriller.
Driver: [Turns the light on] I can't drive like this...

This view of regarding solidarity politeness as encompassing directness is further supported by our findings on the use of mitigating elements in request strategies. Most of these elements (63.8 percent) were used with direct strategies, thus linguistically indicating the speaker's need to indicate solidarity by softening the impact of the bald on-record approach.

Not all uses of the direct style can be considered as exemplifying solidarity politeness. The direct, unmodified form, even if intended as showing solidarity, might be easily misinterpreted as presumptuous. Furthermore, in our data the majority of aggravating devices (66.6 percent) were also used with direct strategies. For the requestee or observer, the effect of directness when used with such elements can often be of unjustified bluntness. Nor, as shown above, is the direct style a generally prevailing one in Israeli society. Nevertheless, the emphasis on common ground in social interaction suggested by our findings can be seen as a dominant interactional style in a society that places a low value on social distance.

Summary

The study of requests in Israeli society was undertaken in an attempt to document variation in requesting behavior in Hebrew and to seek out the social situational variables that account for this variation in actual use. The analysis of about 500 naturally occurring requests, drawn from diverse situations, revealed that Modern Hebrew shares with other languages a rich repertoire of requesting strategies which is fully exploited in acutal use. The data also showed that when all variables are considered together (via a multiple regression analysis), the most important predictors of variance are the types of the request goal, the relative power of the speaker, and the age of the hearer, while neither sex nor relative social distance have a strong predictive value.

The way in which speakers chose to formulate a particular request in a given social situation was shown to be affected by both individual and social factors. Thus, requests from children to adults and those addressed to people in a position of power were found to be less direct than requests made in the reverse situations. Directness tended to rise with increase in familiarity, as well as in the transition from the public to the private domain. Requests in written communication were found to have a distinct, explicit (and direct) pattern, different from the oral one, and such distinct patterns are also revealed for different types of request goals, with requests for action being the most direct and requests for permission the least direct.

We think that in interpreting these findings, it is important to distinguish between the emic and the etic standpoints. From an etic standpoint, these findings can be interpreted as reflecting the distinct, culture-specific inter-actional style of Israeli society. The low value attached to social distance, manifested in language by a relatively high level of directness, suggests that the interactional style of this society is basically *solidarity politeness oriented.* From an emic standpoint, our findings indicate that in Israeli society as elsewhere, variation in requesting behavior is to a large extent determined by social factors inherent in the situation. Thus, while showing the distinct cultural features of Israeli requesting behavior, our findings can also be interpreted as providing yet another example of the interdependence of language and social situations.

Acknowledgments. The research has been supported by the Fund for Basic Research, administered by the Israeli Academy of Science. We are indebted to Elite Olshtain, Robert Cooper, David Gordon, Susan Ervin-Tripp, and Catherine Snow for discussing with us at length various aspects of the study and helping us in understanding the issues involved.

References

Austin, J. (1962). *How to do things with words.* Oxford: Oxford University Press.

Blum-Kulka, Sh. (1982). Learning to say what you mean in a second language: A study of the speech act performance of Hebrew second language learners. *Applied Linguistics, 3*(1).

Blum-Kulka, Sh. (1983). Interpreting and performing speech acts in a second language: A cross-cultural study of Hebrew and English. In N. Wolfson & J. Elliot (Eds.), *Tesol and sociolinguistic research.* Rowley, MA: Newbury House.

Blum-Kulka, Sh., & Olshtain, E. (1984). Requests and apologies: A cross-cultural study of speech act realization patterns (CCSARP). *Applied Linguistics, 5*(3).

Brown, R., and Ford M. (1964). Address in American English. In D. Hymes (Ed.), *Language in Culture and Society.* New York: Harper and Row, 234–243.

Brown, P., & Fraser, C. (1979). Speech as marker of situation. In K. Scherer & H. Giles (Eds.), *Social markers in speech.* Cambridge, England: Cambridge University Press.

Brown, P., & Levinson, S. (1978). Universals of language usage: Politeness pheno-mena. In E. Goody (Ed.), *Questions and politeness* (pp. 56–311). Cambridge, England: Cambridge University Press.

Brown, R., & Gilman, A. (1960). The pronouns of power and solidarity. In T. Sebeok (Ed.), *Style in language.* Cambridge, MA:

Danet, B., & Hartman, H. (1972). On 'protektzia': Orientations toward the use of personal influence in Israeli bureaucracy. *Journal of Comparative Administration, 3,* 405–434.

Danet, B., & Troutzer, L. (1983). *Eve against Eve in the promised land: Sex, speech style and impression formation in an Israeli courtroom setting.* Paper presented at the Second International Conference on Language and Social Psychology, University of Bristol, Bristol, England.

Danet, B. (1985). *Abdication from justice: A study of rule-breaking and redress in bureaucratic encounters*. Manuscript submitted for publication.

Edmonson, W. (1981). *Spoken discourse: A model for analysis*. New York: Longman.

Ervin-Tripp, S. (1976). Is Sybil there? The structure of some American English directives. *Language in Society, 5.*

Ervin-Tripp, S., & Gordon, D. P. (in press). The development of requests. In R. E. Schiefelbusch (Ed.), *Communicative competence: Acquisition and intervention*. Baltimore: University Park Press.

Ervin-Tripp, S., O'Connor, M. C., & Rosenberg, I. (1982). Language and power in the family. In Ch. Kramerae & M. Schulz (Eds.), *Language and power in the family*. Urbana-Champaign, IL: University of Illinois Press.

Fraser, B. (1975). Hedged performatives. In P. Cole & S. L. Morgan (Eds.), *Syntax and semantics* (Vol. 3, pp. 187–210). New York: Academic Press.

Fraser, B. (1981). *On requesting: An essay on pragmatics*. Unpublished manuscript, Boston University, Boston, MA.

Goffman, E. (1967). *Interaction ritual: Essays on face to face behavior*. Gordon City, NY: Anchor Books.

Gordon, A. D. (1943). *Collected works*. Tel-Aviv: Stiebel (in Hebrew).

Gordon, D., & Lakoff, G. (1975). Conversational postulates. In P. Cole & I. Morgan (Eds.), *Syntax and semantics; Vol. 3. Speech Acts*. New York: Academic Press.

Herrmann, T. (1983). *Speech and situation*. Berlin: Springer-Verlag.

Hofstede, G. (1979). Hierarchical power distance in forty countries. In C. J. Lammers & D. J. Hickson (Eds.), *Organizations alike and unlike* (pp. 97–119). London: Routledge and Kegan Paul.

House, J., & Kasper, G. (1981). Politeness markers in English and German. In F. Coulmas (Ed.), *Conversational routine* (pp. 157–185). The Hague: Mouton.

Katriel, T. (1982). *Some communicative aspects of the Sabra ethos*. Paper presented at the Annual Meeting of the Society of Applied Anthropology, Lexington, KY.

Labov, W., & Fanshel, D. (1977). *Therapeutic discourse*. New York: Academic Press.

Lakoff, R. (1973). The logic of politeness: Or minding your P's and Q's. *Proceedings of the Ninth Regional Meeting of the Chicago Linguistic Society* (pp. 292–305). Chicago.

Lakoff, R. (1974). What you can do with words: Politeness, pragmatics and performatives. In *Berkeley Studies in Syntax and Semantics* (Vol. I). Institute of Human Learning, University of California, Berkeley.

Lakoff, R. (1975). *Language and woman's place*. New York: Harper & Row.

Lambert, W., & Tucker, G. R. (1976). *Tu vous usted: A social psychological study of address patterns*. Rowley, MA: Newbury House.

Leech, G. N. (1977). Language and tact. L.A.V.T. paper 46, Trier.

Lieblich, A. (1981). *Kibbutz Makom*. New York: Pantheon Books.

McTear, M. F. (undated). Getting it done: The development of children's abilities to negotiate request sequences in peer interaction. Belfast Working Papers in Language and Linguistics, Belfast.

Morgan, I. L. (1978). Two types of convention in indirect speech acts. In P. Cole (Ed.), *Syntax and Semantics: Vol. 9. Pragmatics*. New York: Academic Press.

Scollon, R., & Scollon, S. (1983). Face in interethnic communication. In I. C. Richards & R. W. Schmidt (Eds.), *Language and communication*, New York: Longman.

Searle, J. (1975). Indirect speech acts. In P. Cole & I. L. Morgan (Eds.), *Syntax and semantics: Vol. 3. Speech Acts*. New York: Academic Press.

Searle, J. (1979). *Expression and meaning*. Cambridge, England: Cambridge University Press.

Snow, C. E. (1979). Conversations with children. In P. Fletcher, & M. Gorman (Eds.), *Language Acquisition*. Cambridge, England: Cambridge University Press.

Snow, C. E. (in press). Parent child interaction and the development of communicative ability. In R. L. Schiefelbusch (Ed.), *Communicative competence acquisition and intervention*. Baltimore: University Park Press.

Chapter 8
In-Group/Out-Group Deixis: Situational Variation in the Verbs of Giving and Receiving in Japanese

Patricia J. Wetzel

Social Deixis

This investigation explores the mechanics of in-group/out-group social deixis in Japanese as it is encoded in the verbs of giving and receiving.

The term *deixis* is defined by Lyons (1977) as follows:

> By deixis is meant the location and identification of persons, objects, events, processes and activities being talked about, or referred to, in relation to the spaciotemporal context created and sustained by the act of utterance and the participation in it, typically, of a single speaker and at least one addressee. (p. 636)

More simply, we might say that the meaning of deictic elements shifts according to the situational context in which they are used. The most obvious examples are items like *here/there, come/go, today/tomorrow*, and elements like the personal pronouns and demonstratives, which vary with the requirements of particular social situations.

Social deixis is a term introduced by Levinson (1983) to describe

> elements that encode the social identity of participants ... or the social relationship between them, or between one of them and persons and entities referred to ... in so far as they are grammaticalized. (p. 89)

Examples of social deixis include polite pronouns and address forms (see Brown & Levinson, 1978), use of which depends on the speaker's social relationship to the addressee or persons referred to.

Lyons (1968) also observes that all deictic phenomena are, by definition, egocentric. That is, the spaciotemporal zero point (the *here* and *now*) of deixis is the speaker's point of view.[1] Social deixis, then, is concerned with elements that encode the social identity of the speaker (Ego) vis-à-vis others in the speech or narrated situation.

---

[1]The notion of Ego as deictic zero point is explored in detail by Benveniste (1958).

The verbs of giving and receiving in Japanese must be recognized as socially deictic insofar as their use depends on the social relationship that exists between the giver and receiver in terms of group membership. However, when faced with the task of describing the social deixis that underlies the verbs of giving and receiving, we are obliged to reconsider the nature of the deictic zero point. Use of the verbs of giving and receiving is tied in not with the relationship of the addressee(s) and others to the speaker (Ego) per se, but to the speaker's (Ego's) *group as defined by the context*. What Bachnik (1982) suggests in her account of Japanese honorifics is that:

> [W]e may perhaps safely assume that the deictic anchor point is Ego in societies where the individual is the basic unit of social organization. But in societies where the basic unit is not the individual, the question of the deictic anchor point and its relation to social organization must be raised, rather than assumed. In Japan, the basic social unit is not the individual, but the primary group. (p. 11)

Among Bachnik's conclusions is that, in Japan, the primary group provides the deictic zero point since the zero point of the speaker is not isomorphic with the speaker (Ego) and since the speaker is part of, but does not encompass, the anchor point. In other words, the anchor point of Japanese social deixis cannot be described as Ego. Ego's identification with group in Japan is such that the group provides the anchor point for socially deictic phenomena.

The social deixis that underlies the verbs of giving and receiving in Japanese may be best termed here as *in-group/out-group* deixis. The contextual and situational factors that go into defining group identity are discussed at greater length below. Recognizing variation in the group boundaries that provide the deictic zero point in Japanese is central to a descriptive account of the verbs of giving and receiving.

Group Identification in Japan: "Uti" and "Soto" Situations

Almost anyone who tries to make sense of his or her observations of Japanese social conduct encounters issues associated with the individual as a member of a group or groups. Nakane (1970) is one of the pioneers in defining the structure of Japanese society in terms that take into account criteria of group formation, internal structures of groups, and the overall structure of society. Nakane begins with the observation that there is an overriding tendency for the Japanese to emphasize situational position in a particular frame.

> [W]hen a Japanese "faces the outside" (confronts another person) and affixes some position to himself socially he is inclined to give precedence to institution over kind of occupation ... When a man says he is from X Televison one may imagine him to be a producer or cameraman, though he may in fact be a chauffeur ... In group identification, a frame such as a "company" or "association" is of primary importance; the attribute of the individual is a secondary matter. The same tendency is to be found among intellectuals: among university graduates, what matters most, and functions the strongest

socially, is not whether a man holds or does not hold a Ph.D. but rather from which university he graduated. Thus the criterion by which Japanese classify individuals socially tends to be that of particular institution rather than of universal attribute. Such group consciousness and orientation fosters the strength of an institution, and the institutional unit (such as school or company) is in fact the basis of Japanese social organization. (pp. 2–3)

Lebra's (1976) estimation of the importance of group identity in Japan also stands in sharp contrast to the emphasis placed on the individual in the West:

> The Japanese may legitimately be characterized as 'other directed.' The sense of identity anchored in group belongingness is thus sustained by going along with peers ... [and] concern for belongingness urges the individual to contribute to the group at the expense of his personal interest. [Thus], for Japanese, legitimate egotism includes nation egotism, company egotism, or family egotism, not individual egotism ... Group identification is so internalized that even the inner experience of an individual tends to have collective implications. (pp. 29–35)

That an understanding of group identity within Japanese society is necessary for successful use of the language has been recognized for quite some time. Nakane points out that group consciousness and group orientation are observable in the Japanese use of the expression *uti* ("inside") to mean place of work, school, office, and the like. There are various group identities that fall under the term *uti*. In conversations between Japanese, the terms *uti-no* or *uti dewa* ("our home's" or "at our home") are frequently used to refer to one's own people and work place. *Uti* may refer to an institution as a whole, or it may refer to the department or section to which the speaker belongs (Nakane, 1970, p. 125).

The use of *uti* to refer to the group that provides social identity in various situations is a well-established phenomenon in Japanese. Sanseido's (1982) *Kokugo ziten* (Japanese Dictionary) includes among its entries for *uti*:

> *uti* (n.) ... c. one's own group, company, etc.
> *uti no syain* 'a member of one's company' ...

"The place that one belongs to" is, of course, situationally dependent, even in the West. But it is not nearly as salient a feature of one's identity in the West as it is in Japan. Lebra (1976) describes the importance of group and the situational dependence of group boundaries in Japan as follows:

> The Japanese are known to differentiate their behavior by whether the situation is defined as *uti* or *soto*. That distinction perhaps characterizes human culture in general, but it is essential in determining the way Japanese interact. Where the demarcation line is drawn varies widely: it may be inside vs. outside an individual person, a family, a group of playmates, a school, a company, a village, or a nation. It is suggestive that the term *uti* is used colloquially to refer to one's house, family or family member, and the shop or company where one works. The essential point, however, is that the *uti-soto* distinction is drawn not by social structure but by constantly varying situations. (p. 112)

The Verbs of Giving and Receiving

The nominal element *uti* is only one among many in Japanese whose use depends upon the in-group/out-group distinction. In fact, direct nominal reference to in-group is probably a far less frequently employed strategy for recognizing in-group and out-group than is the use of a verb form that encodes the in-group/out-group distinction. Among such verb forms are the verbs of giving and receiving.

It is significant that any verb can be used by itself as a complete sentence in Japanese. For example, the verb *kaeru* ("return") is a complete sentence, and the speaker need make no overt reference to a subject. It is said that statements in Japanese typically apply to the speaker unless some other topic is established, while questions typically apply to the addressee. The individual getting up from his or her desk to depart might utter the sentence *Kaeru* ("[I]'m going home"). there is no reason to believe that this sentence applies to anyone other than the speaker, and it is in fact assumed to apply to the speaker since no other topic is mentioned. On the other hand, observing a coworker rising from his or her desk, one might ask, *Kaeru*? ("Are [you] going home?"). This question is assumed to apply to the addressee since there is no indication that it applies to anyone else.

The fact that verbs can stand alone as sentences may account in part for the tendency for in-group and out-group to be encoded more frequently in verbal elements than in nominal elements. That is, context does not always make clear who or what is intended, and a common strategy for specifying arguments in Japanese that does not require nominal reference is the use of verb forms that implicitly refer to in-group and/or out-group—such as the verbs of giving and receiving. Because in-group and out-group are inherently associated with particular sentence roles of the verbs of giving and receiving, these verbs carry implicit reference to in-group and out-group situations.

We can begin by broadly defining each verb in the following way.[2]

1. *kureru*: give to in-group
1a. *kudasaru*: give to in-group (polite: honorific)
2. *ageru*: give to out-group
2a. *sasiageru*: give to out-group (polite: humble)
3. *morau*: get from out group
3a. *itadaku*: get from out-group (polite: humble)

When transfer is perceived to be in the direction of the speaker or speaker's in-group in Japanese, the verbs *kureru/kudasaru* ("give to in-group") or

---

[2]This list includes polite forms of the verbs of giving and receiving, but the role of polite forms in implicitly referring to in-group and out-group is not discussed here. A complete account of in-group/out-group deixis must certainly take into account Japanese honorification (see Wetzel, 1984). However, the set of verbs for giving and receiving can be discussed on their own merits apart from the system of polite forms.

morau/itadaku ("get from out-group") are used. When transfer is in the opposite direction, away from the speaker or the speaker's in-group, the verbs *ageru/sasiageru* are used.

Below are example sentences for the verbs of giving and receiving. Bracketed words in the English translation indicate information not specified in the Japanese. The Japanese postpositions *o* and *ga* which indicate the object and subject in these sentences are glossed as OBJ and SUBJ.

4a. *Hon o   kureru.*
    book OBJ give to in-group.
    "[She] will give [me] a book."

4b. *Mari-san ga   kureru.*
    Mari   SUBJ give to in-group
    "Mari will give [it] [to me]."

4c. *Kureru.*
    give to in-group
    "[She] will give [it] [to me]."

4d. *Kaite   kureru.*
    writing give to in-group
    "[She] will write [it] [for me]."

5a. *Hon o   ageru.*
    book OBJ give to out-group
    "[I] will give [her] a book."

5b. *Mari-san ni ageru.*
    Mari   to give to out-group
    "[I] will give [it] to Mari."

5c. *Ageru.*
    give to out-group
    "[I] will give [it] [to her]."

5d. *Kaite   ageru.*
    writing give to out-group
    "[I] will write [it] [for her]."

6a. *Hon o   morau.*
    book OBJ get from out-group
    "[I] will get a book [from her]."

6b. *Mari-san kara morau.*
    Mari   from get from out-group
    "[I] will get [it] from Mari."

6c. *Morau.*
    get from out-group
    "[I] will get [it] [from her]."

6d. *Kaite   morau.*
    writing get from out-group
    "[I] will get [her] to write [it]."

Let us examine each of these in more detail. Example 4a, *Hon o kureru*, is glossed here as "[She] will give [me] a book," but the Japanese gives information to the effect that some one of us in the in-group will give a book to someone outside the in-group. The giver might be specified, as in 4b, *Mari-san ga kureru* ("Mari will give [it] [to me]"). But no arguments are necessarily specified, as example 4c illustrates: *Kureru* ("[She] will give [it] [to me]"). This sentence, overheard in a Japanese discourse, can effectively be taken to mean "Someone (and we know who) outside the in-group will give something (and we know what) to us, or to some one of us in the in-group (and we know who)." A child who goes in to ask for candy from a group of adults on behalf of her friends might emerge and utter in triumph, *Kureta!* (perfective of *kureru*) ("[They] gave [it] [to me/us]!"). No nominal arguments are necessary to make clear who did the giving, what was obtained, and who benefits from the giving.

Contrast these examples of *kureru* with examples 5a–d, illustrating *ageru*. Sentence 5a, *Hon o ageru*, is glossed as "[I] will give [her] a book," but like the corresponding example with *kureru*, this sentence can effectively be taken to mean "someone in the in-group will give a book to someone outside the in-group." In actual discourse, context provides referents for in-group and out-group.

Similarly, examples 6a–d illustrate the verb *morau*, "get from out-group." Notice that *morau* can only be used in situations when in-group receives from out-group. Certain apparent exceptions to this will be discussed below. However, to describe transfer from in-group to out-group, *ageru* is typically the appropriate verb in Japanese.

The d examples above illustrate another feature of the grammar of the verbs of giving and receiving. *Kaite kureru* can be taken to mean "[She] will do [me] the favor of writing [it]" or, more commonly in English, "[She] will write [it] [for me]." That is, the verbs of giving and receiving occur in combination with verbal elements to describe favors or actions that we might view as beneficial where we in English might say "for me" or "for us."

To give some indication of how often the verbs of giving and receiving are used in discourse, there were 29 of these verbs in a spoken discourse sample of approximately 1950 words.[3] Moreover, all 29 were used in combination with a verbal element like *kaite* ("writing") in the d examples above.

---

[3]The number of "words" in the data sample is estimated here since it is not clear that there is any adequate definition for what a "word" is in Japanese. The estimate is made on the basis of elements being separated by a space in the transcription.

Situational Variations in Group Boundaries

Lebra's (1976) observation that the in-group/out-group distinction is drawn by constantly varying situations is crucial to describing how the verbs of giving and receiving function. Japanese in-group/out-group social deixis differs profoundly from other deictic phenomena in that the bounds of the deictic center shift. Lebra offers the examples of playmates, family, company, and individual person as possible legitimate in-groups. These examples provide an excellent opportunity for describing the circumstances under which a particular in-group provides the deictic center, and how this might be reflected in the verbs of giving and receiving.

Group of Friends/Playmates as In-group

Recall the example offered earlier where the child goes in to ask a group of adults for candy on behalf of her friends. She exclaims on emerging:

7. *Kureta*!
   gave to in-group
   "[They] gave [it] [to us]!"

or

8. *Moratta*!
   got from out-group
   "[We] got [it]!"

The difference between these is similar to the difference between the English *give* and *got*, and will not be pursued here. What is of interest to this investigation is that the in-group is the children who receive the candy, while the out-group is the adults who consented to give the child what she asked for.

When this incident is reported from the adults' point of view later, they, of course, assume the role of in-group giving to out-group, and any one of them might say:

9. *Okasi o   ageta*.
   candy OBJ gave to out-group
   "[We] gave [them] candy."

Notice that nothing in the Japanese tells us whether or not the adults know that the candy was for the child who came in or for her and her friends, nor whether the source of the candy was a single individual or more than one. By the same token, nothing in the child's speech tells us whether she obtained candy from a single individual, or from more than one person, nor whether there was a single recipient or more than one. The Japanese is vague: Whether the makeup of in-group and out-group is one or more than one person is not necessarily salient information. If the little girl had asked for candy for 20 friends, Japanese speakers would be more likely to indicate this at some point since this is a rather large number of children to provide candy for. Otherwise, the makeup of in-group and out-group in terms of number is not necessarily specified. As observers, we can infer what the makeup of in-group and out-group is—information that the participants themselves might not be privy to when the transfer takes place.

Family as In-group

Imagine a family traveling together that gets lost on the streets of a new city, and is told the way by a stranger. Any member of the family might have asked the passerby for directions. But in relating the incident to friends later, Member A says:

10. *Kyoo miti ga   wakaranaku   natte*
    today way SUBJ not understand becoming

    komatte itara, sinsetu na hito   ga
    bothered being kind   person SUBJ

    miti o   osiete kureta.
    way OBJ telling gave to in-group.

    "Today [we] got lost and a kind person told [us] the way."

The family benefited from being told the way and is the in-group, while the stranger is the out-group.

If one member of the family had actively solicited the passerby's help, the incident might be related using the verb *morau*:

11. *Ano hito   ni   miti o*
    that person from way OBJ

    osiete moratta.
    telling got from out-group

    "[I/we] got that person to tell [me/us] the way."

The stranger, then, in relating the same incident to friends, assumes the role of in-group giving to out-group:

12. *Miti o   osiete ageta.*
    way OBJ telling gave to out-group

    "[I] told [them] the way."

Company as In-Group

The following example of company as in-group comes from the author's own experience. It involves a bank customer—an American—who is having difficulty using the computerized cash machine commonly found in Japanese banks. She is approached by a man who has just finished using the adjacent machine. He finishes his own transaction, notices that the American is having trouble, and offers his assistance. He takes the American's cash card, and begins by saying:

13. *Mazu, kotira ni irete*
    first here in putting in

    itadaite . . .
    getting from out-group (humble)

    "First, [we] have you put [it] in here . . . "

This Japanese speaker's use of *itadaite* ("getting from out-group; humble") would be inappropriate in this situation were he an individual having no connection with the bank. His use of this verb is thus a clear indication that he is a bank employee, and the in-group implicitly referred to is the bank he represents.

Individual as In-Group

The ultimate in-group is, of course, the individual. In fact, just as statements using other verbs are taken to apply to the speaker in the absence of evidence to the contrary, so statements using the verbs of giving and receiving are taken to apply to the speaker in the absence of evidence that the in-group is other than the speaker alone. Imagine a situation similar to the one described above involving a family that gets lost in a strange city, but which involves an individual who asks a passerby the way. The scene can be described in the same terms:

10. *Kyoo miti ga wakaranaku natte*
    today way SUBJ not understand becoming

    komatte itara, sinsetu na hito ga
    bothered being kind person SUBJ

    miti o osiete kureta.
    way OBJ telling gave to in-group.

    "Today [I] got lost and a kind person told [me] the way."

If this sentence is heard in isolation, the subject, or in-group, is most likely to be understood as the speaker alone.

Consider now the following example from Kuno (1978, pp. 117–118). Kuno's asterisk denotes unacceptability of the interpretation rather than ungrammaticality.

14. *Taroo-san ga Hanako no uti ni kita*
    Taro SUBJ Hanako 's house to came

    no de, Hanako wa yuusyoku o gotisoo-site
    *0
    NOM since Hanako TOP supper OBJ treat doing

agemasita.
gave

"Since Taro came to Hanako's house, Hanako [*she] made him dinner."

Kuno observes that ellipsis rather than *Hanako wa* in this example is unacceptable if the sentence is to be interpreted as *Hanako* who made dinner. However, Hamada (1983, p. 78) points out that the inference that Japanese speakers are likely to draw from the sentence above without *Hanako wa* is that it was the speaker who treated *Taro* to dinner since he came to *Hanako's* house. That is, when the above sentence is uttered in isolation, it is not the case that it is uninterpretable. Rather, the subject of *ageta* ("gave to out-group") is taken to be the speaker since the speaker is assumed to be in-group when no other group is evident in the situation.

As the above examples illustrate, a group might consist of one individual, or it might consist of an entire group. Often it is not clear, in fact, whether a speaker intends one individual or the group to which that individual belongs in using these verbs. What is of central importance is that Japanese speakers are more likely to distinguish in-group from out-group in many situations than they are to distinguish person.

Deictic Projection

It is by now well-established that signaling empathy—identifying oneself with others in either the speech or the narrated situation—is one of the functions of deictic forms in many languages. For example, one strategy of positive politeness that Brown and Levinson (1978, p. 131) note is to "convey that S [Speaker] and H [Hearer] are cooperators" by including both in the activity. They offer the English example of "Let's have a cookie," where one might take advantage of person categories to include the addressee.

Another way in which English speakers take advantage of deictic projection is when they include themselves in another's experience and ask, for example, "What did we do at school today?" (of a child) or "How are we feeling today?" (doctor to patient).

Lyons (1977, p. 579) calls such uses of deictic expressions in ways that shift the deictic center away from the speaker "deictic projection."

In Japanese, the following are for the most part unnatural:

15. ??*Watakusi ni ageta.*
     I   to gave to out-group
     "??[Someone] gave [it] to me."

16. ??*Watakusi ga   kureta.*
     I   SUBJ gave to in-group

"??I gave [it] [to someone]."

17. *??Watakusi ni   moratta.*
    I   from got from out-group

"??[Someone] got [it] from me."

An exception to this is the case of deictic projection—in a context where the speaker for some reason is viewing the situation from the point of view of someone else. Consider a situation where I gave a friend a sweater as a gift and see him a week later wearing the sweater, full of stains and spills, obviously poorly taken care of. I might then say:

18. *Watakusi ni   moratta seetaa   o*
    me   from got   sweater OBJ

    anna   huu ni kitanaku sityatte ...
    like   that way in dirty   using

    "[Imagine] using the sweater that [you] got from me like that ... "

I can take the perspective of the recipient of the sweater in communicating to him how I, as the giver, interpret his treatment of my gift.

Other examples of deictic projection involve the speaker taking the perspective of others in the narrated situation when neither the speaker nor any member of the speaker's group as defined by the context are involved in the transfer. That is, when the speaker is involved in the transfer, the speaker is normally included in the in-group. When the speaker is not involved in the transfer, the following possibilities arise: (1) If the addressee or addressee's group is involved, the addressee is included in the in-group. Or (2) if neither the speaker nor the addressee is involved, some third person or persons may be the in-group. This usually reflects that the speaker empathizes with whomever is designated as the in-group. As an example of the first of these, imagine that you see your friend carrying a package after a wedding that you yourself did not attend. You might then ask:

19. *Nani o   kureta?*
    what OBJ gave to in-group

    "What did [they] give [you]?"

You, the speaker, are not part of the in-group that received gifts. Rather, this question applies to the addressee, and the out-group can only be a third party—in this case, the couple at the wedding.

Similarly, in asking the friend what she gave to the couple as a wedding gift, you might ask:

20. *Nani o   ageta?*
    what OBJ gave to out-group

    "What did [you] give [them]?"

Again, you, the speaker, are not involved in the transfer, and so in-group includes only the addressee, while out-group is the couple.

The second possibility mentioned above—that some third person might be in-group—again arises only when neither the speaker nor the addressee is involved in the transfer. Imagine relating the following incident to a friend: You met Hanako after a wedding she had attended, and she was given a *furosiki* as a gift by the couple. You might be equally close to Hanako and the couple, and you can relate the incident from either point of view. If you tell the incident from Hanako's point of view, your choice of verb is *kureru*:

21. *Hurosiki o   kureta.*
    furosiki OBJ gave to in-group
    "[They] gave [her] a furosiki."

Of course, you might choose to tell the same incident from the couple's point of view, in which case your choice of verb is *ageru*:

22. *Hurosiki o   ageta.*
    furosiki OBJ gave to out-group
    "[They] gave [her] a furosiki."

Levinson (1983, p. 64) suggests that one form of deictic projection involves shifting the deictic center to the protagonists of narratives. Indeed, Downing (1980, pp. 114–115) notes that Japanese informants frequently employed the donatory predicates in the descriptions of exchanges that she used as data, and she offers the following[4] as an example:

23. *Sore de, ... hurimuite   de   boosi todokete*
    then   turning around and hat   bringing back

    kureta no,   sono hitori no ko ga.   Da   kara, ...
    gave   EXTP that one   boy SUBJ COP since

    sono yoonasi   mitai na   no o,   mittsu agete,
    that Western pear like   COP one OBJ three giving

    "Then he turns around, and brings the hat back for him, one of those boys. So he gives them three of those Western pear-like things."

In its use of the *kureta* ("give to in-group"), this informant's description, Downing stresses, indicates "rather explicitly that she as the speaker was taking the point of view of the boy on the bicycle (the boy whose hat was returned), who had been, up to that point, the hero of the story."

Two other examples of deictic projection arise in data collected for this investigation. Both are from a meeting of a university archery club, the purpose of which was to elect officers for the coming year. In the first example,

---

[4]Both the gloss and the translation of this example are from Downing.

one candidate for president brings up the subject of the elected officers. Judging from his use of *kudasaru* ("give to in-group, hon"), he includes himself among them:

24. *minasan   hazime   ooen-site*
    everyone beginning help doing

    kudasaru
    give to in-group (hon)

    "Everyone will help [us] at first."

The same speaker later sets up a hypothetical situation using the provisional form of the copula *naraba* ("if it is the case") in which club members cannot attend meetings:

25. *Doo site mo   kurabu no hoo dete   korenai*
    no matter what club   coming cannot come

    to   iu   naraba,   zibun no sekinin   de
    QT say COP (prov) self   responsibility COP

    zibun de sore o   mondai o   kaiketu suru nari,
    self   by that OBJ problem OBJ solve   do   or

    mosiku wa ue   no yakuin ni   sore o   site
    or   above   officer from that OBJ doing

    morau   nari site ...
    get from out-group or doing

    "If [you] can't come to the club no matter what, [since] it's [your] own responsibility [you] have to solve that problem for [your]self, or get an officer above [you] to solve [it for you]."

In-group—those who "get an officer . . . to solve [it]"—will not include this speaker, since he himself is running for office, and is describing what he believes to be his role as an officer. For the moment, however, via deictic projection, he has taken the perspective of those club members who find themselves in the situation he describes.

We can thus arrange the person categories in a hierarchy for the likelihood of their being in-group:

First > Second > Third

That is, the speaker, if he or she is a participant in the narrated situation, is the first candidate for in-group. If the speaker is not a participant, the addressee is the next most likely candidate for in-group. And third person is the last on the hierarchy.

Consider now the following sentences from Kuno (1976a):

26. *Tanaka-san wa   Suzuki-san ni hon   o*
    Tanaka   TOP Suzuki   to book OBJ

agemasita.
gave to out-group

"Tanaka gave Suzuki a book."

27. *Tanaka-san wa   Suzuki-san ni   hon   o*
    Tanaka   TOP Suzuki   from book OBJ

    moraimasita.
    got from out-group

    "Tanaka got a book from Suzuki."

According to Kuno, these sentences do not seem to require that *Tanaka* be closer than *Suzuki* to the speaker. In connection with this, he proposes what he calls "empathy-related principles" (p. 252–253), which are:

1. The Ban on Conflicting Empathy Foci: A single sentence cannot have more than one focus of the speaker's empathy.
2. The Speech-Act Participant Empathy Hierarchy: It is not possible for the speaker to empathize with someone else to the exclusion of him- or herself.
   Speaker/Hearer > Third Person
3. The Surface Structure Empathy Hierarchy: Subject > Object > ... > Passive by Agentive

Kuno distinguishes between empathy and actual closeness of the speaker with referents of the subject and dative object. Empathy, he says, refers to "the speaker's identifying himself, in varying degrees, with the participants of an event or state that he describes" (p. 251). In Kuno's framework the speaker's identifying with *Tanaka* is reflected in *Tanaka* occupying the subject position. The person hierarchy, Principle 2, is irrelevant in these examples since there is no first- or second-person involvement in these sentences.

The problem with Kuno's analysis is that he assumes that categories of person are the relevant deictic categories for analyzing Japanese empathy. But compare Kuno's version of the person hierarchy in Japanese with the hierarchy he sets up for English (Kuno 1976b, p. 433):

Speaker > Hearer > Third Person

The very form that these hierarchies take in the two languages should be an indication that there is a two-way opposition overriding the three-way person opposition that he suggests for Japanese. Kuno's

Speaker/Hearer > Third person

hierarchy is less appropriate for describing empathy in Japanese than is the hierarchy:

In-group > Out-group

Constraints on the makeup of in-group and out-group in discourse have already been discussed. One of these is that the speaker or speaker's group, if it is a participant, is typically found in the role of in-group. If neither the speaker nor the speaker's group is a participant, the addressee or addressee's group is the next most likely candidate for in-group.

What happens when neither the speaker nor hearer is a participant in the narrated situation and some other group or individual is set up as the topic of discussion, is that this group or individual is likely to receive empathy—in other words, to be in-group. Recall example 15 above, in which the speaker is assumed to be in-group when no other in-group has been established. Again:

15. *Taroo-san ga   Hanako no uti   ni kita*
    Taro   SUBJ Hanako 's house to came

    no   de,   Hanako wa   yuusyoku o   gotisoo-site
                    *0
    NOM since Hanako TOP supper   OBJ treat   doing

    agemasita.
    gave

    "Since Taro came to Hanako's house, Hanako [*she] made him dinner."

Omission of *Hanako wa* is possible in this example, Hamada (1983) says, if there is a preceding sentence that clearly indicates that *Hanako* is the topic (p. 78):

28. *Hanako wa   me o   tozite*
    Hanako TOP eye OBJ closing

    sakuya   no dekigoto no koto o
    last night 's incident 's thing OBJ

    kangaete ita.
    thinking   was

    "With her eyes closed Hanako was thinking about last night's incident."

29. *Yuugata Taroo-san ga   Hanako no uti   ni*
    evening Taro   SUBJ Hanako 's house to

    kita   no   de   Hanako wa
                            0
    came NOM since Hanako TOP

    yuusyoku o   gotisoo-site   agemasita.
    supper   OBJ treat   doing gave

    "Since Taro came to Hanako's house in the evening she (or Hanako) made him dinner."

This is just what Kuno's second principle implies, but Kuno's principles do not recognize the in-group/out-group deictic distinction, deictic projection, or the relationship of person categories to in-group and out-group.

Conclusion

There are a number of parallels between these Japanese verbs of giving and receiving and other phenomena that fall within the realm of social deixis—such as honorifics (Comrie, 1976) and polite pronouns and address forms (Brown & Gilman, 1960). We can say of all socially deictic phenomena that they reflect the grammaticalization and lexicalization of social information in language structure. Levinson (1983) emphasizes that social deixis is a central concern of linguistics proper, and not simply a matter of sociolinguistic investigation: "Social deixis can be systematically restricted to the study of facts that lie firmly within the scope of structural studies of linguistic systems" (p. 93). The Japanese verbs of giving and receiving should be of interest to anyone investigating the possible range of socially deictic categories, as well as to those who are concerned with how and where socially deictic information is encoded in language. Together with the Israeli data presented in the chapter by Blum-Kulka, Danet, and Gershon (this volume, Chapter 7), the present investigation supports the view that socially and culturally crystallized definitions of interactive situations are reflected in common strategies of language use.

Within the context of this volume in particular, linguistic studies like the present one provide a useful complement to the more psychological-cognitive (e.g., van Dijk, and Hoppe-Graff, Hermann, Winterhoff-Spurk, & Mangold, this volume, Chapters 4 and 5) or social-cultural (e.g., Blum-Kulka et al., in this volume) investigations of the link between language and social situations. The data presented here suggests that Japanese think about and cognitively represent social situations in terms of their group rather than individual identity, a cognitive habit that specifically reflects characteristics of that culture, and manifests itself in situationally dependent language choices not typically found in Western countries. In Bruner's terms (this volume, Chapter 2), the "formats" of interaction in Japan clearly differ from our situation definition strategies. The data discussed here should provide a useful impetus for examining the cross-cultural validity of some of the more specific processing models presented in this volume.

Acknowledgments. I am indebted to a number of people at Cornell University for their contributions of criticism and support during my research for this chapter. They include Sally McConnell-Ginet, Eleanor H. Jorden, Joseph P. Grimes, and Elizabeth Hengeveld. All errors that remain are my own.

References

Bachnik, J. M. (1982). Deixis and self/other reference in Japanese discourse. *Sociolinguistic Working Papers 99*. Austin, TX: Southwest Educational Development Laboratory.
Benveniste, E. (1971). Subjectivity in language. (From *Journal de psychologie 55*.) In

E. Benveniste, *Problems in general linguistics* (pp. 223–230). Coral Gables, FL: University of Miami Press. (Original work published 1958).

Brown, P. & Levinson, S. (1978). Universals in language usage: Politeness phenomena. In E. N. Goody (Ed.), *Questions and politeness* (pp. 56–289). Cambridge: Cambridge University Press.

Brown, R., & Gilman, A. (1960). The pronouns of power and solidarity. In T. A. Sebeok (Ed.), *Style in language* (pp. 253–276). Cambridge, MA: MIT Press.

Comrie, B. (1976). Linguistic politeness axes: Speaker-addressee, speaker-referent, speaker-bystander. *Pragmatics microfiche*, 1.7:A3. Cambridge: University of Cambridge Dept of Linguistics.

Downing, P. (1980). Factors influencing lexical choice in narrative. In W. L. Chafe (Ed.), *The pear stories* (pp. 89–126). Norwood: Ablex.

Hamada, M. (1983). *Referential choices in theme, subject, and ellipsis in written narrative discourse: A case study of Japanese folktales.* Unpublished master's thesis, Cornell University, Ithaca, NY.

Kokugo Ziten. (1982). Tokyo: Sanseido.

Kuno, S. (1976a). The speaker's empathy and its effect on syntax: A reexamination of *yaru* and *kureru* in Japanese. *Journal of the Association of Teachers of Japanese, 9:2 & 3*, 249–271.

Kuno, S. (1976b). Subject, theme, and the speaker's empathy: A reexamination of relativization phenomena. In N. L. Charles (Ed.), *Subject and Topic.* (pp. 417–444) New York: Academic Press.

Kuno, S. (1978). *Danwa no bunpoo* ("The grammar of discourse"). Tokyo: Taishukan Shoten.

Lebra, T. S. (1976). *Japanese Patterns of Behavior.* Honolulu, HI: University Press of Hawaii.

Levinson, S. C. (1983). *Pragmatics.* Cambridge: Cambridge University Press.

Lyons, J. (1968). *Introduction to theoretical linguistics.* Cambridge: Cambridge University Press.

Lyons, J. (1977). *Semantics* (Vol. 2). Cambridge: Cambridge University Press.

Nakane, C. (1970). *Japanese society.* Hammondsworth: Penguin Books.

Wetzel, P. J. (1984). *Uti and soto* ("In-group and out-group"): Social deixis in Japanese. Unpublished doctoral thesis, Cornell University, Ithaca, NY.

Chapter 9
Situational Influences on Perceptions of Accented Speech

Cynthia Gallois and Victor J. Callan

Many writers (e.g., Argyle, Furnham, & Graham, 1981) have pointed to the influence of social situations on every aspect of communication. Rommetveit (1982) has even suggested that the scope of word meanings themselves must include the situations in which the words are used. It is also known that language, language variety, and accent (see Fishman, 1971) and the nonverbal behaviors accompanying speech (see Argyle et al., 1981) change along with the goals, roles, and rules associated with the situation. This chapter describes research in Australia involving perceptions of accented speech, which vary as a function of both the speaker's and listener's social groups and the particular social situation.

Situational Influences on the Perception of Speech

A well-established tradition of research, beginning with the work of Lambert, Hodgson, Gardner, and Fillenbaum (1960), has examined the ways in which language and accent influence listener evaluations of speakers. This research has established in many countries that listeners use language and accent as cues to the group membership of the speaker. Where there is a history of hostility or discrimination, listeners evaluate speakers from disliked or subordinate groups negatively, and members of disadvantaged groups may extend this negative evaluation to speakers using their ingroup language or accent. It appears that virtually anything can serve as a cue to group membership, and thus can influence perceptions of speakers (see Tajfel & Forgas, 1981; Tajfel & Turner, 1979).

In the last decade or so, research on perceptions of language and accented speech has been criticised for failing to take adequate account of situational influences. Situational variables comprise all those aspects of a social encounter that could be altered without changing the essential or identifying characteristics of any of the interactants. Situational variables may include stable features of participants, such as social group membership, but only insofar as these features can affect the relationship between the interactants. In recent work, two major types of situational variables that affect intergroup encounters have been considered. The first type, *macrolevel variables*, involves the general social relations between members of two groups, such as hostility over time, the dominance of one group over the other, and the cultural or linguistic similarity between the groups. The second type, *microlevel variables*, has to do with the immediate encounter, and includes equality or inequality of status and power, formality of the context, and rules for appropriate behavior.

Macrolevel Variables

Giles, Bourhis, and Taylor (1977) have put forward a model of ethnolinguistic vitality which proposes that the survival of a speech community is to a large extent determined by a complex array of macrolevel situational variables, including the status of the group, demographic features (population size, geographic spread), and institutional supports. A minority or nonstandard language variety is more likely to survive if its speakers have economic and social status, are concentrated geographically, have low rates of intergroup marriage, and use their language in school or in government. In addition, multiethnic communities range in language attitudes from total rejection of a minority language, accent, or speech style to favorable opinions toward both a majority and a minority language or variety, depending on the utility of these attitudes to the speakers (Ryan, Giles, & Sebastian, 1982). The macrolevel situation within which a social interaction exists will influence the initial attitudes of listeners toward speakers and their accents. In research on language attitudes, the macrosituation must be described in enough detail to allow perceptions of accented speech to be compared from one study to another.

Microlevel Variables

The theory of speech accommodation elaborated by Giles and Powesland (1975) posits a number of microlevel situational variables, external to the speaker but existing in the interaction, which influence the extent to which one speaker converges in language or accent toward another. For example, speech styles converge or diverge as a function of the formality of the context (Labov, 1972; Rubin, 1968), the physical setting, including interpersonal distance (Jourard & Friedman, 1970), and the topic (Ervin-Tripp, 1964; Fishman, 1971). These variables also influence listener evaluations of convergent or divergent speech (Ball, 1983; Giles & Ryan, 1982), as does the range and strictness of norms within the situation (McKirnan & Hamayan, 1983).

Research on the perception of social situations has isolated a number of central dimensions. They begin with (1) dominance, status, or power, and (2) affiliation or solidarity (Argyle, 1972; Brown & Gilman, 1960). To these dimensions, Mehrabian (1972) added a third: attention, arousal, or involvement. More recently, Wish and his colleagues (Wish, 1979; Wish, D'Andrade, & Goodnow, 1980) have added two more: formality and task structure. In addition, Forgas (1981) has pointed to the special importance of formality and intimacy. Work on speech accommodation and perceptions of accented speech, however, has focused on situations stressing status or solidarity (e.g., Ryan & Carranza, 1975), and on the extent to which the situation is group-centered or person-centered (see Giles & Ryan, 1982).

The emphasis on status and solidarity is derived from the work of sociolinguists (e.g., Fishman, 1971) who have pointed out that one speech variety may be associated with status, achievement, and social mobility (*high language*), while a second variety is connected with feelings of friendliness and solidarity (*low language*), and is more likely to be used in informal, private contexts involving the home and family. Few studies of listener evaluations of speakers have examined status and solidarity. Those that have done so have generally found more favorable perceptions of nonstandard or minority speakers on attributes such as friendliness and helpfulness (Lieberman, 1975; Lyczak, Fu, & Ho, 1976) and in solidarity-stressing situations (Giles & Sassoon, 1983; Ryan & Carranza, 1975).

In their 1979 paper, Tajfel and Turner argued that the salience of the ingroup to a speaker or listener in a particular situation is an important predictor of language attitudes. Recently, Ball, Giles, and Hewstone (1983) have postulated that group salience combines with favorability of attitude toward the outgroup in a nonlinear manner, best described by a cusp catastrophe model, to produce speech convergence or divergence. The degree of group or person salience is determined by such situational features as the number of outgroup members present, language used, level of acquaintance between interactants, and extent of threat to the ingroup (Giles & Ryan, 1982).

As the preceding discussion has indicated, the social, political, and economic macrolevel situation determines the survival, vitality, and prestige of language varieties and accents. In addition, at the microlevel, interactants do not have a single, unchanging attitude to a language or variety. Rather, their perceptions appear to be determined by the dynamics of the particular encounter. The later sections of this chapter summarize the results of three studies that we have conducted in Australia. These studies involve members of four ethnic minority groups: Australian Aborigines, who have a long history of disadvantage, prejudice, and segregation from the Anglo-Celtic majority; Greeks and Italians, who represent the largest immigrant groups from outside Britain and Ireland; and British speakers, who form an ethnic group closely related to the majority and whose speech enjoys high prestige in Australia (Ball, 1983; Seggie, Fulmizi, & Stewart, 1982). Speakers were evaluated in situations that stressed status (school, job interview) or solidarity (home, wedding party) and varied in formality and intimacy. In addition, the studies varied in the extent to which the situation was group-centered or person-centered.

The Macrolevel Situation in Australia

Australia is a multiethnic country, with about one-third of its population made up of immigrants and their children. This feature of the country, along with the establishment by recent Australian governments of a policy of multiculturalism, means that there is a need for sensitivity to cultural differences in many social situations. According to the ideals of multiculturalism, no single ethnic group has a monopoly on the definition of appropriate roles and behavioral rules in social encounters between groups. On the other hand, there is a long history of insensitivity by the Anglo-Celtic majority to cultural differences, and a belief that ultimately ethnic and racial minorities should adopt the attitudes, values, and speech of the majority (Callan, 1983). There remains a subtle level of discrimination, rarely overt or perceived by those who practice it but nevertheless real and felt by those who are subjected to it. No minority group has a language with very high ethnolinguistic vitality and, unlike Canada for example, no minority ethnic group has refused to adopt the majority language. Nonetheless, members of minority groups often use the ingroup language, or what is labeled as the community language, at home, in social and religious situations, and, less often, at work.

A special focus of our research is young adults: Anglo-Australians (children of Anglo-Celtic families who have been in Australia for several generations), the children of immigrant parents, and the more educated children of nontribal Australian Aborigines. Considerably more than their parents, minority young people are educated in the schools of the majority, work with them, and later intermarry with members of the dominant group. English is the language of instruction, and nonstandard varieties of speech are not regarded favorably at school (Ball, 1983; Eltis, 1980). Research in other multiethnic settings (e.g., Lyczak et al., 1976; Ryan & Carranza, 1975) has indicated that young members of minority groups evaluate the speech of the dominant group more highly when the macrolevel situation is of this type.

In contrast to their parents, Greek-Australian and Italo-Australian young people have been educated in Australian schools, are upwardly mobile both socially and occupationally, and have successfully entered the semiprofessional and professional areas of the work force. On the other hand, Australian Aborigines have been much more disadvantaged than any immigrant group, and they have faced strong racial prejudice from the white population (see Rowley, 1970). Aborigines speak varieties of English with distinctive accents (Flint, 1970; Geiselhart, 1978; Sharpe, 1979), which are likely to be regarded unfavorably by Anglo-Australians, especially in situations associated with status and achievement.

Even though they do not use their ingroup language in status-stressing situations, members of ethnic minorities nonetheless associate it with friendliness and solidarity. For example, the home and extended family are highly valued among Greeks, and Greek young people still observe traditions about whom to marry, the role of the family, and the maintenance of ethnic pride through the language. Similarly, Aboriginal language is an important symbol of Aboriginal culture, which also emphasizes the family and group activities (Crowley & Rigsby, 1979), and Aboriginal English is becoming an integral feature of a growing sense of Aboriginality.

Gender of Speaker: Another Macrolevel Variable

Ethnicity is generally seen as a more pertinent speech marker than gender (Giles, 1979), and researchers have tended to use stimulus speakers of only one gender, usually male. This strategy obscures some important features of the perception and evaluation of speakers, and has led to the assumption that the speech of ingroup and outgroup males and females is evaluated in similar ways. There are, however, gender differences in grammatical form and vocabulary for every language group studied (Smith, 1979), and a number of researchers (e.g., Labov, 1972; Trudgill, 1974) have shown that in upwardly mobile social groups, women lead the way in showing a preference for prestige forms. Indeed, Williams and Giles (1978) have proposed that a preference for standard speech may be part of a set of strategies that women employ to gain greater mobility in the male-dominated community. Therefore, in situations that stress status and achievement, young women from subordinate groups may show a stronger preference for standard speech than do men. In addition, there is ample evidence that the speech of women is evaluated differently from that of men by listeners of the same ethnic group (see Kramarae, 1982; Smith, 1979). Our own research (Callan & Gallois, 1982; Gallois & Callan, 1981) has shown that female speakers from ethnic outgroups are evaluated more positively than are males, both by Anglo-Australians and Italo-Australians, and in some cases more positively than either male or female speakers from the ingroup. Speaker and listener gender introduce a number of role-related expectations that are likely to interact with other situational features in influencing perceptions.

Situational Context, Ethnicity, and Gender: Three Australian Studies

The studies described in this chapter all employed a methodology derived from the matched-guise technique (Lambert et al., 1960). Listeners were played audiotapes of speakers presenting content-controlled monologues designed to evoke different types of social situations. In each case the monologue simulated one person in a conversation. Rather than matched guises, we used several speakers from each ethnic group, who were asked to imagine themselves in the situation, and to whom speech and accent were not mentioned. These speakers were later matched across ethnic group for voice quality, dysfluencies, pitch, loudness, and tempo. In this way we were able to obtain samples closer to the speech that the speakers would normally use. Listeners in all three studies rated each speaker in each situation on fourteen adjective scales. Principal axis factor analysis in each case revealed two factors, one associated with status attributes, such as *intelligent, educated, ambitious*, and *powerful*, and one including solidarity-related attributes such as *friendly, helpful*, and *kind*.

Anglo- and Aboriginal Australian Accents in Two Situations

The first study (Gallois, Callan, & Johnstone, 1984) involved male and female speakers of general Australian and Aboriginal English, who presented monologues simulating two situations: one involving a discussion of work and exams, set at school, and one at a wedding reception. The audiotapes were played to three groups of male and female students: urban whites, nontribal Aborigines who lived in a rural area, and rural whites who attended the same school as the Aborigines. All students heard both Aboriginal and white speakers in both situations, but each student heard speakers of only one gender. The results of the study were complex, and only some of them are relevant here.

Students' ratings of the speakers on the status factor showed a significant interaction between situation, ethnicity of speaker, gender of listener, and ethnicity/residence of listener. Figure 9-1 presents this interaction. As expected, female subjects from both white groups gave their highest status ratings to white speakers in the status-stressing situation (school). Aboriginal females, however, did not differentiate significantly in their ratings by either ethnicity of speaker or situation. Urban white subjects of both sexes gave much lower status ratings to Aboriginal speakers than to white speakers, irrespective of the situation. Another four-way interaction, between gender and ethnicity of speaker and listener, revealed that urban whites also rated Aboriginal male and female speakers equally unfavorably, while they favored white male speakers over white females. Other subjects, as Figure 9-1 shows, rated Aboriginal and white speakers more similarly. It would seem that urban white subjects had sufficiently unfavorable views of Aborigines to obscure variables related to the situational context and to the gender of speaker (and the gender-role appropriateness of the situation).

Aboriginal subjects rated their ingroup speakers as positively as white speakers on status-related attributes. Male subjects, in fact, rated Aboriginal speakers significantly higher in the wedding situation. Tajfel (1974) suggested that intergroup social comparisons assist individuals in defining their distinctiveness and ensuring better social identity. Social activities and group and kin relationships are central aspects of Aboriginal culture, and the attention paid to them is reflected in the pragmatics of both Aboriginal

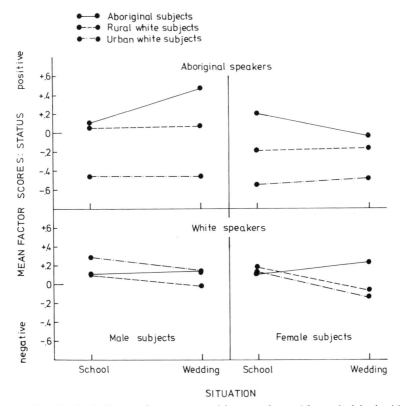

Figure 9-1. Study 1: Interaction among subject gender, subject ethnicity/residence, speaker ethnicity and situation on status ratings. (From Gallois, Callan, & Johnstone, 1984, copyright © Multilingual Matters, Ltd. Reprinted with permission.)

languages and Aboriginal English (Crowley & Rigsby, 1979; Eades, 1982). It is Aboriginal males, in addition, who are most visibly involved in story-telling and rituals. Their ingroup, and the importance placed by it on being competent and successful in group activities, may be particularly salient to young Aboriginal men when they compare their ingroup to whites.

Anglo-Australian and Greek Accents: Status, Solidarity, and Intimacy

The second study (Callan, Gallois, & Forbes, 1983) used a design similar to the first. In this case, however, the speakers were males and females with general Australian or Greek-accented English, and the listeners were Anglo-Australian or second-generation Greek-Australian students. Again, each subject heard speakers of only one gender, but both ethnic groups were rated, as were three situations. The first was a monologue about school work that stressed status and was set in a public context. The second, a family-centered interaction at home, was solidarity-evoking and in a more intimate setting.

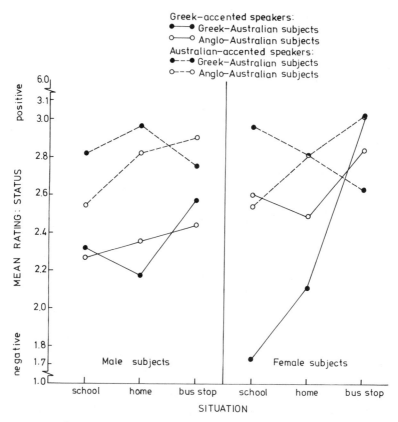

Figure 9-2. Study 2: Interaction among subject gender, subject ethnicity, speaker ethnicity and situation on status ratings. (From Callan, Gallois, & Forbes, 1983. Copyright © 1983 by Sage Publications. Reprinted by permission of Sage Publications, Inc.)

Finally, the third situation was also intended to stress solidarity but was set in a public place, a bus stop. As in the first study, pilot testing indicated that these situations were seen to be of low emotionality and similar naturalness. Once again, the results involved complex interactions, and only some of them will be presented here.

A significant interaction between situation, ethnicity of speaker, and ethnicity and gender of listener appeared for the status factor. This interaction is presented in Figure 9-2. The interaction revealed that all of the male subjects, along with the Greek-Australian females, rated Greek-accented speakers lower than Australian speakers on status attributes in the school and home situations, but not in the bus stop situation. Young Greek-Australian women were the most extreme in their ratings, and seemed to show a particular preference for prestige forms, especially in the school situation, where they gave Greek accents their lowest status ratings. Greek-Australians of both sexes thus appeared to identify with the majority accent and, as others have found, females seemed to form the cutting edge in assimilation.

The situation was the largest influence on Anglo-Australian subjects' ratings, as Figure 9-2 shows. All speakers were rated more favorably in the bus stop interaction, an informal and friendly but public setting. Speakers were rated next most highly on status in the home situation, indicating a preference for others in solidarity-stressing situations. In addition, while they generally downgraded Greek-accented speakers, Anglo-Australians did not do so in the informal bus stop situation.

Previous research contrasting status and solidarity-stressing situations has generally been confounded by the public-private, or intimacy, dimension. Often, the results of research have not supported the prediction that solidarity-stressing situations would lead to positive evaluations of minority groups (e.g., Ryan & Carranza, 1975). Our results suggest that intimate solidarity-stressing situations (e.g., the home) may be susceptible to perceived threat from outgroups. It may be that casual, friendly situations in public (in the present case, at a bus stop) are the least difficult of all for members of different groups to interact in, and may lead to the most positive evaluations (Bergmann & Forgas, this volume, Chapter 13, also suggest that situations of ths kind are least likely to generate anxiety and speech dysfluencies.)

Perceptions of Accented Speech in Person-Centered Situations

Both of the studies described above used a design that directly contrasted speakers of different ethnic groups, as well as different situations. As expected, status-stressing situations generally produced the greatest downgrading of minority speakers by members of the majority. Status-related attributes, too, produced fairly large differentiations among speakers and situations, while solidarity-related adjectives did not (for this reason, these results have not been presented here). In the third study a different design was used. Each subject heard speakers of only one gender and ethnic group (either Australian, British, or Italian). The task was person-centered and emphasized the situational context, which was again a repeated measure. Subjects were 82 male and 96 female university students whose parents and grandparents were Australian-born. They each listened to five speakers, all middle class, who presented monologues simulating conversations in three public situations: a job interview (formal, status-stressing), a parent enrolling children at school (relatively formal, not strongly status- or solidarity-related), and a friend recounting a tennis outing (informal, solidarity-stressing). Pilot testing indicated that these situations were seen as appropriate to middle-class speakers of either gender.

On the basis of previous research and reports of Australian stereotypes about ethnic groups (Callan & Gallois, 1983; Kippax & Brigden, 1977), one would predict firstly that status-related attributes would yield greater

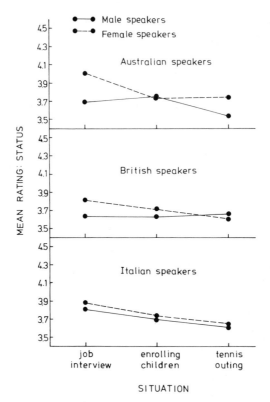

Figure 9-3. Study 3: Interaction among speaker ethnicity, speaker gender and situation on status ratings (rating scale ranged from 1, negative, to 6, positive).

differences in evaluations of speakers than would solidarity-related ones; secondly, that British speakers, especially males, would receive high ratings (even higher than the Australian ingroup) on the status factor, particularly in the job interview situation; thirdly, that Italian speakers, especially males, would receive lower ratings than Australians; fourthly, that differences would be smallest in the informal tennis outing situation; and finally, that situational setting differences would be greatest for the ingroup, Australian speakers. In fact, the results, which are presented in Figures 9-3 and 9-4, were rather different.

The expected interaction between ethnicity and gender of speaker and situation did appear for the status factor ($F(4,332) = 2.53$; $p < .05$), but simple effects tests revealed no differences in ratings by ethnicity in any situation for speakers of either gender. Rather, the situation was the dominant influence on status ratings. Male speakers, especially Australians, were rated lower on status in the tennis outing situation than on either of the other two (all simple effects tests and *post hoc* Newman Keuls tests were at $p < .05$). For female speakers, especially Australians, ratings were higher on status in the

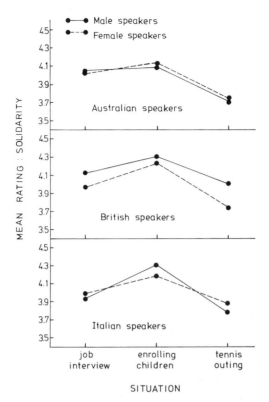

Figure 9-4. Study 3: Interaction among speaker ethnicity, speaker gender and situation on solidarity ratings (rating scale ranged from 1, negative, to 6, positive).

job interview situation than on either of the other two. Female speakers, in addition, received higher ratings than males in the job interview and, in the case of Australians, in the tennis outing situation as well. Overall, as predicted, status ratings of speakers in different situations diverged most for ingroup speakers. Interestingly enough, ingroup speakers were rated relatively highly on the status factor in situations that were stereotypically appropriate to the other sex (job interview for females; enrolling children at school for males).

Results for the solidarity factor also revealed a significant interaction between ethnicity and gender of speaker and situation ($F(4,332) = 2.77; p <$ .05). As Figure 9-4 shows, female speakers were rated as friendlier and more heplful in the enrolling children situation than in either of the other two, and higher on solidarity in the job interview than in the tennis outing. Australian male speakers were rated lower on the solidarity factor in the tennis outing situation than in the other situations, while both British and Italian males were given higher ratings in the enrolling children situation than in the others. Finally, British males were rated higher on solidarity in the tennis outing situation than were Australian or Italian males.

The rather negative ratings given speakers in the tennis outing situation can probably be best explained by reference to its special characteristics. The passage involved some mild complaining, and another group of subjects rated speakers of both sexes from all three ethnic groups as more aroused and less happy in this situation. The high prestige attributed to the British by Australians may have carried the British male speakers through in this case. In general, however, influence of microlevel situational variables was strongest, and the speaker-centered nature of the task served to diminish changes in perceptions caused by social group membership.

Integration and Conclusions

The studies described in this chapter once again highlight the contribution of microlevel situational variables—status, solidarity, public or intimate setting, formality—along with the social group and role relations between speaker and listener (in this case, due to ethnic group and gender), to evaluations of accented speech. Gallois et al. (1984) proposed a model suggesting that the relative importance of microlevel situational factors varies with the level of social distance. Ethnicity and race judgments are made first, and when social distance and prejudice are very great, as they are when urban whites judge Aborigines in Australia, situational variables seem to make relatively little difference to evaluations. As social distance decreases, however, both gender and microlevel variables assume greater importance, especially insofar as they contribute to a sense of threat on the part of the listener. In these cases, as others have noted (see Giles & Ryan, 1982), when the situation is group-centered or group-salient, when status is stressed, or when privacy is involved (as in the home), evaluations of outgroup speakers may become more negative and overpositive evaluations of the dominant group may occur. This result may be particularly likely when the speaker is male and uses dominant nonverbal behaviors (loud voice and low pitch, for example, see Scherer, 1979). On the other hand, when perceived threat is low (solidarity-stressing situation, informal but public context, female speaker, nonaggressive nonverbal behavior), evaluations of outgroup speakers at intermediate levels of social distance may be even more positive than judgments of the ingroup (see Gallois & Callan, 1981). This phenomenon is clearly different from the very positive evaluations of the British by Australians (Ball, 1982; Gallois & Callan, 1981). In that case, social distance is low, stereotypes are positive, and it is male speakers in status-stressing situations who are evaluated so positively. Finally, if the situation is very person-centered, as it was in the third study described here, outgroup speakers at intermediate levels of social distance may be evaluated in the same manner as is the ingroup—in this case, as Giles and Ryan (1982) have suggested, contextual features and nonverbal behavior (other than accent) may be the most important influences on perceptions.

Almost every author in a recent review of language attitudes (Ryan & Giles, 1982) emphasized the need for greater consideration of the social situation (see also Forgas, 1983, for a comprehensive review). Nevertheless, little empirical research has considered situational constraints on language attitudes, and the rather speculative nature of most models in the area reflects this dearth of research. (Several welcome exceptions are represented in this volume; see, for example, Chapter 4 by van Dijk and Chapter 5 by Hoppe-Graff, Hermann, Winterhoff-Spurk, and Mangold.) Our model is a cautious attempt, supported for the most part by our data, to consider macrolevel and microlevel features of the situation and how they influence perceptions.

There is one final consideration. Whatever theoretical model is used, it is important that researchers be very clear about the design and the methodology they employ. Early researchers contrasted speakers of different ethnic groups in the same situation, and thus obtained large differences in listener evaluations as a function of speaker group. Our recent research, on the other hand, like that of many researchers studying social situations, has tended toward the opposite extreme—that is, it has contrasted situations but has not directly contrasted speakers of different groups. The result of this strategy has been to create person-centered situations, where group membership matters much less. A wider variety of research methodologies is needed to take adequate account of the influence of macro- and microlevel situational variables.

As several contributions to this volume so aptly point out, research on the links between language and social situations represents a most promising avenue for cooperation between psychologists and linguists. In that joint enterprise, paralinguistic characteristics of speakers, such as accent, should not be neglected. Accent plays a major role in interethnic communication situations not only in Australia, but in many other countries as well. The study of situational influences on the evaluation of accents could provide us with useful practical knowledge to make such encounters less problematic.

References

Argyle, M. (1972). *The psychology of interpersonal behaviour* (2nd ed.). Middlesex: Penguin.

Argyle, M., Furnham, A., & Graham, J. (1981). *Social situations*. Cambridge: Cambridge University Press.

Ball, P. (1983). Stereotypes of Anglo-Saxon and non-Anglo-Saxon accents: Some exploratory Australian studies with the matched guise technique. *Language Sciences, 5*, 163–183.

Ball, P., Giles, H., & Hewstone, M. (1983). Speech in social encounters: An integrative formalisation. Paper presented at the Second International Conference on Social Psychology and Language, Bristol.

Brown, R., & Gilman, A. (1960). The pronouns of power and solidarity. In T. A. Sebeok (Ed.), *Style and language*. Cambridge, MA: M.I.T. Press.

Callan, V. (1983). Anglo-Australian attitudes toward immigrants: A review of survey evidence. *International Migration Review, 17*, 120–137.

Callan, V., & Gallois, C. (1982). Language attitudes of Italo-Australian and Greek-Australian bilinguals. *International Journal of Psychology, 17*, 345–358.

Callan, V., & Gallois, C. (1983). Ethnic stereotypes: Australian and Southern European youth. *Journal of Social Psychology, 119*, 287–288.

Callan, V., Gallois, C., & Forbes, P. (1983). Evaluative reactions to accented English: Ethnicity, sex role, and context. *Journal of Cross-Cultural Psychology, 14*, 407–426.

Crowley, T., & Rigsby, B. (1979). Cape York creole. In T. Shopen (Ed.), *Languages and their speakers*. Cambridge: Winthrop.

Eades, D. (1982). You gotta know how to talk . . . : Information seeking in South-East Queensland Aboriginal society. *Australian Journal of Linguistics, 2*, 61–82.

Eltis, K. (1980). Pupil's speech-style and teacher reaction: Implications from some Australian data. *English in Australia, 51*, 27–35.

Ervin-Tripp, S. (1964). An analysis of the interaction of language, topic, and listener. In J. Gumperz & D. Hymes (Eds.), *The ethnography of communication*. Menasha, WI: American Anthropological Association.

Fishman, J. A. (1971). *Sociolinguistics: A brief introduction*. Rowley, MA: Newbury House.

Flint, E. (1970). The influence of prosodic patterns upon the mutual intelligiblity of Aboriginal and general Australian English. In S. Wurm & D. Laycock (Eds.), *Pacific linguistic studies in honour of Arthur Capell*. Canberra: Department of Linguistics, Australian National University.

Forgas, J. P. (1981). Affective and emotional influences on episode representations. In J. P. Forgas (Ed.), *Social cognition: Perspectives on everyday understanding*. London: Academic Press.

Forgas, J. P. (1983). Language, goals and situations. *Journal of Language and Social Psychology, 2*, 267–293.

Gallois, C., & Callan, V. (1981). Personality impressions elicited by accented English speech. *Journal of Cross-Cultural Psychology, 12*, 347–359.

Gallois, C., Callan, V., & Johnstone, M. (1984). Personality judgments of Australian Aborigine and white speakers: Ethnicity, sex and context. *Journal of Language and Social Psychology, 3*, 39–57.

Geiselhart, K. (1978). A preliminary study of some vocal stereotypes in Sydney, Australia. Unpublished master's thesis, Macquarie University, Sydney, Australia.

Giles, H. (1979). Ethnicity markers in speech. In K. Scherer & H. Giles (Eds.), *Social markers in speech*. Cambridge: Cambridge University Press.

Giles, H., & Powesland, P. (1975). *Speech style and social evaluation*. London: Academic Press.

Giles, H., & Ryan, E. (1982). Prolegomena for developing a social psychological theory of language attitudes. In E. Ryan & H. Giles (Eds.), *Attitudes towards language variation*. London: Edward Arnold.

Giles, H., & Sassoon, C. (1983). The effect of speaker's accent, social class background and message style on British listeners' social judgements. *Language and Communication, 3*, 305–313.

Giles, H., Bourhis, R., & Taylor, D. (1977). Towards a theory of language in ethnic group relations. In H. Giles (Ed.), *Language, ethnicity and intergroup relations*. London: Academic Press.

Jourard, S., & Friedman, R. (1970). Experimenter-subject "distance" and self disclosure. *Journal of Personality and Social Psychology, 15*, 278–282.

Kippax, S., & Brigden, D. (1977). Australian stereotyping: A comparison. *Australian Journal of Psychology, 29*, 86–96.

Kramarae, C. (1982). Gender: How she speaks. In E. Ryan & H. Giles (Eds.), *Attitudes towards language variation*. London: Edward Arnold.

Labov, W. (1972). *Sociolinguistic patterns*. Philadelphia: University of Pennsylvania Press.

Lambert, W., Hodgson, R., Gardner, R., & Fillenbaum, S. (1960). Evaluational reactions to spoken language. *Journal of Abnormal and Social Psychology, 60*, 44–51.

Lieberman, D. (1975). Language attitudes in St. Lucia. *Journal of Cross-Cultural Psychology, 6*, 471–481.

Lyczak, R., Fu, G., & Ho, A. (1976). Attitudes of Hong Kong bilinguals toward English and Chinese speakers. *Journal of Cross-Cultural Psychology, 7*, 425–438.

McKirnan, D., & Hamayan, L. (1983). *Speech norms and perceptions of ethno-linguistic differences: Toward a conceptual and research framework.* Mimeo, IL: University of Illinois at Chicago.

Mehrabian, A. (1972). *Nonverbal communication.* Chicago: Aldine.

Rommetveit, R. (1982). On meanings of situations and social control of such meaning in human communication. In D. Magnusson (Ed.), *Toward a psychology of situations: An interactional perspective.* Hillsdale, NJ: Lawrence Erlbaum Associates.

Rowley, C. (1970). *The destruction of Aboriginal society: Aboriginal policy and practice.* Canberra: Australian National University.

Rubin, J. (1968). *National bilingualism in Paraguay.* The Hague: Mouton.

Ryan, E., & Carranza, M. (1975). Evaluative reactions of adolescents toward speakers of standard English and Mexican American accented English. *Journal of Personality and Social Psychology, 31*, 855–863.

Ryan, E., & Giles, H. (Eds.). (1982). *Attitudes towards language variation: Social and applied contexts.* London: Edward Arnold.

Ryan, E., Giles, H., & Sebastian, R. (1982). An integrative perspective for the study of attitudes toward language. In E. Ryan & H. Giles (Eds.), *Attitudes towards language variation: Social and applied contexts.* London: Edward Arnold.

Scherer, K. (1979). Personality markers in speech. In K. Scherer & H. Giles (Eds.), *Social markers in speech.* Cambridge: Cambridge University Press.

Seggie, I., Fulmizi, C., & Stewart, J. (1982). Evaluations of personality traits and employment suitability on various Australian accents. *Australian Journal of Psychology, 34*, 345–357.

Sharpe, M. (1979). Alice Springs Aboriginal children's English. In S. Wurm (Ed.), *Australian linguistic studies.* Canberra: Department of Linguistics, Australian National University.

Smith, P. (1979). Sex markers in speech. In K. Scherer & H. Giles (Eds.), *Social markers in speech.* Cambridge: Cambridge University Press.

Tajfel, H. (1974). Social identity and intergroup behavior. *Social Science Information, 13*, 65–93.

Tajfel, H., & Forgas, J. (1981). Social categorisation: Cognitions, values and groups. In J. P. Forgas (Ed.), *Social cognition: Perspectives on everyday understanding.* London: Academic Press.

Tajfel, H., & Turner, J. (1979). An integrative theory of intergroup conflict. In W. Austin & S. Worchel (Eds.), *The social psychology of intergroup relations.* Monterey, CA: Brooks Cole.

Trudgill, P. (1974). *Sociolinguistics.* Harmondsworth: Penguin.

Williams, J., & Giles, H. (1978). The changing status of women in society: An intergroup perspective. In H. Tajfel (Ed.), *Studies in intergroup behaviour.* London: Academic Press.

Wish, M. (1979). Dimensions of dyadic communication. In S. Weitz (Ed.), *Nonverbal communication* (2nd ed.). New York: Oxford University Press.

Wish, M., D'Andrade, R. G., & Goodnow, J. E. II (1980). Dimensions of interpersonal communication: Correspondence between structures for speech acts and bipolar scales. *Journal of Personality and Social Psychology, 39*, 848–860.

Chapter 10
Situational Rhetoric and Self-Presentation

Rom Harré

Language and Self-Presentation

The situational use of language is a major vehicle of strategic self-presentation. It is now some 25 years since Goffman first brought to the attention of social scientists the importance of the ways that we present ourselves in social interaction. In his *Presentation of self* (1959), he clearly distinguished between the performances by which certain practical ends were achieved and the supplementary, or stylistic qualifications of those performances by which the actors displayed the kinds of persons they wished to be taken to be. Going on from his early work, Goffman explored the conventions of language, behavior, costume, and so on, by which that presentation is achieved. However, it has become increasingly clear that the role of language in social interaction is often far more important than that of more visible forms of display (Goffman, 1981). In this chapter I propose to sum up and then develop the work that has been done in recent years on the central role of language in the creation of social order, and the links between language and the social situations within which it is used.

Goffman's early work lacked an important concept, namely that of the moral order in which presentations were performed. Self-presentation is a display of one's self as conforming to a certain image of value, worth, etc. Images of value and worth do not come atomistically, they are parts of social orders. A further advance in our understanding can be achieved when we look for the underlying moral orders from which the values displayed are drawn (see, for example, Elias, 1978, and the later works of Goffman).

In this chapter I shall discuss situational rhetorics. By rhetoric I mean a form of speech or writing that serves to create in the listener or reader a certain impression of the character and the moral qualities of the speaker or writer in a given situation. I use the term "moral quality" in a rather general way, to refer to any attribute of worth, which is to include not only goodness in the ordinary sense, but, in our society, rationality as well. My argument turns on the discovery of rhetorics in the interactive situations of everyday life and the identification and study of the moral properties that these situational rhetorics create. The general theory of social constructionism holds that social realities are created by human symbolic activities and in particular by talk. I shall explore four cases where the analysis of the rhetorics enables us to grasp the reality that is created by the use of it.

Aggro-Talk: The Rhetoric of Aggressive Situations

The early investigation of football hooliganism by Marsh, Rosser, and Harré (1978) revealed a form of talk used both by the fans and by the newspapers to report on the activities of supporters. This talk was characterized by what one can only describe as a "bloodthirsty" vocabulary. The events that occurred in and around football grounds were described in such a way as to make us see them as savage encounters in which severe physical injuries were inflicted on those taking part. The honor to be won was proportional to the bloodiness of the conflict. The fans themselves coined the word 'aggro' to refer to these encounters. It is important to emphasize that this form of talk was used both by the fans and by the newspapers allegedly describing the events in question. As Marsh proceeded with his studies, he became more and more puzzled by the disparity between the kind of happenings which could be observed at football grounds and the way that these happenings were described.

In the vast majority of cases the violence was manifestly ritualized and it was rare indeed for the protagonists of opposing groups actually to come to blows. Far and away the most common interaction was a distant exchange of verbal abuse and threatening postures. One or the other group would retreat from the ground, conceding victory without a tooth being loosened or a drop of blood being spilled. It became clear that the discourse in terms of which these events were "written up" drew on a vocabulary that could not conceivably be treated as literally descriptive. It also became clear that this vocabulary was a rhetoric. It was being used by the fans to redefine symbolic or metanymic events in such a way as to provide a plausible foundation for the claims to honor and worth, which were the rewards for victory. Those who had taken part in successful "fights" were able to rise up the ladder of status, growing in reputation as they went. It became clear that the *social* action in this situation unfolded in terms of the redefined reality. That is, if the social force of aggro was to create and maintain hierarchies of honor, then one's understanding of this necessarily must include the way that the realities were redefined. The role of the newspapers, then, becomes part of the system of confirmation by which the redefined events come, for all practical purposes, to be *the* social reality.

From the vast amount of material he collected, Marsh was able to show that the rhetorical redefinition of reality was bounded by quite strict rules. The introduction into the talk of reference to dangerous weapons, bottles of acid, and so on, was punished by the leaders of the groups, usually by some form of temporary ostracism. Thus, a fine measure of social control was exercised over the redefining process in such a way that the constructed reality conformed to an image of its members as physically tough and engaged in hand-to-hand combat. Marsh has also suggested an interesting corollary to the discovery that aggro-talk is rhetoric. As is well known girls rarely fight, but when they do, they fight much more savagely than boys. Marsh has suggested that this may be another example of the now well-established phenomenon of women and girls drawing on the rhetorics used by men and boys in organizing and maintaining their social orders. Girls borrow the rhetoric but misunderstand it, and treat it as a literal description of how a fight goes and therefore should be managed. The bloodthirsty vocabulary is translated into real action.

Gossip: The Rhetoric of Situational Control

The phenomenon of gossip is, so far as I have been able to ascertain, practically universal among human beings. It is reported in one form or another by both anthropologists and historians almost ubiquitously. Why does it exist? Recently Sabini and Silver (1981) have offered an ingenious suggestion, which assimilates gossip to the kind of situated language-use that is the central concern of this chapter. In aggro-talk social reality is created in terms of which the actors carry on further steps in the creation of their restricted form of social order. As I have suggested in the introductory paragraph, there is another component of social life, namely the moral order, to which the kind of redefinitions that we have seen in aggro-talk are directed. It remains a question, then, how the moral order is maintained and where it is essentially located. Just as aggro-talk defines a situational reality that is present to the actors, gossip defines a reality in which the actors are not immediately present.

Gossip is commentary, critical commentary, upon events which have taken place, or are taking place, elsewhere, and people who are not currently present as contributors to the conversation. Sabini and Silver argue that this activity is necessary to the creation and maintenance of the moral orders within which the action to which the actors are immediately present takes place. Gossip defines the moral world by continuously maintaining and publishing standards of proper speech and action, as well as character and personality display, in a given situation, but it does it offstage, so to speak. If everyone takes part, more or less, in gossip, then the network of promulgations of moral principles includes all the actors, in particular those who, at one time or another, are the subject of gossip themselves. It is rare indeed for an individual to be faced directly with moral reprimand. We only have to notice the grave difficulty that people have in dealing with such relatively harmless moral infractions as ill-

mannered driving or smoking in a no-smoking area. It is very difficult indeed
for one individual to remonstrate with another. One sits suffering a mixture of
embarrassment and indignation, hoping that the stewardness will come by and
notice the offender. It is because of the moral reticence of most of us and the
fact that we are not licensed to make public moral judgments on others, that
gossip plays the enormously important role that it does in stabilizing and
maintaining the moral order. A detailed study of the language of gossiping
remains to be done, but it is already clear that our cognitive definitions of
"proper" behavior in various interaction situations are sanctioned by nothing
more than the threat of rhetorical comments.

File-Speak: The Rhetoric of Character Transcription

Most people simply take it for granted that for all practical purposes, their
person is limited by, and extends only so far as, their physical body, that their
memories are recorded in their own brains, and that their personalities are
displayed on their own faces and by their own actions. Such a view is naive. In
our contemporary world a person is accompanied by an indefinitely extended
penumbra of pieces of paper, many of which are fateful in his or her life
course. This penumbra is made out of the files that follow us and sometimes
precede us throughout our social careers. One has only to think of the process
by which a job selection is normally made in a university, for example. The
selection committee receives, let us say, 30 or 40 files, in which there are pieces
of paper, on which appears a job history, judgment, description, and so on of
the person whose name is on the file. The vast majority of these files are
rejected and the "short list" is made up from the remainder. Only those people
whose names are on the short list appear before the committee and are
credited with having proper social persona. Everyone else has appeared as his
or her file; the fatefulness of the file hardly needs emphasizing. The question
then arises as to the nature of the language in which the files are presented. I
propose to call this language file-speak. Its properties deserve careful and
detailed analysis. The situational influences on file-speak are of crucial
importance in the lives of most modern people. How is file-speak related to
ordinary language?

In a recent study of psychiatric files I was able to show that the language in
which the files were couched has some very special properties. The psychiatric
department whose files I was fortunate enough to be able to study was staffed
by psychiatrists who were (roughly equally) alumni of two famous teaching
hospitals, the Tavistock and the Maudsley. These hospitals taught radically
different psychiatries, one chemotherapeutic, the other psychodynamic. It was
impossible to tell from the language of the files to which school the compiler
belonged, for in every case, without exception, the file was built up in terms of
the language of the patient, not that of the psychiatrist. So at least in
psychiatric files, file-speak begins as ordinary language. But it does not remain
so. A remarkable situational transformation occurs as the file progresses. A

file has an existence and trajectory through the social world, which soon takes it far outside the reach of its subject. A psychiatric file proceeds on its way by a process of retranscription. The complaint that is originally written out in the language of the patient is transcribed into an "official" language, one of the languages of psychiatry. Thus, for example, "feeling miserable" may be transcribed as "displays low affect" to reflect the situational requirements of scientific objectivity embodied in the jargon of psychiatrists.

A striking feature of the transcription process is the psychological and semantic simplification that takes place. The patient's file, condensed into "the letter," appears before another member of the psychiatric profession who may then see the patient and write another file in "patient-language," which is then further transcribed into the return letter to the patient's general practitioner. It became very clear that the two processes of transcription inserted into the trajectory of the file formed a kind of dispersion in which the meaning of the complaint was essentially lost. In returning to the language of the patient after the two transcriptions, it was often difficult to identify traces of the original complaint.

So far as I can see, none of this fascinating process affected the way in which the patient recovered. We know very little about the languages of files. The work that I report on psychiatric files is, I think, the first of its kind in which the file is studied not for its content but for its rhetorical qualities, for the way in which it presents the patient and the psychiatrist, not as people but as types, and for the transformation of these presentations as the rhetorics change. I would very much like to see insurance files, school and university files, and police files subjected to similar studies. Perhaps a general theory of file-speak could be developed on the basis of this work. It seems to be that the situational requirements on file-writers and file-manipulators to live up to their image as objective, detached, and reasonable people has at least as much to do with the language of files as it does with the substantive matters described in them.

In the three cases I have touched upon, the rhetorics of aggro-talk, gossip, and file-speak are distinctive and potent. They define situations and create realities for their speakers, hearers, and readers, realities which are rich in moral content. There is a close relationship, I believe, between moral orders and rhetorics—a relationship which is entirely transparent in the case of aggro-talk, for it is only in the transformation of ritual events into bloody fights that honor is formally created. Thus the moral order of football violence, in which worth is related to victorious accomplishment, exists only by virtue of the rhetorical transformation of the events in question.

Unfortunately, little research has been done on the vocabulary of gossip, specifically on the lists of attributes that are routinely deployed in the discussion of other people and on the kinds of moral judgments that are made of other people's characters and actions. I suspect that serious study in this field would reveal a structure very similar to that which Marsh revealed in aggro-talk, that is, a quite transparent relation between the verbal discourse and the moral order or orders that it sustains. Cross-cultural studies obviously recommend themselves as promising ways to investigate these phenomena. A beginning can be found in Morris's (1980) intriguing analysis of the differential roles of English and Spanish in Puerto Rico, which is to be found in his unjustly neglected *Saying and meaning in Puerto Rico* of 1980.

How we speak has become a popular theme for linguistically inclined social psychologists recently (cf. van Dijk, Gibbs, and Bavelas, this volume, Chapters 4, 6, and 11). I suspect, however, that unraveling the relationship between the rhetorical properties of discourse and the situated moral order or orders implicit in the community will be a difficult and demanding task. The role of the file, for example, is still, to my mind, somewhat obscure. It masquerades as a form of descriptive truth. It functions as a highly potent restriction on the possibilities open to a social actor. This paradoxical feature of files will, I think, prove to be quite central in future studies of the rhetoric and fatefulness of file-speak as a situation-dependent communication register (see also Levin & Snow, this volume, Chapter 3).

Situational Rhetoric in Science

The recent transformation of the sociology of science in the hands of the Paris and Edinburgh schools (see, for example, the work of Latour and Woolgar 1979, Bloor 1976, and Barnes 1977) opens up the intriguing question of the rhetorical qualities of scientific language and its role in the manifestation of the moral order of the scientific community. The stringent morality to which that community subscribes is promulgated in large measure by the way that scientists write. It is astounding to me that this has been only so recently realized. The morality that includes the pursuit of truth, the willingness to abandon theories or hypotheses in the face of contrary evidence, the scrupulous attention to the rationality of discourse, have all until recently been taken to be features of the epistemology of science, that is they have been seen as consequences of a certain conception of knowledge and how it should be garnered. But the authors I have mentioned have been able to show that there are more subtle reasons for the appearance of this rhetoric than the epistemological, reasons that have to do with the display of moral worth within the terms of the situational morality of the scientific community.

I shall make a distinction in this section between what I shall call "scientific rhetoric" and "scientistic rhetoric." In a scientific rhetoric the terminology and the general form of the discourse is the way it is because of certain features of the activities of the community of scientists. A community's scientific standing is taken for granted. In a scientistic rhetoric, however, we find terminologies, modes of expression, and forms of discourse borrowed from the rhetoric of acknowledged science, but employed in the description of work whose similarity to the physical sciences from which the rhetoric is derived is often tenuous and usually remote. It is of considerable interest, I believe, to our understanding of the status of social psychology to see how much of its rhetoric is scientistic rather than scientific—that is, to see it as making claims to a place in a moral order, claims which have by no means been established beyond reasonable doubt.

The Construction of Rationality

We can begin the discussion by asking a commonsense question: Where does the rationality of scientists make its first and most prominent appearance? The answer must surely be "in their writings." But which writings? Scientists write in many different situational contexts, from early drafts and lab notes to the final polished product, the journal paper. It turns out that rationality is most fully and selectively manifested in the logical structures of the discourses which are *published* as science, and sometimes in situations of retrospective descriptions of the process of discovery which form part of the informal autobiographies of scientists.

The deep question, then, is this: To what extent are the rational properties of printed scientific texts reflections of the rationality of scientists' minds rather than mere compliance with situational requirements? It is to this question that Latour and Woolgar have addressed themselves in the fourth chapter of their *Laboratory life* (1979). By a series of close analyses of the moment-by-moment interactions between the members of the scientific team, they show that the rationality of a scientific discourse is the product of a very specific situated social process. There is no ground for reading back into the discourse the cognitive process by which the scientific discovery is made. I can illustrate this by referring to Latour and Woolgar's use of the case of Spencer.

The case of Spencer has become exemplary in the literature since there exists both an article in *Science*, in which the discovery of the effects of the substance bombesin on the central nervous system is represented as the result of a logical deduction, and the original moment-by-moment records of the process by which this discovery was actually made. It emerges quite unequivocally that Spencer "got his idea" by perceiving an analogy between bombesin and another substance neurotensin. However, Spencer himself transforms the events for himself from a tenuous analogy to what he calls a "logical idea." As Latour and Woolgar say (p. 173), Spencer modified his account of the discovery over time. What he did was to transform a weak and illogical connection into a strong logical link. He came to present what was a small step from neurotensin to bombesin as a trial substance into a very large step of massive scientific creativity.

As Bloor (1976) has argued, the social organization of the scientific community embodies a moral order in which retrospective accounts of scientific discoveries are constructed. These accounts transform formally invalid logical structures (e.g., syllogisms) into formally correct forms by the modification of initial premises. In fact, Latour and Woolgar argue (1979, p. 174) that close attention to the local circumstances and chance encounters involved in the appearance of a "new idea" cannot even be expressed as analogical reasoning. In essence, the way in which the emergence of a new finding is written up involves a twofold process of transformation. Local circumstances are transformed into "flashes of intuition" and analogical reasoning is transformed into "tight deductive structure." Why is this done?

To answer this, we must return to the Goffmanesque ideas with which this chapter began. According to Goffman and to amplifications of Goffman's ideas (such as my own development of the concept of "Expressive order," in *Social being*, 1979), a central preoccupation of human beings which structures their social interactions and largely determines the content of those interactions is the presentation of worthy selves. Worth is defined with respect to a locally and situationally valid moral order. It is not too startling an hypothesis to presume that since scientists too are people, they too are concerned with the situational presentation of self in accordance with the principles of the expressive order. Thus, they will seek to present themselves through their activities as beings of value, whose worth is defined with respect to a local moral order, in this case the moral order of the scientific community. The rhetorical processes of transformation described by Latour and Woolgar demonstrate unequivocally the nature of that worth. To have worth as a scientist is, amongst other things, to be rational. But scientific *work* is rarely, if ever, rational. However, in any given situation, a display of science can be so constructed as to manifest just the very worth that the scientific moral order calls for, and that is why the scientists studied by Latour, Woolgar, and others adopt these rhetorical transformations.

Scientistic Impression Management or Psych-Speak: The Situated Identities of Social Scientists

It is possible to show that the moral order of the communities of physical scientists is closely connected to their practice. Scientism is the use of a rhetoric which has an established place in a physical science where it maintains a moral order in its relationship to the scientific processes, in situations or contexts which are in one way or another problematic. The presentation of self in the everyday life of the physical scientist is, so to speak, coordinate with his scientific activities. The most interesting case of scientism, and one of the oddities of contemporary social psychology, is not only its neglect of the subject of rhetoric in, so to speak, its traditional problem area— human interaction—but also in any reflexive analysis of its own activities.

Social psychology is a social phenomenon and its performances are as much shot through with rhetoric as are the activities of football fans. Any social science is under an obligation to turn its own methods and concepts upon itself. What do we notice when we turn the methods of social psychology on the work of social psychologists? Among other things, one is immediately struck by the appearance of rhetorical language devices that are appropriate to the physical sciences, but which a moment's reflection shows are highly problematic in the context of those sciences which are concerned with meanings.

A very simple example, which has been noted often enough, is the very peculiar use of the term *measurement* to describe the empirical description of various social psychological phenomena, such as emotions, personality displays, and so on. Empirical descriptions of such matters can certainly not be considered a measurement in the literal sense, but the role of this term in the rhetoric of self-presentation is entirely obvious. However, much more interesting kinds of rhetorical interventions in the language of social psychology can be found. I have already examined (Harré, 1983) a very interesting example of rhetorical transformations found in the work of J. Turner (1980) on the psychological processes involved in individuals who engage in intergroup conflict. The rhetoric used by Turner is startling in its incongruity with the subject matter of his investigations. Yet its presence has a very straightforward situational explanation in terms of the presentation of an acceptable self in the display of his worth as a being living in accordance with the *general* moral order of the scientific community. It is not difficult to show that the effect of this rhetoric on Turner's own work is a measure of distortion. Thus it becomes a matter for judgment as to whether the deleterious effect of using a rhetoric of this kind on the work itself is outweighed by the rhetorical advantages of overt subscription to the moral order of the physical sciences.

For the purposes of this chapter I turn to another example, which has similar properties. My recent study of mixed rhetoric (Harré & Reynolds, 1984) looked at the interaction between an intentionalist language and a causalist language in the description of the behavior of certain primates. The parallel example I want to look at now is a recent publication on the social psychology of language by Giles and Sassoon (1983). The subject matter of the article is the effect of speakers' accents, social class background, and message style on British listeners' social judgments. The article is written in a fascinating and curious mixture of situational rhetorics, with some examples of extreme scientism coupled with long stretches of ordinary and entirely transparent English. The interplay between these situational rhetorics creates a very curious effect, as the following extract shows:

> In an empirical investigation designed to explore the evaluative consequences of this notion, Ryan and Sebastian ... manipulated information about speakers' social class backgrounds orthogonal to their use of a standard American or ethnic accent in a 2 × 2 within-samples design voice-evaluation study. They found that the independent variables yielded two main effects such that young undergraduate speakers with middle-class backgrounds were preferred over those with lower-class backgrounds, and that standard speakers were evaluated more favorably than Mexican-American accented speakers by Anglo, middle-class informants. Nevertheless, an interaction effect also emerged showing that in general, and particularly for status traits, a sharper differentiation was made between middle- and lower-class non-standard accented speakers than between standard speakers from the two different social backgrounds. The authors argued that "the results for the accented speakers strongly suggest that validating the listeners' hypothesized

assumptions about the speakers' social class assures their derogation. On the other hand, the results suggest that disconfirming these presumed assumptions substantially improves the evaluations of accented speakers" (p. 232). Henceforth, we shall label this the 'Ryan and Sebastian effect.'

In the paragraph just quoted there are striking switches from a causal scientistic rhetoric to an ordinary language/commonsense reasoning rhetoric, so to speak. The sentence "They found that the independent variables yielded two main effects, etc." and the subsequent sentence, " . . . an interaction effect also emerged . . . ," are clearly in the causal mode. However, when Giles and Sassoon approached the authors of the piece whose results they are describing, we find that Ryan and Sebastian have expressed themselves in a quite different rhetoric. For example, they speak of "listeners' hypothesized assumptions," "derogation," "disconfirming these presumed assumptions," and so on, in which a rhetoric of reasons, premises, assumptions, and so on is invoked. Further into the article we find a strong return to the causal scientistic mode. For example, the expression "the dependent measures" appears. These consist of small questionnaires, but the questionnaires are themselves glossed, for example, as "three *control* items, measuring S's perceptions of the three independent variables used in the experiment, that is his social class, accent and formality of speech. These scales were included to check that the manipulations were perceived as intended in the context of the experiment proper, and particularly as the pilot testings had only examined one or two factors at a time." And so on, and so on. Further, the sentence appears: "The control items shall always be last so as not to cue S's into the possible experimental manipulations, but the other four pages were combined in random orders for different S's, so as to counterbalance any possible order effects" (p. 308). These items demonstrate in a striking manner the combination of scientistic and causal elements that make up what I shall now call Rhetoric Mode A.

We note the appearance of the concepts of measure, of independent variable, of experiment, of manipulation, of pilot testings, of factors, of control items, of order effects. All of these terms are drawn from a causal vocabulary and the methodology of the physical sciences. And indeed throughout the article, the term "effect" appears quite frequently where the results of the "experiments" are discussed. However, in the same article, a second rhetoric drawn from a quite different context, which I shall call Rhetoric B, appears. For example, on page 310 we have the following sentences: "More specifically, at what sociolinguistic point does the notion of the speaker disconfirming speech expectations come to listeners' level of cognitive awareness? What motives are invoked and explanations offered for listeners for why it is that certain apparently working-class people speak with RP accents . . . " And so on, and so on. And this is immediately followed by the sentence, "How would such important and differing *causal* attributions mediate impression formation and behavioral actions?" (italics mine).

In Rhetoric Mode B the judgment by a listener on the social class of a speaker is conceived not in terms of cause and effect, but of a mode of reasoning. So the person is conceived as testing an hypothesis, as having a theory, as invoking a motive, as offering an explanation—and, of course, offering explanations and invoking motives have nothing to do with causality. Now, just as we ask why did Spencer rework the fragment of his auto-biography to do with bombesin into the specific form of a logical argument, we might ask why have Giles and Sassoon mixed their rhetorics in this curious fashion. Careful reading of the article suggests that the causal rhetoric, which I have perhaps promiscuously labeled "scientistic," is less appropriate to the phenomena they are describing than is a reasoning and hypothesis-testing way of speaking. We can now turn to social psychology for a Goffmanesque kind of explanation of this piece of situated self-presentation.

The article by Giles and Sassoon is not just a report of a piece of empirical research any more than is the work of Spencer on the effect of certain substances on the central nervous system a report of his experiments with bombesin and neurotensin. In addition, and perhaps importantly, scientific publications are displays of personal moral worth. Giles and Sassoon, in choosing a particular rhetoric, are engaging in a Goffmanesque presentation of self in accordance with conventions appropriate to the situation and the moral order of the community in which this publication plays a part, and that community is the community of social scientists, sociolinguists, and the like. The explanation of the presence of Rhetoric Mode A can be sought in just the same situational conventions of personal manifestation as one looked for in the explanation of Turner's peculiar use of pseudoalgebra in the description of the reasoning processes of those who made unfavorable judgments of people from different ethnic groups.

The list of terms which I have picked out show that the source of the rhetoric is the physical sciences, in which it is entirely appropriate to speak of measures depending on independent variables, and the like. The physical sciences have a well-established moral order in which these terms reflect an engagement by the individual in the moral order of that community, an engagement which, were sociolinguistics to be a physical science, would be entirely coordinate, as it was in the case of Spencer, with the methodology and epistemology of the activity. But what makes the appearance of this rhetoric startling in the Giles and Sassoon paper is its copresence with Rhetoric Mode B. The second rhetoric is, indeed, a rhetoric appropriate to the subject matter, but it lacks the desirable presentational qualities.

The best formulation of all, namely ordinary language, would perhaps have lacked the presentational qualities which the chosen rhetorics both exhibit. Rhetoric Mode B allows us to perceive Giles and Sassoon as beings capable of examining the cognitive processes of their human subjects and is, so to speak, a step or two upmarket from the ordinary language into which the article could have been translated without serious loss of content. The final step to the scientistic rhetoric displays our authors as members of a community to which they do not in fact belong.

Perhaps at this point a little moralizing from *this* author may be forgiven in suggesting that it might be an unwise strategy to opt for the moral order of a community to which one does not belong.

Conclusions

The role of rhetoric, then, is central to a great deal of social interaction. Social personas are not "given" in social interaction, they are constructed. And among the methods by which their construction is achieved is the choice of language. We present and define ourselves in everyday situations, using common rhetorical devices. It seems to me a matter of the greatest scientific interest that the scientific community which busies itself about the study of the social interactions of human beings conceived as subjects, is itself a community of human beings. In the matter of the use of rhetorics for the presentation of selves as people of value and moral worth, social psychologists are no different from the rest of us. This is not a criticism of social psychology; it must count as one of its virtues.

References

Barnes, B. (1977). *Interests and the growth of knowledge*. London: Routledge and Kegan Paul.

Bloor, D. (1976). *Knowledge and social imagery*. London: Routledge and Kegan Paul.

Elias, N. (1978). *The civilizing process*. Oxford: Blackwell.

Giles, H., & Sassoon, C. (1983). The effect of speaker's accent, social class background and message style on British listeners' social judgements. *Language and communication*; Vol. 3, No. 3 (pp. 305–313). Oxford: Pergamon Press.

Goffman, E. (1959). *The presentation of self in everyday life*. London: Allan Lane.

Goffman, E. (1981). *Forms of talk*. Oxford: Blackwell.

Harré, R. (1979). *Social being*. Oxford: Blackwell.

Harré, R. (1983). *Personal being*. Oxford: Blackwell.

Harré, R., & Reynolds, V. (1984). *The meaning of primate signals*. Cambridge: Cambridge University Press.

Latour, B., & Woolgar, S. (1979). *Laboratory life*. Los Angeles: Sage.

Marsh, R., Rosser, E., & Harré, R. (1978). *The rules of disorder*. London: Routledge and Kegan Paul.

Morris, M. (1980). *Saying and meaning in Puerto Rico*. Oxford: Pergamon Press.

Sabini, J., & Silver, M. (1981). *Moralities in everyday life*. New York: Oxford University Press.

Turner, J. C. (1980). Fairness or discrimination in intergroup behaviour? A reply to Braithwaite, Doyle & Lightbown. *European Journal of Social Psychology, 10*, 131–146.

Part IV

Situational Influences on
Communication Problems

Chapter 11
A Situational Theory of Disqualification: Using Language to "Leave the Field"

Janet Beavin Bavelas

Suppose person A has received a gift from a friend who lives in another city. The friend now wants to know, "How do you like the gift I sent you?" A writes the following reply:

1. Thank you so much for the terrific gift. It is something I have always wanted. Whenever I use it I will always think of you. Thanks again.

Person B has also received a gift from a friend, who wants to know, too, "How do you like the gift I sent?" B replies:

2. Yes I received your gift. They say a person gives what he would like to receive. Hopefully one day, I'll be able to return the favor some way or another. Have a nice day.

Or, if the inquiry were made by phone, A might say, in an enthusiastic and pleased voice:

3. Oh, it was really nice. You obviously went to a lot of trouble to pick out something that I like.

While B says hesitantly:

4. Oh, um, it was, ah, not bad . . . [slight laugh].

Disqualification is a dimension that reflects the difference between the two messages in each pair. A's are clear, straightforward, and answer the friend's question. B's are equivocal, contradictory, even evasive. Yet they suddenly make sense when the evoking situations are revealed. A had received a welcome and suitable gift, whereas B's friend had sent a gift so bizarre that it was not possible to tell whether or not it was a joke.

This chapter will describe a research program aimed both at measuring the differences among messages on this dimension and at establishing the situational antecedents of disqualified messages. First, previous descriptions of the phenomenon will be reviewed as background. Then a conflict theory and a measurement procedure will be described. The rest of the chapter will be devoted to experiments conducted to test this theory and to examples of the messages—often strange and amusing but always skillful—produced by normal subjects in our experimental conditions.

Background

There is a tendency in most disciplines dealing with human communication to focus on communication as it "should" be—to gloss it as straightforward and logical, implying that anything else is error or deviance. However, a minority of authors have pointed out that our natural communication is not always thus, and they have not wished to dismiss such occurrences as deviant or erroneous. On the contrary, they have proposed that messages violating certain linguistic standards might still be lawfully related to the social context or situation in which they occur (see also Heikkinen and Valo, and Gibbs, this volume, Chapters 12 and 6).

From their clinical work, Bateson, Jackson, Haley, and Weakland (1956) described "double bind" communication in the families of schizophrenics, proposing that real-life communication can often be paradoxical and that even psychotic utterances make sense if considered in the context of familial communication patterns. Later, members of the same research group variously described "disqualification" as incongruent qualification of a message (Haley, 1959a); incongruence between levels of messages (Haley, 1959b); a contradictory message (Jackson, Riskin, & Satir, 1961); or an indirect negation of what someone else has said, so that statements are not really met (Jackson & Weakland, 1961). Other definitions of disqualification include: not letting a message stand clearly and unambiguously (Weakland & Fry, 1962); a technique that enables one to say something without really saying it (Watzlawick, 1964); and incongruent messages, that is, messages denying each other or, especially, the messages of another person (Sluzki, Beavin, Tarnopolsky, & Verón, 1967). Watzlawick, Beavin, and Jackson (1967) called disqualification communication that invalidates one's own communication or that of the other, for example, "self-contradictions, inconsistencies, subject switches, tangentializations, incomplete sentences, misunderstandings, obscure style or mannerisms of speech . . . etc." (p. 76). Such communications, they propose, are due not to individual pathology but to the social context in which the individual finds him- or herself.

Language philosophers have taken a similar position. Grice's (1975) chapter is already a classic for his proposal that, in natural discourse, "illogical" communication is both common *and* understood by the participants. Our task, he proposed, is to understand how this happens. After Searle (1975) described "indirect speech acts," Nofsinger (1976) developed the logic of indirect responses (e.g., "Do you want to help me with the dishes?" answered by "Do they like porcupines in a balloon factory?"). In a similar vein, Bowers, Elliott, and Desmond (1977) analyzed "devious messages" that do not fulfill semantic demands but work pragmatically (i.e., between users). They went on to outline a class of circumstances that produce such messages.

In social psychology, Wiener and Mehrabian (1968) have described "non-immediacy" in verbal communication, noting that indirect language often serves to remove the user from the object of communication. They also presented experimental evidence that situationally induced negative affect is one factor that will increase non-immediacy in the language describing that situation. This is not, however, typical of the social psychological approach. When faced with incongruent or contradictory messages, social psychologists have usually sought to establish which was the "real" message. In doing so, they are implicitly eliminating the inconsistency by attributing it to unsuccessful deception (e.g., DePaulo & Rosenthal, 1979; Ekman & Friesen, 1969, 1974; Mehrabian & Ferris, 1967).

Theory and Measurement of Disqualification

It is indeed tempting to seek the cause of disqualified messages in the sender, to attribute such "poor" or "unsuccessful" messages to pathology, inability to communicate clearly, some furtive or evasive intention, or just plain error. The theory proposed here suggests that instead of concentrating on intrapsychic causes, we should examine the social situation in which such a message is generated. The consensus of the diverse authors reviewed above can be stated as two broad propositions: (1) There is a standard of direct and clear communication, which is often observed to be violated, and (2) such deviations are explicable in terms of the social context of the message.

We have translated the first proposition into an operational definition using Haley's (1959a) original analysis of disqualification. The second proposition was made specific enough to test by use of Lewin's (1938) conflict model. This model, which was suggested by Tamara Dembo's insightful comments (personal communication, March, 1978) on our early work, will be described first.

A Field-Theoretical Account of Disqualification

Lewin's is an interactionist theory (cf., Ekehammar, 1974), a phenomenological explanation of individual behavior in terms of the social situation or "field" in which it occurs. Lewin often used analogies to physical space and movement, and these can be extended to communicative behavior as well. A situation offers us a choice of possible messages. Some of these can be seen as direct routes—clear messages, conforming to a standard "path." Others are indirect routes, departing to some degree from a direct message. It is interesting that our colloquial terms use the same metaphor: Such messages are not "straightforward" and "direct," but "tangential," "evasive," or "waffling" (probably from "waff" or "waver").

Why would messages ever stray from the straightforward, other than by an error or inability of the sender? To explain this, a second Lewinian concept must be added. If a message is a vector, then its probable effect gives it a *valence*; it is a good or bad thing to say, in the sender's view. For example, most people feel that it is good to pay a sincere compliment, and that it is bad to say something unkind or dishonest. Furthermore, both positive and negative valences show a *goal gradient*, that is, the closer they are, the greater their force on the individual. A positive valence becomes more attractive as it is approached, but a negative valence becomes even more repellent. Obviously, then, messages with positive consequences will be chosen, while those with negative valences will be avoided.

If the situation offers more than one message, all positive, this is an approach-approach conflict. As the individual moves, even randomly, toward any of the choices, it must (according to the model) become more attractive than the others and will quickly be chosen. Thus, such conflicts should be easily resolved. When the alternatives are all negative, this is an avoidance-avoidance conflict, and the same model predicts quite a different outcome: A move in any direction becomes *more* negative, while the alternatives left behind become less so. However, a reversal has the same result so that the individual is trapped—unless it is possible to "leave the field," that is, to avoid all of the negative choices. Thus, if communication is required but all possible messages are negative, they will be avoided and a deflected message will be sent instead, one that "says nothing while saying something, or says something without really saying it."[1]

The Empirical Measurement of Disqualification

Having applied Lewin's theory to communicative behavior, it still remains to place our notion of disqualification in the same theoretical framework. To do this, it is necessary to have a more precise description of what it means for a message to be direct, as a standard by which to measure deflections. Haley (1959a) pointed out that all communication should contain, implicitly or explicitly, four formal elements: *I* am saying *this* to *you* in this *situation*. In other words, there must be a sender, some content, a receiver, and a context. Haley went on to point out that disqualified messages are those that render one or more of these basic aspects unclear.

Here, then, is a standard from which disqualified messages can be seen to depart. We can visualize these four aspects as the coordinates of a target, the

---

[1] Note that such a message should not only be more indirect but should be preceded by a longer latency time than a response to an approach-approach conflict. Evidence for this will be offered below.

center of which is achieved by perfectly direct communication. Other messages avoid this directness, moving off one or more of the dimensions and missing the direct target, because of the consequences.

These four dimensions of directness can be measured by asking the following questions about any message:

1. How clear is this message, in terms of just *what is being said*? (Content)
2. To what extent is this message the *writer's* (or *speaker's) own opinion*? (Sender)
3. To what extent is this message *addressed to the other person* in the situation?   (Receiver)
4. To what extent is this a *direct answer to the* (implicit or explicit preceding) *question*?   (Context)

For example, recall B's thank-you note (message 2):

> Yes I received your gift. They say a person gives what he would like to receive. Hopefully one day I'll be able to return the favor some way or another. Have a nice day.

This message is unclear in content because the sentences do not hold together well and because of its possible double meanings. It avoids giving the sender's opinion by use of "*They* say ... " It refers very little to the friend who sent the gift and, indeed, after the first sentence seems to be addressed to anyone in general. Finally, it obviously changes context by answering a different question to the one that was asked.

We are assuming that, whether or not these four dimensions are truly the essential ones, they will act as a "filter," in that all nuances of disqualification will be drawn to our attention by one or more of them. They will be sensitive to departures from direct communication.

In our procedure, which is described in further detail in Bavelas and Smith (1982), eight to twelve individual lay judges learn to scale sets of messages on these four dimensions, using a magnitude estimation procedure. When each individual's ratings are standardized and averaged with those of the other judges, these scores are highly reliable. For example, five successive groups of judges had a median intraclass correlation of .96 on test sets, and the median r between groups was .95. Since the averaged standard scores still remain essentially Z scores, they have a mean of zero, with higher (positive) values indicating disqualification and lower (negative) values indicating directness. To illustrate, the message above has the following scale values:

Content	Sender	Receiver	Context	Sum
.29	1.02	.55	1.53	3.39

whereas the values for message 1 ("Thank you so much for the terrific gift ... ") are:

−.77	−.88	−.14	−.71	−2.50

This method of scaling was first applied to brief, researcher-written messages, then adapted to those generated spontaneously by our subjects. These include written notes (such as messages 1 and 2), spoken messages (with both verbal and paralinguistic aspects, such as 3 and 4), and face-to-face messages (in which all verbal and nonverbal behavior is captured on videotape). All of these adaptations have gone smoothly; subsequent small groups of lay judges working individually continue to give us reliable and subtle empirical information about the extent of disqualification in a given message. This method is costly, in both the judges' and the supervising experimenter's time, but we remain convinced that these disadvantages are outweighed by the advantages of truly independent and well-focused judgments of each message. Furthermore, these judgments reveal the pragmatic impact of messages on naive receivers, rather than properties of the messages that may only be noticeable to experts.

Experimental Research

All of the experiments to be described here have tested simultaneously both the theoretical model outlined above and the construct validity of the measurement procedure (Cronbach & Meehl, 1955). Our experimental strategy is one of increasingly varied replication, moving along a hypothetical continuum from strict experimental control to more "natural" communication by a series of experiments that partly overlap and partly extend their predecessors. From forced-choice to subject-written to subject-spoken to in-person messages, some of the same and some different situations have been used to explore our hypotheses about the situational antecedents of disqualified messages.

Forced-Choice Experiments

Our first five experiments (cf. Bavelas, 1983) were focused principally on the nature of situations that lead to disqualification rather than on the messages themselves. We therefore used a forced-choice format, in which subjects were asked to imagine a situation and to choose from among the three or four possible replies offered. These replies were written by the researchers and intended to cover all of the possibilities in the situation, including the truth, a lie, and disqualification. Obviously, this is a highly artificial method; yet it can be argued (Bavelas, 1983, p. 133) that all effects of this artificiality would tend to go against our hypothesis.

The first experiment sought to establish whether or not normal subjects would ever choose disqualified responses; to show that the effects were general across situations; and to explore the effects of different instructions on choice of response. We presented avoidance-avoidance conflicts in three different situations: (1) A classmate has just given a very poor presentation and then asks for an opinion, producing a conflict between lying and hurting another's feelings. (2) Someone well-liked has sent a gift that is awful, creating a similar conflict between lying and hurting the person. (3) One friend asks for a job reference about other friend, who worked for you and was incompetent; the conflict is between lying to the former and injuring the latter. In all three situations, we also varied whether the subject was instructed to choose what he or she *would* say versus what he or she *should* say. All possible orders of alternatives were used.

The procedure was as follows: The various combinations of situation, instruction, and order were printed on single sheets of paper, which were randomly permuted and distributed in large classes. Each sheet began as follows:

> Try to imagine the situation described below, as vividly as possible. Then read all the choices and indicate *which you would write* in this situation.
> Remember . . . (1) Try to really put yourself in the situation, and also (2) limit yourself to just the choices given. (3) We are not interested in what you think you *should* say, but in what you think you actually *would* say.

The other instruction reversed point 3 and asked for what the person *should* say. One of three situations followed, for example, the "class" situation:

> Another student in a small class, which meets three times a week for the entire year, has just given a class presentation. It was very badly done—poorly prepared and poorly delivered. After he sits down again, he passes you a note: "How did I do?" You have to jot something down and pass it back to him. Which of the following would you write down?

The alternatives given are shown in Table 11-1, along with their scale values and the frequency with which each was chosen.

Similarly, in the gift and reference situations and in both instructional conditions, the frequency with which a message was chosen varied almost perfectly with the amount of scaled disqualification in the message. This simple experiment eliminated several previously "obvious" possibilities: that subjects would choose randomly; that they would rarely choose disqualified mesasges; that they would choose either the truth or an equally direct lie; and that there would be a difference between what people said they should or would do.

Indeed, since 90% of our 287 subjects chose a message with a positive summed scale value, two unwelcome alternative explanations now suggested themselves. It might be that people rarely communicate directly, regardless of situation, or that our scaling procedure did not in fact measure disqualification. Therefore, our next experiment introduced a control condition in which no conflict was present (i.e., the class presentation was good or the gift was well liked). Using the same procedure, we found that the disqualified message was overwhelmingly but specifically chosen in the conflict situation. When there was no conflict, the straightforward messages were chosen.

However, it could still be argued that no elaborate theory of conflict is

Table 11-1. Amount of Disqualification and Frequency of Choice ("Class" Situation)

Message	Disqualification scale values[a]					
	Content	Sender	Receiver	Context	Sum	f
You did very well. I really liked it.	−.35	−.78	−.38	−.63	−2.14	3
You were terrible; bad job.	−.50	.10	−.32	−.58	−1.30	5
Not well, but don't feel bad about it.	1.02	1.24	.79	−.21	2.84	48
You were braver than I would be!	.02	−.56	−.09	1.42	.79	39

[a]These are standardized scores for the four dimensions of disqualification, as described in the text. Negative values mean that the message is relatively straightforward on that dimension, while positive values indicate disqualification.

Note. Table adapted from Bavelas (1983). Published by permission of Transaction, Inc. from Human Communication Research, Vol. 9, No. 4, copyright © 1983 by Transaction, Inc.

necessary to explain disqualification. Conflict is necessarily unpleasant, and it would be more parsimonious to conclude that *any* simply unpleasant situation leads to indirect communication (i.e., the sender loses control to some degree and is unable to communicate directly). Therefore, unpleasant but nonconflictual versions of the gift and class situations were created. The subject was to imagine having just done very poorly on his or her own presentation, while the person asking had done well; or having forgotten to send a present to the other person, who had sent a welcome gift. Note that in these control versions, the individual might feel miserable, but there is no communicational conflict about lying or hurting the other's feelings. These unpleasant, nonconflictual versions were rated as equally or more unpleasant than the conflictual versions (in which, for example, he or she had done well but the other poorly), yet disqualified messages were rarely chosen. It seems that conflict, and only conflict, leads to disqualification.

Recall that Lewin's theory distinguishes between different kinds of conflict, so that an even more precise test is possible. We had thus far presented avoidance-avoidance conflicts, where all direct messages were negative. So we introduced an *approach-approach* conflict, in which a choice must be made between pleasant but mutually exclusive messages. For example:

> Someone you work with arrives at a staff meeting. She is wearing a new dress and also has a new hairstyle. Both are great—she really looks good. She sits down next to you and passes you a note: "How do I look?" You are going to write a note and pass it back to her. Of the choices below, which would you write?
>
> > I think your dress is really nice.
> > I think your hair looks great that way.
> > You've changed!

In the *avoidance-avoidance* version, the dress and hair both look awful, and the first two alternatives say so; the third alternative was the same as in the approach-approach conflict. In this and a second situation, the disqualified alternative was the predominant choice in the avoidance-avoidance conflict but was seldom chosen in the approach-approach conflict; see Table 11-2 for sample results.

In this series of five forced-choice experiments offering 30 different messages, those scaled as highly disqualified were chosen specifically in avoidance-avoidance conflicts. It is important to emphasize that, although disqualified, these are not "poor" messages. Each is the best choice in a bad situation; lying is worse, as is injuring someone needlessly. Indeed, Turner, Edgley, and Olmstead (1975) point out that a hurtful truth to a person one cares about is a relationship lie: "Is it honest to tell someone a truth that would sever or greatly jeopardize your relationship with a person if that is honestly not what you want to do? ... In other words, being truthful and honest at all times may have consequences which are neither truthful nor honest ... (p. 83).

Table 11-2. Frequencies of Choice in Approach-Approach vs. Avoidance-Avoidance Conflicts ("Staff" Situation)

Message	Disqualification Scale Values[a]					f[b]	
	Content	Sender	Receiver	Context	Sum	+/+	-/-
I think your hair looks great that way. OR I don't think your hair looks good that way.	-.56	-.47	.03	-.61	-1.61	26	5
I think your dress is really nice. OR I don't think your dress suits you.	-.53	-.47	-.94	-.36	-2.30	6	4
You've changed!	1.09	.92	.91	.97	3.89	8	31

[a]Scale values for the approach and avoidance versions of messages were virtually identical and are averaged here.
[b]Frequencies of choice in approach-approach (+/+) vs. avoidance-avoidance (-/-) versions. Chi-square for the first two versus the third (disqualified) message = 26.47, $df = 1$, $p < .001$.
Note. Table adapted from Bavelas (1983). Published by permission of Transaction, Inc. from Human Communication Research, Vol. 9, No. 4, copyright © 1983 by Transaction, Inc.

Since the disqualified messages avoid both untruths, they should be seen as a good solution to a difficult problem.

Subject-Written Messages

The next series of experiments (Bavelas & Chovil, in press) focused on *how* subjects solved these problems, that is, on messages actually written by them rather than chosen from ones written by us. It might be that people choose disqualified messages when they are offered but would never think to write them spontaneously. If so, our theory would have a very limited scope. Moreover, we were curious about these messages—what would they be like, and would the scaling method detect differences among them?

Consequently, we presented conflict (and control) situations to subjects and asked them to write a brief response. Four different situations were used: (1) A note to be written to a fellow student following a bad (vs. good) class presentation. (2) A telegram to be sent by the subject in the role of a Member of Parliament who must address an issue on which his or her constituency is badly divided (vs. completely in agreement); the conflict is to avoid alienating one side or the other. (3) A thank-you note to be written to a friend who has sent a gift so bizarre that it is unclear whether or not it is intended as a joke (vs. welcome and well-suited); the conflict is whether to treat the gift as serious or as a joke, either of which may be wrong and therefore offensive. (4) A car ad to be written for a car that must be sold but is in bad (vs. good) condition; the conflict is between lying and betraying one's own self-interest.

These four experiments were conducted successively, with a total of 70 subjects seen individually, randomly assigned to the conflict or control situation. All messages from each situation were given to judges to scale, with no indication of the experimental condition under which they were written.

For example, 18 subjects were individually given the following written instructions by an experimenter (who did not know which condition was contained therein):

> Try to imagine the situation described below as vividly as possible. Please write your actual reply in the space provided.
> Remember . . . (1) Try to place yourself in the situation. (2) We do not want what you think is the "proper" reply, instead we would like your own *actual* response.
> Your car, a 1966 Volkswagen Bug, is in bad (*or* good) condition but you need to sell it because you are really short of money. Write the ad for the newspaper describing the general running condition of the car. (Three lines were provided for the ad.)

These 18 messages, retyped exactly as written and arranged in random order, were scaled by the judges, who were given an edited version of the situation and question so that they had no idea that the messages came from two different conditions. These messages are presented in Table 11-3, along with scale values and *t*-tests of the differences between the two conditions. The two sets of messages differed significantly on all four dimensions and their

Table 11-3. Subject-Written Messages and Their Scale Values ("Car Ad" Situation)

	Content	Sender	Receiver	Context	Sum
Nonconflict condition					
MUST SELL: 1966 V.W. BUG. EXCELLENT CONDITION. RUNS GREAT. ONLY 5000 MILES ON IT. BEST DEAL IN THE CITY! PLEASE PHONE SOON—THIS DREAM WILL GO FAST!	-.60	-.48	-.59	-.62	-2.29
For Sale! 1966 Volkswagon Bug in good operating condition. Any reasonable offer. Please phone xxx-xxxx	-.67	.03	-.85	-.77	-2.26
1966 VW—good running condition, new brakes, new tires OFFERS—PHONE 321-1234 after 5 p.m.	-.67	.51	-1.00	-1.03	-2.19
have to sell my good old buddy '66 VW Bug. Excellent runner, good milage and good bargain!!	.19	-1.26	-.60	-.48	-2.15
Must sell 1966 VW Bug, good running condition, very good on gas. No reasonable offer will be refused.	-.20	-.04	-.50	-.90	-1.64
VOLKSWAGEN FOR SALE BODY AND ENGINE IN GOOD CONDITION. ONE OWNER, MUST SELL BEFORE DEC 15 PHONE_____ ASK FOR MARK	-.16	-.35	-.64	-.39	-1.54
For Sale—66 VW Bug, good condition, lady driven, must be sold quickly, asking about $800 cash, good mileage on highways	-.73	-.17	-.02	-.24	-1.16

Advertisement					
FOR SALE 66, VOLKSWAGON BEETLE GOOD RUNNING CONDITION EASY ON GAS IDEAL SECOND CAR	-.65	.08	.63	-1.02	-.96
Bargain! Student needs to sell much loved VW. This 1966 Bug is a great old car. Perfect for a mechanical tinkerer.	.60	-.96	.75	1.17	1.56
Conflict condition					
For sale a 1966 V-W bug in excellent running condition. Price is right for an egar (sic) buyer in need of transportation.	.22	.16	-.37	-.84	-.83
For sale: 1966 Volkswagen Bug, in running order, but would need some minor repairs.	.05	.69	.09	-.15	.68
For sale a 1966 Volkswagen bug, it is in poor running condition, but just needs some tender loving care and a mechanic (sic) mind.	.46	.19	.92	-.72	.85
1966 Volks Bug—student must sell to survive summer, needs some body work, but mechanically o.k.	.55	-.39	.35	.50	1.01
Want to sell 1966 Bug, good body but some engine trouble—needs work.	.06	.40	.36	.28	1.1
VW Beetle, 1966. Needs work. $500. 592-1626 after 5:30 p.m.	-.58	.67	-.01	1.33	1.41
1966 VOLKSWAGEN BUG AS IS QUICK SALE FOR CASH PHONE _____	.92	.76	-.87	1.87	2.68

Table 11-3. *Continued*

	Content	Sender	Receiver	Context	Sum
MECHANIC'S DREAM—1966 Volkswagen—best year of the bug—however needs some bugs removed by caring mechanic. Sacrifice at $2500.xx.	.47	.13	1.41	.73	2.74
FOR SALE 1966 VOLKSWAGEN. VERY CHEAP. PERSON WHO LIKES WORKING ON CARS WOULD BE WISE TO BUY THIS CAR.	.74	.03	.95	1.28	3
t-tests nonconflict $\bar{x}$ =	-.32	-.29	-.31	-.48	-1.40
conflict $\bar{x}$ =	.32	.29	.31	.48	1.40
t =	2.98	2.66	1.99	2.47	4.88
(one-tailed) *p* <	.005	.01	.05	.025	.0005

Note regarding means:
  The conflict and nonconflict means are often "mirror images" with signs reversed, as above. This apparent coincidence arises because the message scores are standardized for each judge, then averaged across judges. Since judge agreement is very high, averaging leaves them as a set of standard scores which usually add to zero. When this is true, any partition into halves will produce means that add to zero.

sum. Thus, although each message is different, and the subjects often invented details not supplied to them, the property of disqualification can be measured in each, and this measurement shows the predicted difference between conditions. Note that all but one message in the control condition had negative sums, and all but one in the conflict condiiton had positive sums.

The disqualified messages are ingenious and systematic ways of neither admitting the car's real condition nor clearly misleading the prospective buyer. In each case, the sender could if challenged say that he or she had not actually said the car was in good condition. It is interesting that the message closest to a direct lie (the first of the conflict-condition group) is fairly clear, having a low negative sum. Even so, the second sentence gives a hint that is inconsistent with the first, which is why the value on the content dimension is positive. A perfect lie should be perfectly clear.

The control messages give a baseline of the amount of clarity that can be expected in this format. Compared to these, the ones with high (positive) values on the *content* dimension are ambiguous ("as is") or contradictory (e.g., containing "but " or "however"). Those low on the *sender* dimension contain some personal reference ("my good old buddy"), whereas the high ones avoid this and seem to stand at arm's length from their own statement ("Needs work"). (In other situations, where the format permits fuller expression, a key difference on the sender dimension is the presence or absence of a first-person pronoun.) The *receiver* dimension revealed an unexpected tactic by which the writer narrowed the implicit audience of "anyone reading car ads" to a "mechanic" or "a person who likes working on cars." Finally, the stipulated context of the ad is often avoided in that the general running condition of the car is not described, and other questions are answered instead ("very cheap," "good body").

In all four experiments, the differences on each dimension (and the sum) were in the predicted direction. This difference was always significant for the context dimension, usually significant for the content dimension, and occasionally for the sender and receiver dimensions. (This apparent priority of dimensions has been consistent in all of our subject-generated messages.) By whatever means, these messages managed to steer a careful course away from either outright fraud or full revelation. Indeed, they were much richer and more imaginative than those we had written and offered to subjects in the first series.

Subject-Spoken Messages[2]

By now we were eager to see (and hear) what the addition of a nonverbal channel would do. Not only would the theory be extended further toward

---

[2]These and the face-to-face experiments will be described in a forthcoming article by J. B. Bavelas, N. Chovil, J. Mullett, and A. Black, provisionally entitled "Truths, lies, and alternatives: Disqualification in verbal and nonverbal channels."

naturalistic situations, but new ways to disqualify would be available in paralinguistic tone, stress, fluency, etc. Furthermore, these may or may not be congruent with the verbal component of the message.

So the next three experiments were similar to those above but were conducted "live" over a telephone connection, with an experimenter in another room. The situations used were two of the old standbys, the class presentation and the bizarre gift, plus a new one (suggested by an earlier subject during debriefing), which will be described here. There were always two experimenters, only one of whom was seen in person by the subject. This experimenter gave the following instructions:

> What you will be doing is having a telephone conversation with another person. The other person is next door in the other room. This conversation will be recorded.
>
> Imagine that you work in a grocery store, and you know that Tuesday is the day they sell off all the old meat at a reduced price. Some of it is very old and of poor quality (*or, in the control condition*, This is just to make sure it doesn't accumulate; it is all fresh and good quality meat).
>
> On this particular Tuesday, the telephone rings. You answer it, and it is someone who saw the sale of the meat at a reduced price advertised in the newspaper. They have never shopped at your store, so they have called to get some information before coming to the store.
>
> Try to keep your response brief. When I leave the room, imagine that the phone has just rung, pick up the receiver, and say "Hello." The other person will be on the line.

When the subject had said Hello, the other experimenter said:

> "Hello, I've never been to your store before, and I was wondering, the meat that is on sale today, is it good?"

The subjects' replies were transferred to a master tape in random order and scaled by the judges as usual. Transcriptions, scale values, and *t*-tests are given in Table 11-4.

All subjects in the conflict condition reported that they had felt "on the spot"; this was reflected in significant differences in disqualification in both content and context, as well as in the sum. The extent to which subjects put themselves into this situation is noteworthy. As the messages show, they often added their own details and new information. Furthermore, subjects in the conflict condition acted as though their bind were real: They were not really employees torn between honesty to a stranger and loyalty to an employer (or the risk of losing a job). Yet none were totally truthful *or* deceptive. All statements about the quality of the meat were highly ambiguous verbally ("It's fairly fine," "It's the usual") and/or nonverbally (e.g., the paralinguistic hesitancy in the third and fifth messages in the conflict group in Table 11-4).

Furthermore, this experiment was conducted in tandem with the bizarre-gift situation, using the same 12 subjects but with the conditions reversed. A subject who had been randomly assigned to the control condition for the gift inquiry was then presented with the conflict condition in the meat market, and vice versa. Yet both experiments showed strongly significant effects. This virtually eliminates any explanation other than the immediate situation, because the clear and straightforward messages given in the control condition in Table 11-4 were generated by the same people who had given messages significantly disqualified on every dimension just a few minutes earlier. (Messages 3 and 4 at the beginning of the chapter are samples of control and conflict messages in this gift situation.)

All of the above experiments had used the device of telling subjects about a situation in which something was said to be good or bad (e.g., some meat, a gift, a car, a presentation, or an employee). The subjects had not merely repeated back what they were told, but had generated their own unique messages. Still, "in real life," information about which we must respond does not usually come to us already encoded. Therefore we next presented subjects with uncoded information from which they had to draw their own inferences, including the fact that a conflict existed. For example, one of these two experiments revived the employee reference situation, in which the subject in the role of a personnel officer is asked by a friend for a reference about another friend. The subject was given an "Employee Reference Form" with a mixture of either excellent and good *or* borderline and poor ratings on 13 items such as "knowledge of job" and "attitude toward supervisor." The other situation gave detailed information about the car to be sold. Both situations produced significant differences as predicted. Subjects had apparently inferred their bind and "escaped" it by disqualification.

Finally, spoken messages offer the opportunity to test another prediction from Lewin's conflict theory, namely, that avoidance-avoidance conflicts will take longer to resolve. The latency between the question asked and the message given in reply should be longer in these situations, presumably because the subject is approaching—and then avoiding—the various alternatives. In these five experiments involving a total of 48 subjects, the mean latency time was always longer for the conflict than for the control conditions; this difference was significant in three of the experiments. These means are less than 1 second in the control versus 1½ to 3 seconds in the conflict conditions. Although such latencies may be the closest we can come to observing the psychological process that Lewin proposed, some caution is needed in interpreting them. They are perfectly consistent with a conflict theory, but they do not establish it exclusively. A less intrapsychic interpretation would be that such pauses are simply another paralinguistic aspect of the message contributing to its ambiguity, especially on the sender dimension. Certainly our judges noticed these hesitations and saw the messages as less clear in part because of them.

Face-to-Face Messages

We have recently begun the extension of this research to face-to-face interaction in which all verbal and nonverbal channels are available. Such messages (on videotape) can be reliably scaled by judges (by now our eighth

Table 11-4. Subject-Spoken Messages and Their Scale Values ("Meat Market" Situation)

	Content	Sender	Receiver	Context	Sum
Nonconflict condition					
It's good quality meat, yes.	-1.35	-.47	-.37	-1.09	-3.28
It sure is, it's top-grade A meat.	-1.02	-.64	.47	-1.15	-2.34
Yes, it's very good quality.	-.20	-.68	.29	-1.15	-1.74
[We] wouldn't be selling bad meat, you'd only bring it back.	-.92	.68	-1.26	.02	-1.48
Oh yes, it's all very fresh. We just put it on sale to reduce inventory.	-.11	.31	-.53	-.52	-.85
Um, I can be...be reasonably assured that it's good. I haven't had any fault with...with the meat there before. If you...if you find something, um, has gone bad like the chicken, ah, it can be exchanged.	-.65	-.57	.71	-.03	-.54
Conflict condition					
I think it's quite good, yes, for the price.	.66	-1.09	.59	-.11	.05
Well, it is on sale because it has been in the store for awhile but that doesn't mean that it's bad.	.09	.15	-.42	.31	.13

I, well, yes it is good meat, the, ah, I uh . . . I'd like you to realize though that it . . . ah, is day-old meat or older so that it may not have some of the color that, uh, the meat that you would find cut freshly today . . . so and it's, um, not top-quality meat, it's . . . There's nothing wrong with the meat but it's not your, um, cross your standing rib roast or your sirloin steaks that are on sale but it's all, um . . . there's nothing at all wrong with it, but the color may have gone out of it.	.36	.49	-.71	.77	.91
Oh, it's, it's fairly fine, yes.	1.07	.10	1.02	.41	2.6
Um . . . ah, the reason why they're selling is because it's, um, it's a little bit old.	.65	1.43	.15	1.29	3.52
It's the usual.	1.43	.27	.99	1.25	3.94
t-tests nonconflict $\bar{x}$ =	-.71	-.23	-.12	-.65	-1.71
conflict $\bar{x}$ =	.71	.23	.27	.65	1.86
t =	5.08	1.12	.91	4.08	4.38
(one-tailed) *p* <	.0005	n.s.	n.s.	.005	.005

group since the beginning of the project). Our first experiments using this technique were also successful: When an experimenter playing the role of a fellow student asked in person how her class presentation had been, subjects in the conflict condition produced messages that were significantly more disqualified on all four dimensions (and their sum) than those in the control condition. If this effect replicates across other situations, as has been true of the previous series, then the whole will form a coherent pattern of evidence for our theory.

Conclusions

These final "visual" experiments will be the last variation on the basic paradigm used so far, in which normal adult subjects have solved hypothetical situational conflicts by disqualified messages. We have shown that such messages can be elicited even in experimental conditions and that the eliciting situation is a good explanation—and predictor—of such messages. When the situation presents only messages that are negatively valenced yet communication is required, the sender will "leave the field," at least communicationally, by avoiding direct communication. This avoidance can be measured as disqualification, which amounts to "saying nothing while saying something."

Current and Future Research

For the remainder of the project, three major new lines will be developed. First, Jennifer Mullett is obtaining spoken messages from children in order to study the development of their ability to disqualify (as well as to perceive the interpersonal conflict in a situation). We suspect that children are much more skillful communicators in these situations than their popular image of tactlessness would imply. There is an important theoretical issue involved here: Linguists and psychologists have tended to see language acquisition as a purely cognitive process, whereas it is surely manifest and functional almost entirely in social situations (see Chapter 2 by Bruner in this volume). Children must learn not only to represent such situations by language but also to *solve* them by their speech acts.

Returning to adults, a second interest is the relation of this model to the nonverbal "leakage" model that dominates deception research (e.g., Ekman & Friesen, 1969). These models vary in two significant respects. Deception research classifies messages dichotomously, as "truth" or "lying" with no alternative such as disqualification. It is assumed that people intend to lie, but that the truth is revealed by nonverbal leakage. In contrast, we do not see disqualified messages as "leaky" versions of a lie but rather assume that the message sent is the one intended—an inseparable package delivered on all channels, with none having priority over, or less control than, any other. Our evidence to date implicitly supports this interpretation. In the forced-choice experiments, subjects chose not to lie. In the written-message experiments, subjects had the full control of a purely verbal channel and, again, disqualified in preference to lying. Furthermore, disqualification occurs equally across channels; the transcribed verbal portions of our spoken and visual messages are not lies but disqualifications. Another problem with most deception research is its inattentiveness to the situations in which the messages are elicited. These are highly varied and questionably comparable (cf. Knapp & Comadena, 1979), and since the messages themselves are seldom reported, it is impossible to connect the actual language and the social situation with any precision.

Finally, we are beginning to gather naturally occurring messages in order to show that the theory extends past hypothetical situations in the lab. Rather than creating avoidance-avoidance conflicts by the use of confederates and deceptive experiments, we are looking around for actual instances of such conflicts, and their communicative sequelae. For example, televised political campaigns and real letters of reference are promising possibilities. The problem will not be finding disqualifications; it will be the methodological problem of making the same firm connection between situation and communication as has been possible in the experimental work to date.

Implications

If we step back from this particular project and phenomenon, what are the broader implications for the study of language and discourse, especially in natural settings?

First, language is a precise interpersonal act. The messages we call disqualified initially appear to be vague or faulty communication, to be dismissed or reinterpreted. Yet they are systematic and lawful, in two senses: Their "nonstraightforwardness" can be measured with precision and can be shown to vary with specific changes in the situation. We believe that the same is true for many aspects of natural language that at first appear to be careless, impenetrable, even nonsensical versions of what "should" have been said: the politician's double-speak, the militarist's euphemisms ("preventative retaliation"), the mental patient's verbal symptoms, or the amiable meaninglessness of polite conversation. We should resist glossings or inferences that assume that a different (better) message was intended and focus instead on the actual message.

Second, that focus should also include the situation, as the inescapable context that shapes our language, the context in which it is embedded and therefore best understood. This position is different from (but not incompatible with) a purely cognitive approach. In the latter, language is seen as the mirror of thought, as a representation of the situation, but not part of it. We would add that the language used is an integral part of the situation as well. It is elicited by, reactive to, and aimed at affecting the situation. Thus, especially when natural language is studied, because the situation is not of our making nor in our control, its particulars must be recorded along with the language of interest. As noted above, the situational and cognitive approaches are not mutually exclusive, so long as the analysis does not isolate language from its social context or abstract it from its uses and users.

Acknowledgments. This program of research has been generously supported since 1977 by the Social Sciences and Humanities Research Council of Canada, and by the Univeristy of Victoria. I would also like to acknowledge my excellent collaborators, Nicole Chovil, Jennifer Mullett, and Al Black.

References

Bateson, G., Jackson, D. D., Haley, J., & Weakland, J. (1956). Toward a theory of schizophrenia. *Behavioral Science, 1*, 251–264.

Bavelas, J. B. (1983). Situations that lead to disqualification. *Human Communication Research, 9*, 130–145.

Bavelas, J. B., & Chovil, N. (in press). How people disqualify: Experimental studies of spontaneous written disqualification. *Communication Monographs*.

Bavelas, J. B., & Smith, B. J. (1982). A method for scaling verbal disqualification. *Human Communication Research, 8*, 214–227.

Bowers, J. W., Elliott, N. D., & Desmond, R. J. (1977). Exploiting pragmatic rules: Devious messages. *Human Communication Research, 3*, 235–242.

Cronbach, L. J., & Meehl, P. E. (1955). Construct validity in psychological tests. *Psychological Bulletin, 52*, 281–302.

DePaulo, B. M., & Rosenthal, R. (1979). Telling lies. *Journal of Personality and Social Psychology, 37*, 1713–1722.

Ekehammar, B. (1974). Interactionism in personality from a historical perspective. *Psychological Bulletin, 81*, 1026–1048.

Ekman, P., & Friesen, W. V. (1969). Nonverbal leakage and cues to deception. *Psychiatry, 32*, 88–106.

Ekman, P., & Friesen, W. V. (1974). Detecting deception from the body or face. *Journal of Personality and Social Psychology, 29*, 288–298.

Grice, H. P. (1975). Logic and conversations. In P. Cole and J. L. Morgan (Eds.), *Syntax and semantics* (Vol. 3). New York: Academic Press.

Haley, J. (1959a). An interactional description of schizophrenia. *Psychiatry, 22*, 321–332.

Haley, J. (1959b). The family of the schizophrenic: A model system. *Journal of Nervous and Mental Diseases, 129*, 357–374.

Jackson, D. D., Riskin, J. V., & Satir, V. M. (1961). A method of analysis of a family interview. *Archives of General Psychiatry, 5*, 321–339.

Jackson, D. D., & Weakland, J. (1961). Conjoint family therapy: Some considerations on theory, technique, and results. *Psychiatry, 24* (supplement to No. 2), 30–45.

Knapp, M. L., & Comadena, M. E. (1979). Telling it like it isn't: A review of theory and research on deceptive communications. *Human Communication Research, 5*, 270–285.

Lewin, K. (1938). The conceptual representation and measurement of psychological forces. *Contributions to Psychological Theory, 1* (4, Serial No. 4).

Mehrabian, A., & Ferris, S. R. (1967). Inference of attitudes from nonverbal communication. *Journal of Consulting Psychology, 31*, 248–252.

Nofsinger, R. E., Jr. (1976). On answering questions indirectly: Some rules in the grammar of doing conversation. *Human Communication Research, 2*, 172–181.

Searle, J. R. Indirect speech acts. (1975). In P. Cole and J. L. Morgan (Eds.), *Syntax and semantics* (Vol. 3). New York: Academic Press.

Sluzki, C. E., Beavin, J., Tarnopolsky, A., & Verón, E. (1967). Transactional disqualification: Research on the double bind. *Archives of General Psychiatry, 16*, 494–504.

Turner, K. E., Edgley, C., & Olmstead, G. (1975). Information control in conversations: Honesty is not always the best policy. *Kansas Journal of Sociology, 11*, 69–89.

Watzlawick, P. (1964). *An anthology of human communication: Text and tape.* Palo Alto, CA: Science and Behaviour Books.

Watzlawick, P., Beavin, J., & Jackson, D. D. (1967). *Pragmatics of human communication: A study of interactional patterns, pathologies, and paradoxes.* New York: W. W. Norton & Co.

Weakland, J. H., & Fry, W. F., Jr. (1962). Letters of mothers of schizophrenics. *American Journal of Orthopsychiatry, 32*, 604–623.

Wiener, M., & Mehrabian, A. (1968). *Language within language: Immediacy, a channel in verbal communication.* New York: Appleton-Century-Crofts.

Chapter 12
Slips in Interaction: The Psychopathology of Everyday Discourse

Hannele Heikkinen and Maarit Valo

Introduction

A girl happens to bump the handbag of an elderly lady so that the bag falls to the floor. The girl hastens to say: *"That's all right!"*

Slips like this happen quite often in everyday interaction. In fact, they are not strictly slips of the tongue but slips in interaction. What are these slips, where do they come from, and what can they tell us about the process of discourse production? In this chapter, we shall analyze some common forms of interaction slips, with particular emphasis on the role that various situational features play in their production. We shall suggest that just as the analysis of slips of the tongue can tell us something about the process of language production, interaction slips reveal much about the process of producing discourse and the planning and performance of larger verbal interaction sequences. We shall suggest that interaction slips in the *sequence* of a discourse may be due to the undermonitoring of overroutinized discourses, while slips in the *content* of conversations may be due to the overmonitoring of nonroutine, problematic discourse features (see also van Dijk on situational influences on discourse, this volume, Chapter 6).

Slips of the Tongue Versus Slips in Interaction

Slips of the tongue have been studied widely within linguistics (see, e.g., collections of papers by Cutler, 1982; Fromkin, 1973, 1980) and they have been discussed from various points of view, such as aphasia, linguistic changes, or the psychological reality of a linguistic theory. Slips of the tongue, which are unintended utterances of a speaker, may be classified in various ways. They can, for example, be errors in the sequence of speech sounds, such attributed to the Rev. W. Spooner himself, would be "You hissed all my mystery lectures" instead of "You missed all my history lectures." Or, slips of the tongue may result in substitutions of whole words by others. Malapropisms, or word substitutions in which the target word and the slip are phonologically related, are an example of these. If Finnish *identtiset kaksoset* ("identical twins") is changed into *indefiniittiset kaksoset* ("indefinite twins"), the speaker is committing a malapropism.

It has been claimed that slips of the tongue may throw light on the linguistic programming of human beings. They have been used as evidence in the discussion of the characteristics and processes of our speech production mechanism. It is argued that these malfunctions in the mechanism are one way of making inferences about the nature of the otherwise inaccessible processes involved. We base our arguments on a similar view. However, we have found that there are aspects of slips in everyday communication that have not been much discussed in the current literature. First, we have noticed that the situational point of view has been neglected. It is clear that everything the speaker hears or sees may inadvertently slip into his or her utterance. These slips, caused by factors outside the current linguistic plan, have not been paid much attention to (however, see Harley 1983). Also, the role of the discourse history, and the thoughts and images evoked by the situation and their associations for the speaker, have not been discussed much since Freud wrote his *Psychopathology of Everyday Life*. We see all these factors, which have been considered as not strictly linguistic and therefore not worth discussing, as important.

We have also noticed that slips involve larger entities than words or sentences. For example, slips may occur in turn-taking or in anticipation of a conversational move. Thus, we have tried to show that speech planning really involves much more than the mere planning of linguistic structures. We have based our arguments on slips that happen in everyday interaction and have thus expanded the notion of slip. However, we have excluded from our study those *social blunders* that are related to other than linguistic behavior or are not under the immediate control of the participants themselves. These include slips such as forgetting the name of the person addressed, forgetting what one is supposed to say when making a speech, various flaws in appearance, and so on. Such social blunders have been collected and analyzed (see Gross & Stone, 1964) and their consequences have been studied. In our analysis, we are primarily concerned with the conveyance of the intended message: how the interaction is affected if the intention of one participant is not transmitted to the other because of some inadvertent action.

The slips we discuss in the present chapter are slips that do not seem to be purely linguistic or purely behavioral in character. They are slips that in some way distort the fluent flow of interaction, and accordingly, we call them *slips in interaction*. We discuss them mainly from the point of view of interaction planning, focusing on the sorts of things a human being has to consider when planning a discourse. Our approach perhaps reflects a general, if gradual, change of paradigm within the speech and language sciences: There has been a shift from the study of language as a structure toward the study of language as a means of communication (see, e.g., Sajavaara & Lehtonen (1980)). In our analysis we hope to make use of some of the current knowledge within linguistics, psycholinguistics, communication research, and social psychology.

Slips and the Components of a Speech Situation

Example 1. A colleague of the authors is leaving the office for the Christmas holidays late in the afternoon. She intends to wish us a merry Christmas, but says instead *"Good night!"*

It is our assumption that slips like the one above tell us something about the planning of discourse. For example, it seems clear that the speaker in the above example was not substituting one word for another but one greeting for another. The planning procedure can apparently handle entities such as "greetings" as well as words and sentences; it is not purely linguistic in character.

Every speech situation includes a number of components (see, e.g., Brown & Fraser, 1979). The planning of an interaction has to include such factors as the structural rules of the conversation, the topic, the register, etc., to name but a few. The relevant components of a situation, according to Hymes (1972), may be symbolized by the word SPEAKING: setting, participants, ends, art characteristics, key, instrumentalities, norms of interaction and interpretation, and genre (see also Ervin-Tripp, 1969, 1972; Goffman, 1964). In the following we try to show that the speaker must consider each of the components in interaction planning, and what kind of slips may follow if some of the factors are left unattended. It should be emphasized that we are not attempting to classify interaction slips, and that in fact we consider their strict classification and analysis highly problematic. Rather, we emphasize that slips can be due to a wide range of factors, and that they reflect the actual nature of the planning and processing involved. The examples we discuss are taken from our data of spontaneous Finnish conversation material. Most of our examples are recorded from casual encounters.

Every community determines its norms of interaction and also its norms of interpretation, suitable for a particular speech situation. We suggest that the management of interaction involves primarily two aspects. First, the participants have to consider the sequential organization of the conversation: e.g., opening, closing, sequencing, turn-taking, etc. Second, the participants have to take into account the correct conveyance of their intention: to assure that the content of the utterance, or the message they wish to convey, is correct (cf. the "housekeeping" or "management" moves vs. "substantive" moves by Weiner & Goodenough, 1977). This includes choice of topic, register, manner, etc. It seems clear that slips may occur in both cases. They are described in more detail below.

The Sequential Organization of Conversation

A great deal of casual conversation is automatized. The verbal elements of the interaction form a fairly closed class, and the rules can be applied to several speech situations (see, e.g., Weiner & Goodenough, 1977). For example, opening and closing moves can be seen as fairly automatic speech (vs. novel speech): They do not leave much room for the speaker to exercise his or her creativity. Opening and closing phases of a casual conversation are *inter-actional rituals* or *conversational routines* (cf. Coulmas, 1981; Goffman, 1967; Saville-Troike, 1982). Phases of routinized conversation seem to be rather prone to slips:

> Example 2. A speaker who usually meets the office cleaning woman in the morning happens to meet her in the afternoon and greets her: *"Good morning!"* instead of "Good afternoon." The inadequate greeting was triggered by the presence of the other participant whom she was accustomed to associating with mornings.

> Example 3. A speaker meets an acquaintance in the street. There is a moment of silence when neither of the participants says anything. Then the speaker says, *"I'm fine thanks!"* The speaker was anticipating the moves of the conversation by triggering the response she had planned in case she was asked "How are you?"

> Example 4. A speaker with a bad cold meets her friend, who is quite well and healthy. At the end of the conversation, the friend says, "Get well soon!" The speaker responds with *"You too!"* (It is idiomatic in Finnish to answer almost any wish with "kiitos samoin," meaning "you too," the use of which in this case was extended erroneously.)

We think that these slips, which are fairly common, can be explained precisely by their taking place in routine speech. The structure of repeated acts, such as casual conversations or telephone conversations, is well-known to all members of a particular community. Thus, the generic outline of the conversation is so well-rooted in the mind of an adult speaker that there is no need to pay special attention to it—neither to its planning nor to its production. Also, in casual encounters there is often a greater need to keep the smooth flow of interaction going than to "make sense": It is the speech act itself which becomes the communicative goal in this kind of phatic speech. Phatic communication is perhaps more relevant to the self-image of the interactants. The image of the fluent interactant is highly desirable, and clumsiness or awkwardness gives an unfavorable impression (see, e.g., Laver, 1975). These seemingly careless slips in greetings can be compared to word substitutions that occur with very familiar words: the substitution of *knife* for *fork*, or *Tuesday* for *Thursday*, etc. (see Heikkinen, 1983).

It has been suggested that pauses are used to plan speech; that is, smaller speech chunks (see, e.g., Butterworth, 1980, and Bergmann and Forgas, on speech dysfluencies, this volume, Chapter 13) are planned during the silent phases. Speech routines in day-to-day interaction may be seen to serve a similar purpose. It seems probable that the existence of such routinized speech may give the speaker time to concentrate more on the planning of the content of his or her forthcoming moves and on situation-specific characteristics of the discourse. In example 3 above, the speaker could not tolerate a longer silence and she was "plugging a conversational gap." Similar pressures may also lead to disqualified messages (e.g., Bavelas, this volume, Chapter 11). Longer pauses are usually interpreted as inconvenient, and indeed, it may be that the intrusions illustrated in the above examples show a certain sensitivity and communicative skill: The one who is more concerned tries to save the situation but sometimes slips like the speaker in example 3. Naturally, the tolerance of pauses varies, both individually and as regards different cultures (see, e.g., Lehtonen & Sajavaara, in press), and can also cause cross-cultural problems.

We would also like to emphasize here the inseparability of the speaker, the listener, and the environment in the interaction-planning process. When managing a conversation, one is not only planning one's moves, but also making predictions and guesses about what the other speaker is going to say. This fact is clearly reflected in slips involving turn-taking.

> Example 5. A (answering the telephone): Hello.
> B: Can I speak to the assistant, please.
> A: I'll see whether she's in.
> B: *Yes, just a moment*—I mean thank you.

The speaker answers with a phrase that the other person could (perhaps even should) have used. In a way, she steals the content of the other person's message. The speaker had predicted that the other person was going to react by saying "Just a moment," and when this was not the case, she used it herself, in a way repeating the message already uttered. This kind of behavior can be named *perseverative*.

> Example 6. A speaker is going on an important visit and she is rather nervous. When she meets her hostess at the door she blurts out: *"Welcome!"*

> Example 7. A speaker has gone to a ladies room where the bolt on the door is out of order. Another person rushes in. After a moment of acute embarrassment, the person who was first in says: *"Sorry I didn't notice ... "*

> Example 8. A woman is celebrating her fiftieth birthday. After receiving many congratulations during the day, she finally says, when welcoming a new guest: *"Many happy returns!"*

In these examples, whole turns—both the timing and the content—are stolen. For example, in an embarrassing situation the speaker may react too quickly and anticipate the other participant's turn. This kind of reaction seems to be related to an intolerance of pauses of interaction.

If we adhere to the view that the components of the speech situation—the participants and the environment—are really inseparable, it is easy to see how this can be analogized to a play. This idea has been expressed by Goffman

(1956) as well as by Firth (1935), who used the expression "knowing one's lines." Moves in routinized conversations are really largely determined by the society, by the situation type, and by the role of the interactant—not by the speaker himself.

Finally, slips connected with the structure of the conversation show that we plan not only such units as *tone groups* or *phonemic clauses*[1] at a time, but also larger entities. It is fairly evident that we have larger plans imprinted in our memory, e.g., *social episodes* (Forgas, 1982) or *scripts* (Schank, 1977). That is, we know how to do certain tasks, such as having dinner in a restaurant, buying and selling, attending a meeting, and so on. These larger plans obviously involve the storage of some verbal responses in the memory as well. The mental lexicon, or the inner storage for words, does not consist only of words in the literal sense, but also of phrases, greetings, etc., that can be handled as a whole. Similarly, we also have stored the knowledge of how to manage a casual conversation: what to say first, how to take turns, etc. This knowledge of interaction structure parallels our knowledge of the syntactic structure of sentences.

The Content of Conversation

The structure of conversations is usually culturally and situationally regulated, and to some extent predictable. The content of conversations, in contrast, is much more unpredictable, and depends on the unique variables present in the situation. Speakers have to consider who they are talking to, what kind of register they will use, what topics will be dealt with, what manner the message is delivered in, etc. There are no ready-made patterns for every situation—the exact properties have to be planned as the situation progresses. Thus, the choices of topic, register, and manner are usually not automatized but have to be submitted to more conscious control. We suggest that these things are monitored more carefully and therefore it may be that fewer slips occur in this aspect of communicative performance. The *communicative repertoire* or *speech repertoire* (Gumperz, 1964; Hymes, 1967) includes a varying number of registers and styles, and the speaker can choose from these—more or less consciously—the most suitable ones for the specific situation and the goal. A wrong selection can be a slip. These slips are often interpreted as social blunders, i.e., there is greater danger for embarrassment and insult. However, they are slips in the sense that they are temporary lapses and not deliberately brought about. They do not result from the communicative incompetence of the speaker. Every one of us probably commits them every now and then.

---

[1]A phonemic clause is a production unit consisting of a single intonation contour and one primary stressed syllable, and characterized by preceding and following pauses (see, e.g., Boomer & Laver, 1968).

What are the goals and principles according to which people behave in conversations? Grice's (1975) *maxims of conversation* seem to be concerned with content and its conveyance. He presumes that people share such principles as amount of information, truthfulness, relevancy, and unambiguity. According to Grice, these maxims can be violated. Nevertheless, he seems to regard conversation as an exchange of information and he presumes that the speakers act according to principles that ensure the effective transmission of some piece of information. The function of conversations is of course much wider and the information that is exchanged in casual encounters is rarely the kind that could be expressed in logical propositions. In what follows we discuss the three kinds of slips connected with the planning of conversational content: topic, manner, and register slips.

Topic

Topics are culturally, situationally, and individually determined, and certain topics have to be avoided within certain cultures or subcultures or in the company of certain people. As the proverb says, "Name not a rope in the house of a man who hanged himself." Thus there are taboo topics. But it is a peculiar and also in a way a very human failing that if one is trying hard to avoid a taboo topic, there seems to be a great danger that it will find its way into the conversation. Hidden ideas, even dimly conscious thoughts and impressions, may surface:

Example 9.   At a birthday party, a guest is making a speech to an 85-year-old lady. He addresses her as *"our deceased friend."*

Example 10.   A speaker visits her friend who is in hospital because of jaundice. She wants to cheer up her friend by telling her that she looks much better—the whites of her eyes are not at all yellow anymore. She starts: *"The yellow of your eyes ..."*

It is obvious that yellowness was an unsuitable subject to mention and the situation deteriorated due to the unfortunate slip. It can be claimed, and Freud probably would, that there is much hidden in slips like these and that they may not be as innocent as they look. It is probably also familiar to all of us that gossip of some sort will sometimes be involuntarily revealed by a slip. There are also taboo words, as well as taboo topics, in every culture and community. Slips of the tongue, for example, tend to be discomforting if they result in even slightly daring words or connotations. If a lecturer keeps talking about *orgasms* instead of *organisms*, his audience will be either amused or embarrassed. We suggest that the slips involved in the taboo area result from the fact that the taboo topic or word is paid too much attention, i.e., the speaker tends to monitor his utterance, hoping to avoid making blunders, and therefore, since the subject is "too present," it is also brought into the actual utterance.

Manner

By manner (cf. *key* in Hymes, 1972; or *mode of discourse* in Hasan, 1977), we mean the way in which the speaker conveys his or her intention: being polite, ironic, friendly, angry, etc. The speaker may fail to convey the message correctly by committing any kind of slip which the addressee interprets as disturbing or impolite.

> Example 11. A customer in a spectacle shop is trying to tell the owner politely that she is not going to buy the spectacles she intended to, after all. She pays special attention to being polite. She intends to say something like "I'm sorry but I think I won't be taking these..." She begins "*Fortunately*, I've decided not to take these..." The slip might have sounded rather offensive, had it not been that the owner had a sense of humor.

> Example 12. A nurse is examining a patient.
> Nurse: "Do you feel any pain here?"
> Patient: "Yes."
> Nurse: "*That's good.*"

In the latter example, the nurse was inadvertently giving a habitual response, which she undoubtedly often used, and extending a reaction toward positive news to a case in which the news was negative. The manner of the discourse was changed since her remark sounded inconsiderate. This slip shows that it is impossible to discuss slips from the point of view of one interactant only: Both the addresser and the addressee are required to define the slip.

Register

The register of the discourse varies according to the parameters of the situation (e.g., the status and role of the interactants) and the topic. The selection of correct register is probably carried out rather automatically once one sees one's addressee. However, there are temporary lapses out of register. These include, for example, use of the wrong form of address (in Finnish the use of the second-person pronoun sinä, French *tu* instead of *te*, French *vous* to an elderly person is such a slip) and other kinds of involuntary behavior that is inappropriate, e.g., too familiar.

> Example 13. In a public library, an elderly, dignified woman is looking for a certain book. The librarian is going to get it for her, and informs her: "*Wait a sec!*" Immediately the librarian realizes that the expression was far more familiar than she intended.

> Example 14. A teacher urged her adult students (whom she did not know well) to hurry up, using the baby-talk expression "*Kipi, kipi,*" which she was accustomed to use with her children.

Such register slips may be seen as violations of Ervin-Tripp's (1972) alternation rules: Where there is a possibility of choice, as in address, there is also a possibility of a slip. The continuous repetition of one kind of register may lead to a miscarried extension of it when an exception comes along. These slips happen especially in service encounters.

In the slips above, the social status or the role of the addressee was seemingly not considered, although the speaker must have been aware of them. These kinds of slips are related to such action slips as putting one's knife into one's mouth during a formal dinner, even if one knows perfectly well how to behave; the slip is not caused by the social incapability of the person, but may be interpreted as such.

The Interplay of the Interactants

It is fairly easy to define a slip from the point of view of the speaker, and argue that it is a failure to convey one's intention, or to achieve the goal one has set. When discussing the receiver of the message, it is somewhat harder to define what happens. *Slips of the ear* have been discussed in the literature (see, e.g., Garnes & Bond, 1975): A slip like this happens when the addressee hears *slip of the ear* as *snip of the ear*, for example. But what is a slip from the point of view of a receiver in interaction? Could it be a wrong interpretation of the addresser's intention, due to the ambiguity of the message, for example a wrong interpretation of nonverbal cues? In this section we will discuss some cases of nonverbal communication. For example, a nonintentional gesture can be interpreted as a communicative one:

Example 15. A lecturer happens to glance at his watch toward the end of his lecture. The students perceive this as a sign that the lecture is about to be finished, and start to move restlessly.

Example 16. Two persons are sitting on a bus. The one who is sitting on a window seat closes the zipper of her bag. The other person interprets this as a sign that the first is getting off the bus, and rises from his seat to let her pass.

Which one is slipping, the person who gives "wrong" signs or the one who reads them? "Slip" is not necessarily a meaningful term in these examples. Possibly these examples indicate only the fact that nonverbal communication is by and large ambiguous, and the same gestures can be either nonintentional or a means of communication.

The following example also illustrates the erroneous interpretation of a nonverbal cue:

Example 17. It is the first lecture of a course.
Student (in a nasal, drawling voice): "When do we have the exam?"
Lecturer (thinking that the student is bored and has a negative attitude toward the course, starts, jokingly, in the same kind of voice, but realizes simultaneously that the student was using her normal voice mannerism): "Well, we'll decide on it later..."

The lecturer interprets the paralinguistic feature incorrectly, and behaves accordingly, but realizes her slip. The accommodation of the lecturer toward the vocal behavior of her student was intentional, but she quickly realized that it was ill-chosen. Once again, we argue that it is really the inherent ambiguity of the social situation which leads the speaker to plan a move that can be interpreted as a slip. The concept of slip has to be defined within the conceptual framework of the interaction.

In addition to intentional accommodation, in everyday interaction there is also unconscious accommodation to the other interactant. People tend to adapt to various properties of the verbal and nonverbal behavior of others in a communicative situation. Every speech situation is a common ground for the participants in this sense. The features that tend to be accommodated include register, dialect, average speech rate, and pausing, to name but a few (see, e.g., Giles & Smith, 1979; Street & Giles, 1982). Too much convergence, however, can be interpreted as insulting or patronizing, especially when there is convergence toward features that are not prestige ones. Clearly, this kind of extreme accommodation may be a slip. It is regarded as grossly impolite to adopt another participant's speech defect, as in the following:

> Example 18. A student has a temporary job. His employer speaks a variant of Finnish that is considered to be a lower prestige pronunciation, in which *t* is substituted for *d*. One morning, the student greets his employer with exactly the customary expression and pronunciation of his.

It is typical of slips that the original goal of the interactional situation is not reached. The failure to reach the goal may have two kinds of consequences, either humorous or embarrassing. We assume that slips in interaction are (by definition) always noticed. If the situation is comfortable or familiar, the slips can be treated as jokes. On the other hand, they can cause tragicomical or even painful associations:

> Example 19. A woman meets her sister, who has just been widowed. She intends to comfort the widow and says with a sobbing voice: *"Congratulations . . . "*

> Example 20. A journalist makes a telephone call to reach a member of a communal council. The voice of a woman answers and tells him that the man he wants to talk to died six months ago. The journalist ends up with: *"Oh well, I'll call him again later!"*

As the consequences also show, a slip usually effects the interaction in some way, but the actual results cannot be predicted. They depend on the interplay of the interactants: It is for them to decide whether they will go on, drop the subject, or end their relationship altogether.

Slips and Discourse Planning

It is necessary to emphasize that the boundary between a slip and an error is by no means clear. In most cases "we know what we know," but there are certain borderline cases. Intuitions about language cannot be classified into strict categories of "correct/incorrect." This is shown by the fact that grammatical intuitions can be manipulated (Leiwo, 1983) or by the fact that blends are often regarded as acceptable words of one's language (Heikkinen, 1983). There is both interindividual and intraindividual variation as regards linguistic acceptability. For instance, in malapropisms it is very difficult to know whether a person commits a slip or a consistent error. Also, as regards certain interaction slips, you don't know whether the person knows he or she should not have said something or not. Sometimes you simply dare not ask.

Goffman (1981) distinguishes between "knows better" errors and "does not know better" errors, and classifies hesitations and slips into the "knows better" ones. This, of course, is related to the communicative skill of the person. In the same way that the rules of language are acquired during childhood and adolescence, so it is with the rules of conversation and interaction. Thus a person acquires skills in sequencing a conversation, in turn-taking, in topic-choosing, and in registers, etc. The definition of a slip, thus, has to be a flexible one: What is a slip in adult behavior may be only the lack of a skill in children's discourse. Topics are a clear example: Children tend to discuss the characteristics of another person's appearance very openly, to the annoyance of their parents.

Above, we have discussed slips descriptively from the point of view of interaction. Slips can also be approached from the perspective of general motor behavior. Human beings evidently have a capacity to plan their behavior and also to see whether their behavior is relevant. The *planning* and *monitoring* functions are also reflected in slips. Both slips of the tongue and slips in interaction can be anticipatory in character: Speakers can anticipate their own lines, the other participant's replies, the ends of the situation, etc. Thus it is necessary to assume a planning phase; otherwise such anticipations as the following would be impossible.

> Example 21. A young man is going to buy a hot dog. Contrary to his usual habit, he plans to take mustard on his hot dog. He starts the interaction with the vendor: "*Mustard, please!*"

Slips in interaction can also be perseverative: A speaker may continue to be influenced by a feature of an interaction situation that is no longer relevant.

> Example 22. A saleswoman in a shop has to answer the telephone repeatedly, giving the name of the shop: "Jack's Photo Shop." A customer comes into the shop. The saleswoman addresses the customer: "*Jack's Photo Shop.*"

Anticipation and perseverance are general properties of the planning procedure that have been revealed by research carried out within speech sciences on, e.g., coarticulatory processes. Such procedures as *activation* of the material and *selection* of the most appropriate expression must also be included in the process of interaction planning. Many of our examples are cases of wrong selection, e.g., greetings that are inappropriate for the situation.

Tentatively, we conjecture two sources for slips in interaction. First, they are related to the degree to which one monitors his or her interaction behavior. We would like to suggest that routine behaviors are prone to slips precisely because they are usually performed without hesitation. Usually these slips are also related to the fact that there is something slightly unusual or unexpected in the situation. Some of the variables of the situation are changed. For example, if one usually meets a person in the afternoon, the greeting "Good afternoon" becomes associated with him, and the same greeting is triggered when he is met in the morning.

On the other hand, monitoring may be too intensive (cf. Bergmann & Forgas, this volume, Chapter 13). That is, a topic may be so strongly present in the mind that it comes through whatever the subject or the situation. Taboo topics are an example of this. Also, people may develop a sort of mental block for various words, phrases, or ways of communicating; these blocks may also result in slips. When lecturing about slips, for example, it is sometimes very hard to keep in mind which of the utterances is the one containing a slip.

The quantity of slips, or the probability of a slip occurring, can increase for various reasons. On the level of interaction planning, the amount of monitoring of one's utterances can affect the number of slips. On the level of the physiological state of the speaker, it is self-evident that any kind of slip will tend to occur more often when the speaker is exhausted, inattentive, or under the influence of alcohol. The third factor that increases the amount of slips is the situation itself. Some unexpected element in the situation may lead to a slip. It is also obvious that all these factors are interrelated: The amount of monitoring is related to the physiological state of the speaker and to the situation; the unexpected elements in the situation can affect the interaction-planning procedures, so that decision-making concerning utterances has to be made hastily and cannot be checked properly, and so on.

Conclusion

As noted above, there are slips of several kinds and they can be classified and categorized in terms of several standards. We would like to emphasize, however, that there are no clear-cut boundaries between slips of various kinds, such as slips of the tongue, slips in interaction, and action slips (cf. Norman, 1981). Deviations in linguistic or communicative behavior all arise from the processes and plans of action of human beings. The boundary between a slip and an error is not clear either. The boundary line is not invariable either interindividually or intraindividually: There are situational effects that may have a decisive influence on communicative behavior.

Finally, slips in interaction imply certain things about the nature of models constructed to describe human communicative behavior (cf. van Dijk, this volume, Chapter 6). First, a model should take into account the fact that planning involves entities larger than sentences. This can be seen by considering that the utterance of a speaker may be influenced by turn-taking planning, topic, the role of the other participant, etc.—all factors not directly concerned with the planning of an utterance as such. Second, the linguistic component should not be treated as separate from nonverbal procedures. Slips in interaction seem to support the view that we must include the planning of nonverbal elements in the model. Third, the planning of communicative behavior is not done in a serial, or hierarchical, manner. Serial models of speech processing, which are based on the linguistic point of view and regard the processing of speech as a stepwise flow of different (linguistic) levels, have been criticized recently elsewhere (see, e.g., Marslen-Wilson & Komisarjevsky Tyler, 1980). Also, slips in interaction reflect the parallel nature of interaction planning: The speaker has different kinds of material storages and different kinds of incoming information, and he or she uses all this data in more or less parallel fashion, that is, simultaneously (for a preliminary formulation of such a model, see Hoppe-Graff et al., this volume). For example, the probability of a slip is increased if there are several factors favoring it (cf. slips discussed by Freud in which there are often linguistic resemblances between the slip and the target item and additional causes related, for example, to the individual himself). Fourth, more attention should be paid to the difference between automatic and novel speech production. It seems natural to propose that some aspects of speech production are more automatized than others. For instance, we presume that outlines of casual conversations and outlines of sentences are examples of such automatisms. Thus, they do not require as much conscious planning as those factors that have to be planned specifically in each unique speech situation. Automatisms are prone to slips due to undermonitoring, while novel situations are in danger of overmonitoring. Fifth, we argue that the idea of a single largest or smallest planning unit (such as a script or segment) is irrelevant: Planning takes place within schemata of varying size, which are by no means predetermined when we start an act. A large plan, for example, would be to have coffee in the cafeteria. This plan is vague and would be submitted to various kinds of alterations and completions as we go on. These could include having a conversation with the saleslady, choosing a table, meeting a friend, deciding whether or not to start a conversation, choosing a topic, selecting the register, and finally formulating the "grammar" of the actual utterances. But as we plan, we are always ready for intrusions and changes: We may be influenced by the other participants, by overheard conversation, and so on. Speech and interaction planning is both using one's own mental storage and employing the incoming information to formulate a plan. The planning unit as such does not exist: It is flexible, and it is perhaps more justifiable to discuss the planning *process* than a unit.

We would like to propose a view of the interaction process as a holistic happening. Speech production is always interaction and language cannot be distinguished categorically from other behavior. In interaction we cannot separate the speaker from the hearer or either of them from the situation: they are one. In interaction we cannot separate "linguistic" knowledge from the "knowledge of the world": They are one. We cannot separate the inner happening (e.g., the knowledge) from the outer happening (e.g., incoming information): They are one. What we learn about the communicative rules of our society, how we store the knowledge mentally, and how we use the knowledge are all intimately woven together. Slips in interaction constitute one illustration of this.

References

Boomer, D., & Laver, J. (1968). Slips of the tongue. *British Journal of Disorders of Communication, 3*, 2–11.

Brown, B., & Fraser, C. (1979). Speech as a marker of situation. In K. R. Scherer & H. Giles (Eds.), *Social markers in speech*. Cambridge: Cambridge University Press.

Butterworth, B. (1980). Evidence from pauses in speech. In B. Butterworth (Ed.), *Language production I*. London: Academic Press.

Coulmas, F. (Ed.) (1981). *Conversational routine*. The Hague: Mouton.

Cutler, A. (Ed.) (1982). *Slips of the tongue and language production*. Berlin, New York, Amsterdam: Mouton.

Ervin-Tripp, S. M. (1969). Sociolinguistics. In L. Berkowitz (Ed.), *Advances in experimental social psychology* (Vol. 4). New York: Academic Press.

Ervin-Tripp, S. M. (1972). On sociolinguistic rules: Alternation and co-occurrence. In J. J. Gumperz & D. Hymes (Eds.), *Directions in sociolinguistics*. New York: Holt, Rinehart and Winston.

Firth, J. R. (1935). The technique of semantics. In *Papers in linguistics: 1934–1951*. London: Oxford University Press.

Forgas, J. P. (1982). Episode cognition: Internal representations of interaction routines. In L. Berkowitz (Ed.), *Advances in social psychology* (Vol. 15). New York: Academic Press.

Fromkin, V. (Ed.) (1973). *Speech errors as linguistic evidence*. The Hague: Mouton.

Fromkin, V. (Ed.) (1980). *Errors in linguistic performance: Slips of the tongue, ear, pen and hand*. London: Academic Press.

Garnes, S., & Bond, Z. (1975). Slips of the ear: Errors in perception of casual speech. In *Papers from the Eleventh Regional Meeting of Chicago Linguistic Society*. Chicago: Chicago Linguistic Society.

Giles, H., & Smith, P. M. (1979). Accommodation theory: Optimal levels of convergence. In H. Giles & R. N. StClair (Eds.), *Language and social psychology*. Oxford: Basil Blackwell.

Goffman, E. (1956). *The presentation of self in everyday life*. Garden City, NY: Doubleday Anchor Books.

Goffman, E. (1964). The neglected situation. *American Anthropologist, 66*, 133–136.

Goffman, E. (1967). *Interaction ritual*. Garden City, NY: Doubleday Anchor Books.

Goffman, E. (1981). *Forms of talk*. Oxford: Basil Blackwell.

Grice, H. (1975). Logic and conversation. In P. Cole & J. L. Morgan (Eds.), *Syntax and semantics 3: Speech acts*. New York: Academic Press.

Gross, E., & Stone, G. P. (1964). Embarrassment and the analysis of the role requirements. *American Journal of Sociology, 70*, 1–15.

Gumperz, J. J. (1964). Linguistic and social interaction in two communities. *American Anthropologist, 66*, 137–153.

Harley, T. A. (1983). *A critique of top-down independent levels models of speech production: Evidence from non-plan internal speech errors*. Unpublished manuscript. University of Dundee, Department of Psychology.

Hasan, R. (1977). Text in the systemic-functional model. In W. V. Dressler (Ed.), *Current trends in text-linguistics*. Berlin: Walter de Gruyter.

Heikkinen, H. (1983). Errors in lexical processing. In H. Ringbom (Ed.), *Psycholinguistics and foreign language learning*. Publications of the Research Institute of Åbo Akademi Foundation. Turku: Åbo Akademi.

Hymes, D. (1967). Models of the interaction of language and social setting. *Journal of Social Issues, 23*, 8–28.

Hymes, D. (1972). Models of the interaction of language and social life. In J. J. Gumperz & D. Hymes (Eds.), *Directions in sociolinguistics*. New York: Holt, Rinehart and Winston.

Laver, J. (1975). Communicative functions of phatic communication. In A. Kendon, R. M. Harris, & M. R. Key (Eds.), *Organization of behaviour in face-to-face interaction*. The Hague: Mouton.

Lehtonen, J., & Sajavaara, K. (in press). The silent finn. In M. Saville-Troike & D. Tannen (Eds.), *The functions of silence*. Norwood, N.J.: Ablex.

Leiwo, M. (1983). On grammatical intuition. In F. Karlsson (Ed.), *Papers of 7th Scandinavian Conference of Linguistics 2*. University of Helsinki: Department of Linguistics.

Marslen-Wilson, W., & Komisarjevsky Tyler, L. (1980). The temporal structure of spoken language understanding. *Cognition, 8*, 1–71.

Norman, D. A. (1981). Categorization of action slips. *Psychological Review, 88*, 1–15.

Sajavaara, K., & Lehtonen, J. (1980). The analysis of cross-language communication: Prolegomena to the theory and methodology. In H. W. Dechert & M. Raupach (Eds.), *Towards a cross-linguistic assessment of speech production*. Frankfurt: Verlag Peter D. Lang.

Saville-Troike, M. (1982). *The ethnography of communication: An introduction*. Oxford: Basil Blackwell.

Schank, R. G. (1977). Rules and topics in conversation. *Cognitive Science, 1*, 421–444.

Street, R. L., Jr., & Giles, H. (1982). Speech accommodation theory. In M. E. Roloff & C. R. Berger (Eds.), *Social cognition and communication*. Beverly Hills, CA: Sage Publications.

Weiner, S. L., & Goodenough, O. R. (1977). A move toward a psychology of conversation. In R. O. Freedle (Ed.), *Discourse production and comprehension I*. Norwood, NJ: Ablex.

Chapter 13

Situational Variation in Speech Dysfluencies in Interpersonal Communication

Günther Bergmann and Joseph P. Forgas

Introduction

In this chapter we shall deal with the problem of speech dysfluencies, particularly stuttering, in interpersonal communication. We shall suggest that features of social situations and the communicative anxiety they generate in speakers have a major influence on various speech dysfluencies in general, and stuttering incidence in particular. We will also propose a preliminary model linking features of social situations through the mediating factors of communication responsibility and need for control to the occurrence of speech dysfluencies.

Our approach is based on the belief that the time has now arrived to link existing research on characteristics of social situations in cognitive social psychology with research on speech disturbances. Recent advances in the social psychology of situations (Argyle, 1984; Argyle, Furnham, & Graham, 1981; Forgas, 1982) can contribute much to the explanation of stuttering as a phenomenon of interpersonal interaction (Krause, 1982; Muller & Duckworth, 1983). Similarly, research on the incidence of stuttering can make an important contribution toward answering the question of what factors make a social situation difficult. It seems worthwhile to point out at this stage that many traditional theories of stuttering are organic or intrapsychic in orientation, and tend to ignore the social character of this phenomenon. Physical interventions, including surgical procedures that remove a small piece of the tongue, were commonly accepted treatments for stuttering in the not too far distant past. Even today many theories of stuttering are entirely nonsocial, emphasizing affective or physiological problems (Krause, 1982).

Before embarking on this enterprise, it is perhaps in order to illustrate our major message with a personal observation. While conducting an experiment with stutterers (Bergmann, 1983b), an unexpected and quite interesting effect was noticed. The aim of the experiment was to study stutterers' production of prosodic features in a reading task. Because high-quality sound recordings were essential for the subsequent digital speech analysis, the stutterers were to be recorded in a sound-isolated booth. There was no direct contact, either visual or auditory, with the experimenter. Subjects even received their instructions from a tape recording, and spoke into a microphone.

Surprisingly, some subjects did not stutter at all during the various reading tasks. When the subjects were asked after leaving the booth to describe their experiences during the experiment, they again stuttered in their customary way. Eventually, the experimental arrangement was changed, and a co-experimenter sat with the subjects face-to-face in the booth. His only function was to follow the text as the subjects read. Once this procedure was adopted, stuttering again occurred at a level which was usual for the subject's normal interactions, and the experiment could be completed as planned.

Toward a Model of Situational Variation in Speech Dysfluencies

From this observation, as well as from the extensive literature on stuttering, it is clear that stuttering is a phenomenon that is often specific to interpersonal interaction. There is considerable self-report evidence from stutterers documenting that they do not stutter when speaking alone. Several studies show that stuttering is drastically reduced when stutterers speak to children or animals. On the other hand, stuttering is particularly frequent in demanding interpersonal situations, such as speaking to an audience, speaking to persons of authority, speaking to strangers, or speaking on the telephone. What links such situations to speech dysfluencies? Except for the last situation (speaking on the telephone), all of the above situations were also shown to be difficult or problematic for nonstutterers as well (cf. Argyle et al., 1981). Empirical research on speech anxiety also suggests that not only stutterers, but normally fluent speakers as well produce more speech dysfluencies in these situations.

It would be a grave mistake to assume that there is a direct, one-to-one relationship between particular situations and the occurrence of speech dysfluencies. The matter is of course much more complex. We must take into account at least three aspects of a communicative encounter if we wish to link situations to speech dysfluencies. The first aspect is *situation perception*, or the way a person perceives and cognitively represents a particular social episode, and we shall have more to say about this later. The other two subjective aspects are *message content* and the perceived *consequences of the communication*. These three aspects must always be considered in conjunction. For example, stuttering frequency could be very high even in an episode generally considered easy, such as a conversation with a friend, if the content of the message is emotionally important. Communication with a stranger, normally a "difficult" episode, may in turn cause no problems if the message content is neutral and no further interaction is expected.

Of course, certain episodes are problematic irrespective of message content.

Speaking to a person in authority is always difficult, but particularly so when active disagreement has to be expressed. Such encounters requiring assertiveness occupy a special place in our communicative repertoires, as Argyle et al. (1981) and others have shown. The third parameter of communication situations is perceived consequences. As this essentially involves the speaker's expectations and estimates of likely positive and negative outcomes, ultimately the self-image of the person is also at stake.

These three aspects of communication—episode definitions, message content, and perceived consequences—mediate the extent to which a person will experience subjective ego involvement, communication responsibility, and the need for control in a communicative encounter. We shall suggest here that the perception and interpretation of the social situation, influencing subjective communication responsibility, and need for control may ultimately have a major impact on the incidence of speech dysfluencies. The communicators' beliefs, expectations, and past experiences in similar situations will play a crucial role in how a specific communicative encounter is interpreted. Our model is represented in a somewhat simplified form in Figure 13-1. We shall devote the rest of this chapter to considering the various lines of evidence supporting this formulation, including some of our own empirical data.

The Social Character of Stuttering

There is considerable evidence indicating that speech dysfluencies such as stuttering are strongly dependent on a range of social and cultural factors. There appear to be important differences in the incidence of stuttering across cultures, and the competitiveness of a particular society seems directly related to the frequency of stutterers. As Bloodstein (1975) observed, stuttering as a disorder seems to be "a significant comment on the culture that produces it. To say that there are many stutterers in a given society is apparently to say that it is a rather competitive society" (p. 97). And later, "The probability that stuttering is related to environmental pressures for achievement and conformity of some kind appears to represent one of the fundamental pieces of information we have gained about its causation" (p. 103).

The immediate social milieu, such as the family, and the style of childrearing in particular also seem to be related to the emergence of childhood stuttering (Krause, 1982). High expectations of a child by ambitious parents, upward social mobility, and great emphasis on communicative competence are paradoxically some of the family characteristics that may play a role in the etiology of stuttering in childhood. There is some as yet controversial evidence suggesting that affect suppression, and negative reactions to the communicative endeavours of the child, also play a critical role in the etiology of stuttering, and a later predisposition to speech anxiety (Krause, 1982; Motsch, 1979).

Once stuttering as an enduring speech disturbance is firmly established, the

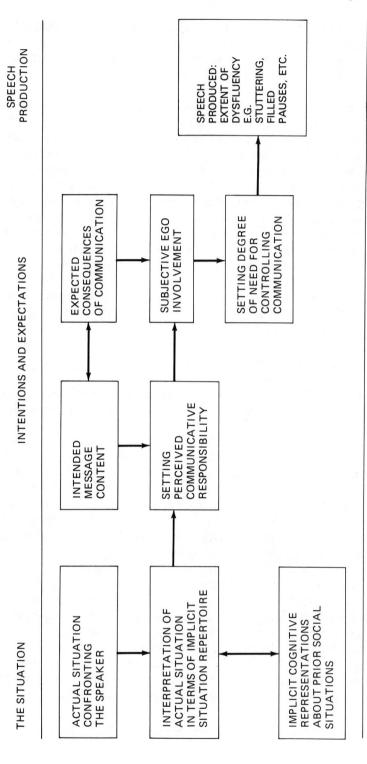

Figure 13-1. A hypothetical model linking situational variables to the occurrence of speech dysfluencies. From Forgas, 1978, copyright © Academic Press. Reprinted with permission.

role of social factors, particularly the character of specific social situations, continues to play an important role in its regulation. There have been many attempts in the past to develop a taxonomy of social situations in which stuttering occurs. Although these attempts have generally been unsuccessful, it is clear that stuttering does not occur every time a stutterer speaks. On the contrary, it is highly dependent on contextual factors. Even some very severe stutterers show no symptoms 75% of their total speaking time (Bar, 1973). The interactive routines of particular individuals thus naturally play a major role in influencing stuttering frequencies.

Firstly, stuttering frequency seems to depend on the speaking modality. Most stutterers produce less stuttering in an oral reading task than in spontaneous speech (Kroll & Hood, 1976; Van Riper, 1971). Stuttering is also reduced when reading meaningless materials such as syllables or numbers (Bloodstein, 1975; Sheehan, 1958). Other studies, (e.g., Bardrick & Sheehan, 1956) showed that emotionally loaded words produced more stuttering than either ordinary communication or nonsense material. These findings are consistent with the view that stuttering incidence is related to the degree of subjectively experienced communicative responsibility on the part of the speakers. Communicative responsibility (and stuttering) is clearly reduced when the spoken material is either meaningless or is not the speaker's own communication.

Thus, the extent of stuttering depends not only on the meaningfulness or propositionality, but also on the affective loading of the communicational content. We have seen so far that social and cultural factors play an important role in the etiology and incidence of stuttering. We shall now turn to a more detailed consideration of the influence of social situations on stuttering incidence.

Situational Variations in Stuttering

There are several studies showing that stuttering varies depending on the characteristics of the surrounding social situation. For example, Van Riper (1971) reports that the identity of the communication partner has a noticeable effect on stuttering frequency. Stuttering incidence was found to decrease across situations in the following order: speaking to an audience, speaking to a stranger (one of the opposite sex is particularly demanding), speaking to a therapist, speaking to a close friend, and speaking alone. Other situational features, such as status differences, sexual composition of the dyad, and behavior setting, may also influence the occurrence of stuttering. Unfortunately, research is not always unequivocal on these various points, probably because the stutterers' subjective perception and interpretation of a confronting situation are more important in eliciting stuttering behavior than the objective features of the situations commonly studied. In the next section, we shall briefly survey the available evidence on the links between specific situational features and stuttering.

Speaking Alone Versus Speaking to Others

The alleged reduction or even absence of stuttering when speaking alone is a particularly intriguing proposition, which would of course be in strong accord with a social-situational account of this disturbance. Wingate (1976) examined the evidence for this assertion in some detail. He reviewed several studies, and concluded that this pattern was only true for a minority of stutterers. Hahn (1940) observed 52 stutterers reading aloud when they believed themselves to be alone, and noted that all but three of them stuttered even in this situation.

In another study, Razdol'skii (1965, cited in Wingate, 1976) compared stuttering frequency for children and adults when alone and speaking in a social interaction situation. Only 11 out of the total of 125 subjects did not stutter when speaking alone. However, most subjects did in fact stutter much less when speaking alone, and the size of this effect was also found to be age dependent. Preschool children showed nearly as much stuttering when speaking alone. Most of the school-age children in turn stuttered noticeably less when alone, and most of the teenagers and adults in fact stuttered significantly less in the isolated speaking situation. A drastic reduction (but not complete elimination) of stuttering in isolated speaking by adults has been confirmed by several studies (Hahn, 1940; Porter, 1939; Steer and Johnson, 1936; Svab, Gross, & Langova, 1972). We may count the observation recounted at the beginning of this paper (cf. Bergmann, 1983a) as a further example supporting this suggestion. These results are consistent with the view that a person's increasing sophistication in differentiating between social situations with increasing age may be intimately related to the incidence of stuttering.

Nevertheless, the apparent persistence of stuttering in isolated speaking situations reported by Wingate (1976) requires additional explanation. For one thing, demand characteristics in these studies might have caused the stutterers to expect observation by an anticipated audience. Even without such demand characteristics, an isolated stutterer can still modify the relevant situational components by subjectively representing an audience, or by heightened monitoring of his or her own speech. The importance of self-monitoring and attempts at control has been frequently noted in stuttering research (Krause, 1982). We may then conclude that stuttering frequency seems to be specifically associated with the social nature of the situations, although the removal of an audience does not reliably result in its complete elimination.

The Effects of Audience Size

The size of the audience is one of the few situational factors in regard to stuttering that has received considerable attention. Porter (1939) found increasing frequencies of stuttering with audiences of one, two, four, and eight listeners. Further studies tended to generally confirm this finding (Dixon,

1955; Hahn, 1940; Shulman, 1955; Siegel & Haugen, 1964). These studies have been criticized on the ground that they confound two possibly quite distinct sources of stuttering: a person's expectation of difficulty with an audience of a particular size, and his or her actual reactions to a real audience. When a stutterer is informed that he or she will have to speak to a certain number of listeners, this information alone may generate a certain degree of speech anxiety based on past experiences with similar audiences. The actual reactions to a real audience may be largely preempted by such subjective expectations.

In testing the role of such expectations, Young (1965) found no systematic effect of audience size on stuttering frequency when speakers had no prior knowledge or expectation of the kind of audience they were to address. These results confirm that subjectively anticipated difficulties in speaking, rather than the objective characteristics of situations, are largely responsible for determining stuttering frequency, a distinction about which we shall have more to say later.

The Effects of the Identity of the Listeners

Size of the audience is not the only situational variable affecting stuttering. Stuttering frequency is also affected by the identity of the listeners. Ramig, Krieger, and Adams (1982) studied the speaking behavior of stutterers and nonstutterers to children. They were able to show that stuttering frequency decreased by more than half when their subjects spoke to a child instead of to the adult experimenter. It seems reasonable to assume that these differences may be even greater in natural situations, where the obvious anxiety associated with an experimental setting would be further reduced.

There is also considerable evidence suggesting that stuttering incidence is reduced when speaking to animals. Taken together, these various observations substantiate the view that communication responsibility and anxiety about the success of a communicative encounter play an important role in stuttering. Stuttering seems to decrease when the evaluative potential of the audience (children and animals vs. adults) decreases.

Situational Influences on Stuttering: An Experimental Demonstration

The following experiment, recently conducted by Bergmann, also suggests that stuttering may be regarded as a phenomenon closely tied to the features of the interpersonal situation. This study grew out of research the major aim of which was to examine stutterers' production of prosodic features in various reading tasks (Bergmann, 1983a, 1983b). It was in the context of these studies that we observed the phenomenon that stuttering was drastically reduced when subjects were seated alone in an acoustic booth for the purpose of recording. When the situation was made more "social" by placing an otherwise passive coexperimenter in the same booth with the subject, the usual level of stuttering returned.

In order to explore this effect more systematically, we introduced several further variations into the experimental setting. Six male stutterers (ages 17 to 38) performed a reading task, first reading a fable in the isolated reading situation without a coexperimenter. Afterwards they were interviewed about their reactions to the experiment. About four weeks later the same subjects returned to the laboratory, and they again performed the same reading task, this time in a nonisolated speaking situation with a coexperimenter also sitting in the booth. A second interview was conducted afterwards.

The number of dysfluent syllables was counted from audio recordings for each condition using a categorization scheme proposed by Bergmann (1984). This classification scheme is based on the systems of Johnson, Darley, and Spriestersbach (1963) and Zerbin (1973), and on the standard definition of stuttering proposed by Wingate (1964, 1977). According to this scheme, stuttering events may be subdivided into the following four categories. (1) Repetitions: Any repeated syllable is counted. In the case of whole words repeated, only one repetition is counted. (2) Prolongations: Consonants and vowels may both be prolonged, predominantly in initial word positions. (3) Blocks and pauses: Speech blocks, often associated with visible struggle behavior, and pauses are calculated in the same category since they cannot be unequivocally differentiated on the basis of audio recordings. (4) Filled pauses and interjections: Filled pauses are defined as nonword interjections like "ah," "ehm," etc., often used by normally fluent speakers as well. Other interjections may consist of nonspeechlike sounds, and words not originally contained in the text. Word reversions may also be listed in this category.

According to this scheme, every stuttering symptom is only listed once in any one of these categories. We shall not differentiate between these four categories in our analyses, since it cannot be assumed that these categories are diagnostic of subgroups of stutterers or of different kinds of stuttering behaviors. Since the fable first read by subjects contained 130 syllables, a section of the interview of the same length was selected for evaluation. This section was taken from the middle of the interview. In Table 13-1, the absolute values of stuttering frequency in these different situations can be compared. Absolute values without further conversions are used since they express most clearly the differences between these situations.

As Table 13-1 clearly shows, there was a very noticeable difference in stuttering between the isolated speaking situation and the following interview (interpersonal communication situation). Five of the six subjects stuttered hardly at all during the isolated reading task. Only Subject 1 showed substantial stuttering. The increase in stuttering in the postexperimental interview cannot be fully explained by the differences in the material (fable vs. speaking about one's own experiences). As the right-hand side of the table shows, the same stutterers reading the same material also produced a significantly higher rate of stuttering when a coexperimenter sat with them in the booth. While there is a difference in stuttering rate as a function of the material (reading vs. speaking), the major effect illustrated by Table 13-1 is

Table 13-1. Number of Dysfluent Syllables in Each of Four Different Speaking Situations

Subject number	Isolated speaking (fable)	First interview	Nonisolated speaking (fable)	Second interview
1	27	42	33	49
2	3	21	21	19
3	0	11	6	11
4	2	32	18	29
5	0	27	28	32
6	2	24	19	22
Mean Values	5.7	26.2	20.8	27.0
Mean Values Without Subject 1	1.4	23.0	18.4	22.6

between isolated vs. interpersonal speaking situations. We must also remember that the nonisolated speaking situation created here is much more restrictive than normal everyday interactions.

How can we interpret these findings, in the light of other experimental evidence available about situational influences on the incidence of stuttering? It seems most likely that the situations summarized in Table 13-1 differed in terms of the subjectively experienced communicative responsibility of the speakers. In a completely isolated, nonsocial situation, communication responsibility is minimal: There is no immediate reaction to what is said, and the material itself is not personally relevant. When another person shares the same space, communication responsibility is likely to be dramatically increased. Even though the message is not personally relevant, the onus is now on the speaker to communicate it clearly and effectively to another individual who is monitoring this performance. Finally, the face-to-face interviews represent the highest level of communication responsibility. Here, the speaker is both personally involved in the message, and his or her performance is directly evaluated by an attentive audience. The data in Table 13-1 generally support such an interpretation.

Communication responsibility is directly related to the degree of subjective involvement experienced by a person. If the consequences of a communication are highly important for a person's self-image, the need to control one's own behavior and performance is also increased. This seems to be a crucial factor in stuttering. The perceived need to control one's own communicative behaviors increases anxiety, which in turn may contribute to a breakdown of speech control, and result in stuttering.

The same kind of process applies not only to stutterers, but also to normally fluent persons. For example, overmonitoring, linked to communication anxiety, may also be responsible for the "interaction slips" discussed by Heikkinen and Valo (this volume, Chapter 12). The main link between situational characteristics and the incidence of various speech dysfluencies is the subjectively experienced communication responsibility. The resulting anxiety will be directly related to the speaker's degree of personal involvement in the situation, his or her anticipation of others' possible reactions, and the relevance of those reactions to the person's self-image (cf. Spielberger, 1975).

Before further elaborating the central role that communication responsibility plays in mediating between situational factors and stuttering, we need to look at the way interaction situations are conceptualised and described in psychology. On the basis of such description schemes, to be summarized in the next section, we should be able to better understand the process linking situations to speech dysfluencies.

Psychological Aspects of Situational Difficulty in Everyday Interaction

Everyday social life largely consists of routine, recurring interactions. Most verbal encounters are carried out according to well-known, and consensually shared interaction rules. Members of a particular culture or subculture usually possess a clear and unambiguous cognitive representation of the interaction episodes commonly practiced in their milieu, and these representations can even be readily quantified (cf. Forgas, 1979, 1982). The study of everyday situations is a relatively new development in psychology, although it has considerable historical roots in the work of psychologists such as Brunswik, Lewin, and Kantor, and sociologists such as Thomas, Wolff, and Waller. But it was the recent reformulation of personality psychology (cf. Mischel, 1968, 1977, 1979) that forced a turning away from ideas of intrapsychic causation toward more interactionist approaches to the explanation of behavior (Ekehammar, 1974; Endler & Magnusson, 1975, 1976; Frederiksen, 1972; Lazarus & Launier, 1978; Magnusson, 1971, 1981; Pervin, 1976; Pervin & Lewis, 1978).

Psychologists are of course not the only ones interested in descriptions of situations. Linguists such as Hymes (1967, 1972) suggested, for example, that three elements are fundamental to situation perception: the environmental setting of the interaction, the characteristics of the participants, and the purpose of the interaction. Somewhat similar schemes were developed by Giles and Powesland (1975), and by Brown and Fraser (1979), who proposed that communicative situations are constituted of such main components as scene (divided into subelements such as purpose and setting) and participants (again divided into subelements). Others such as Barker (1968) developed extensive taxonomic systems of interactions in terms of the physical behavior setting in which an encounter occurs.

There is also considerable descriptive research on the specific characteristics of "difficult" situations. In their study of interaction difficulty in a student population, Bryant and Trower (1974) found that two major situational characteristics, initial contact with strangers (particularly of the opposite sex) and intimate social encounters, created the greatest difficulty. In a study by Richardson and Tasto (1976), seven factors of a social-anxiety inventory were extracted. The first four involved situational elements such as fear of disapproval or criticism from others, fear of social assertiveness and high visibility, fear of confrontation and expression of anger, and fear of heterosexual contact.

In an extensive research project on shyness, Zimbardo (1982) found that 40% of the United States population (60% in Japan and 40% in Israel) describe themselves as "shy." The most difficult situations eliciting shyness are those threatening the esteem and optimal performance of the individual. Foremost among these are situations that can be characterized as "social, novel, or evaluative; situations that require assertiveness, that make the person the focus of attention, or that place the person in a lower status vis-a-vis others" (p. 474). These are exactly the same situational characteristics that were also found to elicit stuttering and other speech dysfluencies.

In a recent comprehensive review, Argyle et al. (1981, pp. 328–329) summarized seven types of common difficult situations that are described in the literature with some consistency. (1) Situations requiring expressions of *intimacy* are problematic particularly if they involve contact with relative strangers in an initial encounter, or if partners are members of the opposite sex. Situational difficulty further increases if the communication involves self-disclosure or expression of affect. (2) Situations demanding *assertiveness*, or the active expression of disagreements or conflicting interests, are commonly found to be difficult. Situational difficulty is even greater if the partner is a person of higher status or authority. (3) Being the *focus of attention* of a group of observers is especially demanding. Such situations include speaking in front of an audience, being tested, performing at a job interview, as well as being visibly different from other people in physical appearance (for example, being handicapped). Jeger and Goldfried (1976) showed, for example, that qualitatively different sources of attention, such as a live audience, a camera, or simply a mirror, can all greatly affect speech anxiety. (4) Situations involving *complex social routines* that are highly formalized and ritualized are also difficult, particularly for people who are not familiar with the interaction rules. Marriage or funeral ceremonies or court proceedings often have such a ritualistic character, and most people never acquire enough practice to become familiar with such situations. (5) Situations involving *failure or rejection* are considered difficult by Argyle et al. (1981) if a person's self-esteem, self-image, and confidence in front of others is threatened. (6) Situations where potential or actual physical *pain* or injury is a possibility are by definition difficult, as are (7) situations involving *loss* or bereavement, for obvious reasons which require no further comment.

These approaches to situation description tend to suffer from one major shortcoming as far as the potential explanation of speech dysfluencies is concerned. They tend to emphasise the objective, directly observable characteristics of situations to the relative neglect of how persons engaged in an encounter subjectively perceive and react to the episode. Even something as tangible as the possibility of physical pain or injury is not necessarily related to perceived difficulty. Experiencing pain partly depends on subjective evaluation and attributions (Leventhal & Everhart, 1979; Mason, 1974). The same can be said for situations involving loss. Loss is not stressful per se, but only if it is perceived and interpreted as a personal loss (e.g., Lazarus & Launier, 1978). The real difficulty of a communicative encounter cannot be established in terms of such objective, a priori characteristics. The actor's subjective reactions and interpretations play a crucial role in determining whether difficult situations will in fact elicit anxiety or not.

On the face of it, most of the seven types of difficult situations described by Argyle et al. (1981) are likely to be difficult because they entail some danger to the actor's self-image: They are situations characterized by a heightened sense of communication responsibility. But we do not have any evidence about how people subjectively interpret such encounters. This problem of the subjective as opposed to the objective antecedents of stress has been extensively discussed (e.g., Bergmann, in press; Lazarus & Launier, 1978) with respect to coping research. We shall now turn to a consideration of more subjective, cognitively based studies of features of difficult situations.

Subjectively Perceived Characteristics of Situations

Several researchers have attempted in recent years to construct empirical taxonomies of interaction situations based on people's perceptions of them. Wish and Kaplan (1976), for example, used a multidimensional scaling method (MDS) to analyse people's perceptions of hypothetical interactions. They found that five bipolar dimensions defined such representations: cooperative/competitive, intense/superficial, formal/informal, equal/unequal, and task-oriented/non-task-oriented. Others adopted a more idiographic strategy. Pervin (1976), for example, carried out an intensive analysis of the perceived situational repertoires of a few selected individuals, using a factor-analytic methodology.

Yet another strategy was used by Price and Bouffard (1974). These authors asked their subjects to rate the appropriateness of a variety of behaviors (e.g., read, sleep, talk, eat, run) in a variety of different situations (e.g., on a date, in a restaurant, etc.). By summarizing the appropriateness ratings of all behaviors for a given situation, something like an empirical measure of situational difficulty or restrictiveness may be calculated. Price and Bouffard (1974) found that situations that are private are least governed by behavioral prescriptions. As we have seen in the above review of the stuttering literature, it is precisely in these situations that stuttering is least common, and perceived communication responsibility is at its lowest.

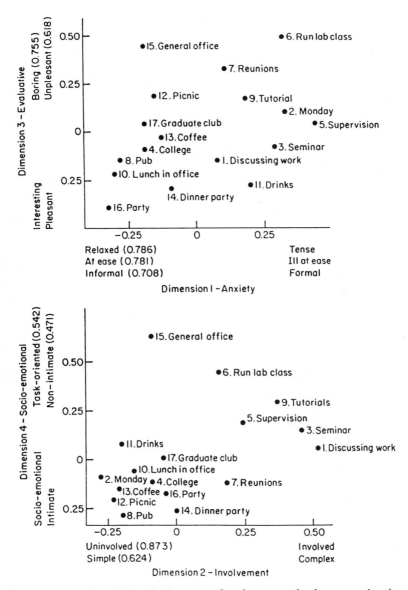

Figure 13-2. A model of the episode space of an intact academic group, showing the the bipolar scales used in the labeling of the four episode dimensions. (From Forgas, 1978, copyright © Academic Press. Reprinted with permission.)

In some of our own research (Forgas, 1979, 1982), we attempted to expand these techniques in order to discover the links between situation perception strategies and a variety of personal and cultural characteristics, again using MDS procedures. We found that it is indeed feasible to construct empirical representations of social interaction episodes in terms of how people perceive them, and that such representations are quite stable over time. An important finding was that people naturally perceive such epsiodes almost exclusively in terms of affective, connotative characteristics. It is not the objective situation, but people's subjective feelings about a situation, that ultimately determine how they think about it. Frequently, very different encounters (e.g., a formal ceremony and a tutorial) may be seen as almost identical to each other, in terms of how a person feels about these encounters. Both episodes are restrictive and highly regulated, and are performed with a lack of self-confidence, despite their very different surface characteristics.

It is precisely these subjective reactions to situations that play a crucial role in mediating communication responsibility, speech anxiety, and ultimately stuttering. To give an example of the kind of subjective episode classifications we found in our research, a model of such an episode "space" is shown in Figure 13-2. This happens to be the perceived episode space of an academic group, consisting of graduate students, faculty members, and other staff (Forgas, 1978). As Figure 13-2 shows, these episodes are perceived relative to each other in terms of how this group of people feels about them. Extending this idea to the problem of stuttering, we may predict that episodes seen as demanding, involved, and unpleasant (at a supervision session, running a lab class, etc.) would be associated with greater communication anxiety than relaxed, uninvolved, and positively evaluated encounters (e.g., morning coffee, in the pub).

In further investigations, it turned out that perceptions of episode domains are also significantly influenced by the enduring personal characteristics of a person. People who had particularly low scores on social-skills measures tended to see social episodes in terms of a single, dominant anxiety dimension. More skilled, self-confident, and extroverted individuals had a more complex and more critical evaluative episode perception style (Forgas, 1983). These findings can again be extended to the problem of stuttering. If we conceive of stuttering not as a fixed trait but as a more or less enduring personal predisposition, then the actual incidence of stuttering frequency should be dependent on a person's way of perceiving and interpreting the social encounters he or she participates in. It is such subjective representations that in turn influence communication responsibility and ultimately precipitate speech disturbances in stutterers as well as in normally fluent speakers.

Speech Dysfluency in Normally Fluent Speakers

We should perhaps begin this section by asserting that stuttering should not be seen as an isolated category on its own, but as one extreme on a continuum of speech dysfluencies ranging from the superficial to the severe. Without an extensive review of the relevant literature to substantiate this point (Adams & Runyan, 1981; Gregory, 1979; Johnson et al., 1963; Stäcker, Bergmann, & Kriebel, 1982; Van Riper, 1971; Williams, 1957), let us just refer to two commonly accepted truths. First, most normally fluent people do in fact display some degree of speech dysfluency depending on the situation they find themselves in. Second, stuttering itself occurs in a wide variety of manifestations, from the minor to the extremely serious (Krause, 1982). There is thus no real ground for assuming that stutterers are categorically different from fluent speakers.

What can we learn from the dysfluencies of normal speakers? Early research mainly dealt with the problem of classifying speech dysfluencies (cf. Mahl & Schulze, 1964). Mahl (1956) classified interruptions of continuous speech into the following categories: interjections (e.g., "ah"), repetitions, stuttering events, omissions, sentence incompletion, tongue slips, and intruding incoherent sounds. As this list suggests, there is a great deal of arbitrariness in deciding where speech dysfluency ends and interactional dysfluency (cf. Heikkinen & Valo, this volume, Chapter 12) begins. Mahl (1956) developed ratio measures of these various disturbances in relation to the total number of words spoken. Mahl and Schulze (1964) then further differentiated between "ah" disturbances (interjections) and all other categories that they saw as influenced by different processes.

There is some support for such a distinction. When normally fluent people were asked to provide impromptu as well as rehearsed explanations of cartoons, Goldman-Eisler (1961) concluded that unfilled pauses were related to cognitive factors in language production, whereas filled pauses seemed to have a more emotional origin. In terms of a situational model, we would expect that filled pause rate would be more sensitive to situational characteristics than unfilled pause rate, at least for nonmanifest stutterers.

Others, such as Boomer (1963), introduced different classification schemes. He labeled stuttering, slips of the tongue, and incoherent sounds as articulation errors; omission, sentence change, and sentence incompletion as editorial corrections; and finally, "ah" interjections and repetitions as filled pauses. Despite their various advantages, few of these classificiation schemes possess empirically confirmed validity (Maclay & Osgood, 1959; Panek & Martin, 1959; Rochester, 1973), mainly because they are inadequately anchored to the various variables and processes influencing speech production.

The incidence of silent, unfilled pauses in normal speech presents us with even greater problems of classification and interpretation, since they represent the interaction of numerous phonetic, syntactic, and pragmatic variables (cf. Feldstein & Welkowitz, 1978; Rochester, 1973; Scherer, 1979; Siegman, 1978). Studies attempting to show a correlation between personality traits and unfilled pause rate have generally yielded equivocal results. Rochester (1973), in his literature review, concluded that when significant differences are found, high-anxiety speakers display fewer filled and unfilled pauses than do low-anxiety speakers. On the contrary, Scherer (1978) found emotional stability to be positively correlated with fewer filled pauses. As with most language phenomena, social and cultural background also play an important role here. Scherer (1978, 1979) pointed to the importance as socioeconomic status and nationality in influencing these behaviors. Comparing German and American speakers, he found that Americans produce more speech dysfluencies (non-"ah" ratio, in Mahl & Schulze's classification).

As with so many other behaviors, the study of the interaction of personal characteristics and situational features proved to be a more appropriate strategy in explaining unfilled pauses (Ekehammar, 1974). Helfrich & Dahme (1974) used the repression-sensitization dimension of Byrne (1964), and found that sensitizers showed an increase in long silent pauses only in threatening situations, whereas there were no differences in positively valued situations. These authors proposed an explanation in terms of self-presentation strategies, suggesting that sensitizers use the rather noticeable long pauses to appeal for support. Repressers, generally described in the literature as having a strong need to control their emotional state (e.g., Krohne, 1978), tend to avoid such displays to mask being affected by the situation.

Stäcker and Kriebel (1983) also looked at the situational and cognitive factors influencing speech dysfluences in normally fluent speakers, based on a model of stuttering constructed by Stäcker, Bergmann, and Kriebel (1982). From a total of 200 male subjects, extreme groups were selected on the dimensions of "speech anxiety" (using a German version of Lamb's speech anxiety inventory; cf. Kriebel, 1984), and "need for control" (using a German version of the "order" and "impulsivity" scales of Jackson's Personality Research Form; cf. Angleitner, Stumpf & Wieck, 1976). Speech dysfluencies in the categories "filled pauses," "prolongations and blocks," "repetitions," and "syntactical reversions" were calculated from samples of 1,000 syllables of spontaneous speech about a "personally relevant problem or event in one's life." Three situational contexts were also varied: (1) neutral situation, (2) speaking after frustration (i.e., after receiving negative feedback about speech performance), and (3) controlled speaking (instruction to imagine the presence of an audience, and to speak carefully to create a good impression).

As the summary of results in Figure 13-3 shows, there was a small tendency for an increase in filled pause rate in the most difficult controlled speaking situation, mainly for subjects who scored low on the dimension "need for control." This is consistent with the results of Helfrich and Dahme (1974). Concommitantly measured physiological variables also indicated increased arousal in the controlled speaking situation.

Figure 13-3 also shows an interesting interaction between the types of dysfluencies produced, and the personality dimension of need for control. Across all situations, highly controlled subjects produced more prolongations and blocks than low-controlled subjects, whereas low-controlled subjects produced more reversions. The increase in prolongations and blocks on the part of the highly controlled subjects can be interpreted as an attempt to control one's speaking, but in the end failing because of the severe interruptions to fluency thus produced. These findings also have some relevance to the explanation of stuttering, which is also often marked by the predominance of blocks. Blocks and prolongations of longer duration can be seen as failures of correction trials (repetitions) (cf. Bergmann, 1982; Stäcker, Bergmann, &

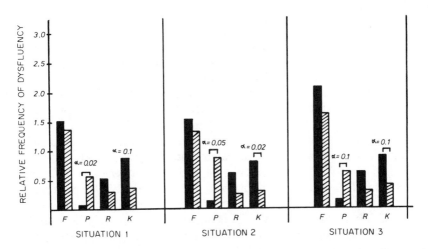

Figure 13-3. Relative frequencies of speech dysfluencies as % of syllables spoken in three experimental conditions: Situation 1: spontaneous speech—neutral, Situation 2: speaking after frustration, Situation 3: speaking in front of an imaginary audience. F = filled pauses; P = polongations and blocks; R = repetitions; K = reversions; number of subjects N = 15; Chi-square test of significance. (Adapted from Stäcker and Kriebel, 1983, p. 30, with permission of the authors.)

Kriebel, 1982), and speakers with a strong need for control show this type of dysfluency more frequently. Stuttering is thus to some extent a phenomenon produced by a heightened need to monitor and control speech performance in given situations.

Communication Responsibility, Need for Control, and Speech Dysfluencies

It is now time to once again return to our initial model proposed at the beginning of this chapter, and to survey the various pieces of evidence supporting it. Throughout the foregoing discussion, we focused on the crucial role of subjective cognitive representations about situations as crucial in the generation of communicative responsibility, need for control, and, ultimately, stuttering. It is highly remarkable that some of the effective therapeutic techniques also seem to essentially rely on modifying a client's situation perception strategies (see, e.g., Gregory, 1979).

Distraction from the interpersonal characteristics of an encounter seems to be a common feature of many therapeutic aids. Instrumental speech aids, such as metrical pacing, auditory masking, and delayed auditory feedback, were often found to improve the fluency of stutterers directly and very drastically. One likely explanation is that these aids reduce the interactional character-istics of the communication (Fiedler & Standop, 1978; Krause, 1976). Similar processes may also account for the improvements achieved with such techniques as shadowing, speaking in chorus, and even singing, where stuttering normally does not occur. In all of these techniques, clients are brought to subjectively define the speaking situation as noninterpersonal.

A somewhat paradoxical effect, amenable to a similar explanation, has been observed in situations involving the diagnostic recording of stuttering frequency. When stutterers are overtly recorded while reading a prepared text in a clinical interview (facing a tape recorder), stuttering frequency is reduced when compared to covert recording. This counterintuitive effect is small in size but significant, and has been replicated twice (Howie, Woods, & Andrews, 1982; Ingham, 1973). The effect can be interpreted in terms of the subjective redefinition of the speaking situation by the stutterer. When speaking into a tape recorder, the subject may see his or her speech as mediated by the machine. Thus, distance from the communication partner is established, reducing the subjectively experienced communication responsibility and need for speech control.

Most of the evidence of reduced stuttering frequency in isolated speaking situations can be accounted for in similar terms (Bloodstein, 1975; Eisenson & Horowitz, 1945; Fiedler & Standop, 1978; Krause, 1976; Stäcker et al., 1982). Speaking alone or speaking to children and animals are examples of situations where need for control and responsibility for the communication are minimized.

This view is also supported by another quite distinct line of evidence. It has been shown repeatedly that stutterers exhibit quite unrealistic expectations concerning the reactions of their interaction partners (Gendelmann, 1977; Motsch, 1979). Such a tendency to expect negative evaluations might load even otherwise neutral speaking situations and create anxiety. In attempting to avoid the expected negative assessments, stutterers apparently engage in a desperate (and ultimately futile) effort to control their speech performance. The resulting anxiety is the immediate antecedent of stuttering (Van Riper, 1971; see also Sheehan, 1970; Wischner, 1952). The role of cognitive situation-interpretation processes in this cycle is extremely important (Berg-mann, 1982; Kamhi & McOsker, 1982; Stäcker et al., 1982).

The great importance of control, particularly the control of affective expression in stuttering, has been well documented in the research by Krause (1980, 1981, 1982). Among other things, Krause found that stutterers use reduced expression of affect even in the nonverbal modalities. Stutterers also tend to occupy more speaking floor time than their partners, even when they are not stuttering. Krause interpreted these manifestations as symptoms of a chronically defensive coping strategy, particularly oriented toward avoiding expression of affect. As a result, even situations not commonly seen as demanding may require considerable feats of affect control for stutterers.

It must be emphasized once again that the activation of these strategies is typically dependent on subjective definitions of situations. We saw earlier that interaction situations are perceived by people largely in terms of affective, connotative characteristics such as evaluation, self-confidence, involvement, or intimacy. These dimensions are clearly and unequivocally related to our notion of subjective communicative responsibility. Just as an individual's concept of self-efficacy (Bandura, 1977) is situationally variable, his or her perceived sense of communication responsibility is subject to the same situational constraints.

Conclusions

We argued in this chapter that the occurrence of speech dysfluencies in otherwise fluent speakers, as well as the incidence of more serious speech disturbances such as stuttering, are regulated by a similar set of variables. On the basis of our review of the literature on speech dysfluencies, as well as recent social psychological research on cognitive representations of situations, we proposed a model that would link situation perception via the mediating variables of communicative responsibility and need for control to the incidence of speech dysfluency. We realize that our model represents only one of many possible pathways from situation appraisal to speech production. We believe, however, that it has the major advantage of focusing attention of the subjective representations that speakers have of a communicative encounter, a hitherto largely ignored variable in stuttering research.

The second important feature of our model is that it places major emphasis on the cognitive processes linking situation perceptions to speech. Whereas in the past, speech disturbances have been explained largely in terms of physical, physiological, or affective factors, the cognitive processes that undoubtedly play a role received less than sufficient attention. As Bloodstein (1975) suggested, stuttering "develops readily in circumstances in which speech pressures are unusually heavy, the child's vulnerability to them unusually high, or the provocations in the form of communicative difficulties or failures unusually frequent, severe or chronic" (p. 301). In this respect, we believe that our approach is in line with the most recent developments in research on language and social situations (e.g., Chapter 1, Forgas; Chapter 4, van Dijk, and Chapter 5, Hoppe-Graff, et al., this volume).

The model also has the crucial advantage that empirically testable hypotheses may be derived from it. In the first instance, it would be of considerable interest to establish whether there is a specific link between stuttering severity and biased perceptions of interaction episodes, just as such a link between low social skills and episode perception was established by Forgas (1983). We would indeed expect such distortions in the situation-perception strategies of stutterers on the basis of the research reviewed here. Once such a link is established, some therapeutic implications would immediately follow. Intensive training in situation representation and interpretation skills, using the well-tried methods of social skills therapy (cf. Argyle, 1980; Trower, Bryant, & Argyle, 1978), could produce considerable improvement in conjunction with other, more symptom-oriented therapeutic methods. We hope that the present chapter will contribute in some small measure to greater interest in the study of the situational genesis of speech dysfluencies by future researchers.

Acknowledgments. The authors are grateful for the helpful suggestions of Dr. Reinholde Kriebel, and financial assistance from the German Research Foundation (Deutsche Forschungsgemeinschaft).

References

Adams, M. R., & Runyan, C. M. (1981). Stuttering and fluency: Exclusive events or points on a continuum? *Journal of Fluency Disorders, 6*, 197–218.

Angleitner, A., Stumpf, H., & Wieck, T. (1976). Die "Personality Research Form" von Jackson: Konstruktion, bisheriger Forschungsstand und vorläufige Ergebnisse zur Äquivalenzprüfung einer deutschen Übersetzung. *Wehrpsychologische Untersuchungen,* (Ed.: Bundesministerium der Verteidigung, Ministry of Defense), Heft 3/76.

Argyle, M. (1980). Interaction skills and social competence. In P. Feldman & J. Oxford (Eds.), *The social psychology of psychological problems.* London: Wiley.

Argyle, M. (1981). The experimental study of the basic features of situations. In D. Magnusson (Ed.), *Toward a psychology of situations: An interactional perspective* (pp. 63–83). Hillsdale, NJ: Erlbaum.

Argyle, M., Furnham, A., & Graham, J. A. (1981). Social situations. Cambridge: Cambridge University Press.

Bandura, A. (1977). Self-efficacy: Toward a unifying theory of behavioral change. *Psychological Review, 84*, 191–215.

Bar, A. (1973). Increasing fluency in young stutterers vs. decreasing stuttering: A clinical approach. *Journal of Communication Disorders, 6*, 247–258.

Bardrick, R. A., & Sheehan, J. G. (1956). Emotional loadings as a source of conflict in stuttering (abstract). *American Psychologist, 11*, 391.

Barker, R. G. (1968). *Ecological psychology.* Stanford, CA: Stanford University Press.

Bergmann, G. (1982). Der Beitrag apparativer Sprechhilfen für Theorie und Therapie des Stotterns. *Die Sprachheilarbeit, 27*, 278–288.

Bergmann, G. (1983a). Incidence of stuttering in different prosodic contexts: Verse and prose reading in stutterers and nonstutterers (abstract). *Folia phoniatrica, 35*, 105–106.

Bergmann, G. (1983b). *Prosodic disturbances in stuttering.* Paper presented at the Interdisciplinary Symposium on the Suprasegmentals of Speech "Prosody—Normal and Abnormal," Zürich, Switzerland.

Bergmann, G. (1984). Vorschläge für eine kontrollierte und standardisierte Diagnostik des Stotterns. *Die Sprachheilarbeit, 29*, 167–176.

Bergmann, G. (in press). Streß und Coping: Psychologische Forschungsansätze. In K. R. Scherer, H. G. Wallbott, F. Tolkmitt, & G. Bergmann (Hrsg.), *Die Streßreaktion: Physiologie und Verhalten.* Göttingen: Hogrefe.

Bloodstein, O. (1975). A handbook on stuttering. Chicago: National Easter Seal Society for Crippled Children and Adults.

Boomer, M. R. (1963). Speech disturbance and body movement in interviews. *Journal of Nervous and Mental Disease, 136*, 263–266.

Brown, P., & Fraser, C. (1979). Speech as a marker of situation. In K. R. Scherer & H. Giles (Eds.), *Social markers in speech* (pp. 33–62). Cambridge: Cambridge University Press.

Bryant, B., & Trower, P. (1974). Social difficulty in a student sample. *British Journal of Educational Psychology, 44*, 13–21.

Byrne, D. (1964). Repression-sensitization as a dimension of personality. In B. Maher (Ed.), *Progress in experimental personality research* (Vol. 1) (pp. 169–219). New York: Academic Press.

Dixon, C. C. (1955). Stuttering adaptation in relation to assumed level of anxiety. In W. Johnson (Ed.), *Stuttering in children and adults*. Minneapolis: University of Minnesota Press.

Eisenson, J., & Horowitz, E. (1945). The influence of propositionality on stuttering. *Journal of Speech Disorders, 10*, 193–197.

Ekehammar, B. (1974). Interactionism in psychology from a historical perspective. *Psychological Bulletin, 81*, 1026–1043.

Endler, N. S., & Magnusson, D. (Eds.) (1975). *Interactional psychology and personality*. London: Wiley.

Endler, N. S., & Magnusson, D. (1976). Toward an interactional psychology of personality. *Psychological Bulletin, 83*, 956–974.

Feldstein, S., & Welkowitz, J. (1978). A chronography of conversation: In defense of an objective approach. In A. W. Siegman & S. Feldstein (Eds.), *Nonverbal behavior and communication* (pp. 329–378). Hillsdale, NJ: Erlbaum.

Fiedler, P. A., & Standop, R. (1978). *Stottern*. München: Urban & Schwarzenberg.

Forgas, J. P. (1978). Social episodes and social structure in an academic setting. *Journal of Experimental Social Psychology, 14*, 434–448.

Forgas, J. P. (1979). Social episodes: The study of interaction routines. London: Academic Press.

Forgas, J. P. (Ed.) (1981). Social cognition: Perspectives on everyday understanding. London/New York: Academic Press.

Forgas, J. P. (1982). Episode cognition: Internal representations of interaction routines. In L. Berkowitz (Ed.), *Advances in experimental social psychology* (pp. 59–101). New York: Academic Press.

Forgas, J. P. (1983). Social skills and the perception of interaction episodes. *British Journal of Clinical Psychology, 22*, 195–207.

Frederiksen, N. (1972). Toward a taxonomy of situations. *American Psychologist, 27*, 114–123.

Gendelmann, E. G. (1977). Confrontation in the treatment of stuttering. *Journal of Speech and Hearing Disorders, 42*, 85–89.

Giles, H., & Powesland, P. F. (1975). *Speech style and social evaluation*. London: Academic Press.

Goldman-Eisler, F. (1961). A comparative study of two hesitation phenomena. *Language and Speech, 4*, 18–26.

Gregory, H. H. (Eds.) (1979). *Controversies about stuttering therapy*. Baltimore: University Park Press.

Hahn, E. F. (1940). A study of the relationship between the social complexity of the oral reading situation and the severity of stuttering. *Journal of Speech Disorders, 5*, 5–14.

Helfrich, H., & Dahme, G. (1974). Sind Verzögerungsphänomene beim spontanen Sprechen Indikatoren persönlichkeitsspezifischer Angstverarbeitung? *Zeitschrift für Sozialpsychologie, 5*, 55–65.

Howie, P. M., Woods, C. L., & Andrews, G. (1982). Relationship between covert and overt speech measures immediately before and immediately after stuttering treatment. *Journal of Speech and Hearing Disorders, 47*, 419–422.

Hymes, D. (1967). Models of the interaction of language and social setting. *Journal of Social Issues, 23*, 8–28.

Hymes, D. (1972). Models of the interaction and social life. In J. J. Gumperz & D. Hymes (Eds.), *Directions in sociolinguistics: The ethnography of communication*. New York: Holt, Rinehart & Winston.

Ingham, R. A. (1973). A comparison of covert and overt assessment procedures in stuttering therapy outcome evaluation. *Journal of Speech and Hearing Research, 18*, 346–354.

Jeger, A., & Goldfried, M. (1976). A comparison of situation tests of anxiety. *Behavior Therapy, 7*, 252–255.

Johnson, W., Darley, F. L., & Spriestersbach, D. C. (1963). *Diagnostic methods in speech pathology*. New York: Harper & Row.

Kamhi, A. G., & McOsker, T. G. (1982). Attention and stuttering: Do stutterers think too much about speech? *Journal of Fluency Disorders, 7*, 309–324.

Krause, R. (1976). Probleme der psychologischen Stottererforschung und Behandlung. *Zeitschrift für Klinische Psychologie und Psychotherapie, 24*, 128–143.

Krause, R. (1980). Stuttering and nonverbal communication: Investigations about affect inhibition and stuttering. In H. Giles, W. P. Robinson, & P. M. Smith (Eds.), *Language: Social psychological perspectives* (pp. 261–266). Oxford: Pergamon.

Krause, R. (1981). *Sprache und Affekt*. Stuttgart: Kohlhammer.

Krause, R. (1982). A social psychology approach to the study of stuttering. In C. Fraser & K. R. Scherer (Eds.), *Advances in the social psychology of language* (pp. 77–122). Cambridge: Cambridge University Press.

Kriebel, R. (1984). *Sprechangst*. Stuttgart: Kohlhammer.

Krohne, H. W. (1978). Individual differences in coping with stress and anxiety. In C. R. Spielberger & I. G. Sarason (Eds.), *Stress and anxiety* (Vol. 7) (pp. 233–260). Washington, D.C.: Hemisphere.

Kroll, R. M., & Hood, S. B. (1976). The influencing of task presentation and information on the adaptation effect in stutterers and normal speakers. *Journal of Communication Disorders, 9*, 95–110.

Lazarus, R. S., & Launier, R. (1978). Stress-related transactions between person and environment. In L. A. Pervin & M. Lewis (Eds.), *Perspectives in interactional psychology* (pp. 287–327). New York: Plenum.

Leventhal, H., & Everhart, D. (1979). Emotion, pain, and physical illness. In C. E. Izard (Ed.), *Emotions in personality and psychopathology* (pp. 28–54). New York: Plenum.

Maclay, H., & Osgood, C. E. (1959). Hesitation phenomena in spontaneous English. *Word, 15*, 19–44.

Magnusson, D. (1971). An analysis of situational dimensions. *Perceptual and Motor Skills, 32*, 851–867.

Magnusson, D. (1981). Wanted: A psychology of situations. In D. Magnusson (Ed.), *Toward a psychology of situations: An interactional perspective* (pp. 9–32). Hillsdale, NJ: Erlbaum.

Mahl, G. F. (1956). Disturbances and silences in patient's speech in psychotherapy. *Journal of Abnormal and Social Psychology, 53*, 1–15.

Mahl, G. F., & Schulze, G. (1964). Psychological research in the extralinguistic area. In T. A. Sebeok, A. S. Hayes, & M. C. Bateson (Eds.), *Approaches to semiotics* (pp. 51–124; see p. 57 ff.). The Hague: Mouton.

Mason, J. W. (1974). Specifity in the organization of neuroendocrine response profiles. In P. Seeman & G. M. Brown (Eds.), *Frontiers in neurology and neuroscience research*. Toronto: University of Toronto.

Mischel, W. (1968). *Personality and assessment*. New York: Wiley.

Mischel, W. (1977). The interaction of person and situation. In D. Magnusson & N. S. Endler (Eds.), *Personality at the crossroads: Current issues in interactional psychology* (pp. 333–352). Hillsdale, NJ: Erlbaum.

Mischel, W. (1979). On the interface of cognition and personality. *American Psychologist, 34*, 390–405.

Motsch, H. J. (1979). *Problemkreis Stottern*. Berlin: Marhold.

Muller, D. J., & Duckworth, M. (1983, July). *Why isn't there more research in the social psychology of stuttering*. Paper presented at the Second International Conference on Social Psychology and Language, Bristol.

Panek, D. M., & Martin, B. (1959). The relationship between GSR and speech disturbance in psychotherapy. *Journal of Abnormal and Social Psychology, 58*, 402–405.

Pervin, L. A. (1976). A free response description approach to the study of person situation interaction. *Journal of Personality and Social Psychology, 34*, 465–474.

Pervin, L. A., & Lewis, M. (Eds.) (1978). *Perspectives in interactional psychology*. New York: Plenum.

Porter, H. V. K. (1939). Studies in the psychology of stuttering: XIV. Stuttering phenomena in relation to size and personnel of audience. *Journal of Speech Disorders, 4*, 323–333.

Price, R. H., & Bouffard, D. L. (1974). Behavioral appropriateness and situational constraint as dimensions of social behavior. *Journal of Personality and Social Psychology, 30*, 579–586.

Ramig, P. R., Krieger, S. M., & Adams, M. R. (1982). Vocal changes in stutterers and nonstutterers when speaking to children. *Journal of Fluency Disorders, 7*, 369–384.

Richardson, F. C., & Tasto, D. L. (1976). Development and factor analysis of a social anxiety inventory. *Behavior Therapy, 7*, 453–462.

Rochester, S. R. (1973). The significance of pauses in spontaneous speech. *Journal of Psycholinguistic Research, 2*, 51–81.

Scherer, K. R. (1978). Personality inference from voice quality: The loud voice of extraversion. *European Journal of Social Psychology, 8*, 467–487.

Scherer, K. R. (1979). Personality markers in speech. In K. R. Scherer & H. Giles (Eds.), *Social markers in speech* (pp. 147–209). Cambridge: Cambridge University Press.

Sheehan, J. G. (1958). Conflict theory of stuttering. In J. Eisenson (Ed.), *Stuttering: A symposium*. New York: Harper & Row.

Sheehan, J. G. (1970). *Stuttering: Research and therapy*. New York: Harper & Row.

Shulman, E. (1955). Factors influencing the variability of stuttering. In W. Johnson (Ed.), *Stuttering in children and adults*. Minneapolis: University of Minnesota Press.

Siegel, G. M., & Haugen, D. (1964). Audience size and variations in stuttering behavior. *Journal of Speech and Hearing Research, 7*, 381–388.

Siegman, A. W. (1978). The tell-tale voice: Nonberbal messages of verbal communication. In A. W. Siegman & S. Feldstein (Eds.), *Nonverbal behavior and communication* (pp. 183–243). Hillsdale, NJ: Erlbaum.

Spielberger, C. D. (1975). Anxiety: State-trait-process. In C. D. Spielberger & I. G. Sarason (Eds.), *Stress and anxiety* (Vol. 1) (pp. 115–143). New York: Hemisphere.

Stäcker, K. H., & Kriebel, R. (1983). *Analyse und Modifikation von Sprechunflüssigkeiten*. Unpublished research report, research project granted by Deutsche Forschungsgemeinschaft, University of Essen.

Stäcker, K. H., Bergmann, G., & Kriebel, R. (1982). Sprechflußstörungen. In G. O. Kanter & F. Masendorf (Hrsg.), *Brennpunkte der Sprachheilpädagogik und Leseforschung* (pp. 1–50). Berlin: Marhold.

Steer, M. D., & Johnson, W. (1936). An objective study of the relationship between psychological factors and the severity of stuttering. *Journal of Abnormal and Social Psychology, 31*, 36–46.

Svab, L., Gross, J., & Langova, J. (1972). Stuttering and social isolation: Effect of social isolation with different levels of monitoring on stuttering frequency. *Journal of Nervous and Mental Disease, 155*, 1–5.

Trower, P., Bryant, B., & Argyle, M. (1978). Social skills and mental health. London: Methuen.

Van Riper, C. (1971). The nature of stuttering. Englewood Cliffs, NJ: Prentice-Hall.

Williams, D. (1957). A point of view about stuttering. *Journal of Speech and Hearing Disorders, 22*, 390–397.

Wingate, M. E. (1964). A standard definition of stuttering. *Journal of Speech and Hearing Research, 6*, 91–100.

Wingate, M. E. (1976). *Stuttering: Theory and treatment.* New York: Irvington.

Wingate, M. E. (1977). Criteria for stuttering. *Journal of Speech and Hearing Research, 20*, 596–607.

Wischner, G. J. (1952). An experimental approach to expectancy and anxiety in stuttering behavior. *Journal of Speech and Hearing Disorders, 17*, 139–154.

Wish, M., & Kaplan, S. J. (1976). Perceived dimensions of interpersonal relations. *Journal of Personality and Social Psychology, 33*, 409–420.

Young, M. A. (1965). Audience size, perceived situational difficulty, and stuttering frequency. *Journal of Speech and Hearing Research, 8*, 401–407.

Zerbin, R. (1973). Erfassung der Symptomatik Stotternder. *Die Sprachheilarbeit, 18*, 174–185.

Zimbardo, P. G. (1982). Shyness and the stresses of the human connection. In L. Goldberger & S. Breznitz (Eds.), *Handbook of stress: Theoretical and clinical aspects* (pp. 466–481). New York: Free Press.

Chapter 14
Epilogue: On the Situational Nature of Language and Social Interaction

Joseph P. Forgas

Language is the most important medium of human social interaction. Our use of language represents a crucial link between the collective, cultural, and cognitive individual domains in our everyday lives. Language as a system of communication is collectively created, maintained, and modified, yet it is our individual cognitive understanding of its symbols and the situations in which it is appropriate to use them that qualifies us as fully fledged members of a society. The role of language in symbolizing and abtracting our essentially situational interactive experiences has been well recognized at least since Mead (1934). The other side of this connection, the way that situational knowledge regulates language use, has only been investigated since the emergence of sociolinguistics as an independent field of study. The contributions in this volume bear witness to the considerable importance of this subject, and the advances made in our knowledge about situated language use in recent years.

Yet we are still very far from having an integrated theory linking situations to language. It is only recently that psychological methods and theories have been brought to bear on this problem. What are the major conceptual issues facing us? How is research likely to develop in the future? The aim of this final brief chapter is to present a recapitulation of the volume, and some admittedly speculative answers to questions such as these.

How Is Language Situational?

Although it is generally well accepted nowadays that language is a situation-dependent communication device, the exact nature of this link is rarely specified. Traditionally, there have been two major alternatives to the scientific study of language: We may view language as primarily a self-contained and closely structured system of signals, or we may look at it as a living communication system, inseparable from the everyday contexts in which it is used. At least since de Saussure (1915), we have had a very clear statement of this dychotomy, implicit in his famous distinction between "langue," the language code shared by a community of speakers, and "parole," the actual communicative use of that code. It is now commonly accepted that communication systems such as language "have a real existence only in the social and cultural settings in which they appear," and that for "further progress on certain key issues of linguistic theory a meticulous examination of occasions of human interaction is necessary" (Wurm, 1976, pp. 363–366).

This is indeed a recognition which many of the contributions to this book clearly bear witness to. The idealized language code, de Saussure's "langue," or Chomsky's "pure form" in the mind of the ideal "speaker-hearer," does not in itself constitute an adequate system of human communication. "Knowing a language perfectly" (Chomsky, 1965, p. 3) also involves knowing the situational rules of when, how, and what to say and do. Without these essentially social skills (Forgas, 1983b), the idealized speaker-hearer in complete possession of the language code would nevertheless remain a "cultural monster," incapable of effective communication (Hymes, 1967, p. 639; Bell, 1976). Despite the growing dominance of research on pragmatics, the study of language-as-used, there is still considerable confusion about the sense in which language may be regarded as "situational."

Indeed, there are at least two aspects to the argument that language and the social situations in which it is used are inseparable from each other. The first one is philosophical, and has to do with the theory of meaning. It is essentially based on a radical criticism of the Cartesian, rationalist notion that words and sentences carry immanent meanings that can be detached from the contexts in which these messages are used. The roots of an alternative conceptualization can be found in the writings of George Herbert Mead, William James, Vygotsky, Wittgenstein, and many others who were primarily concerned with the collective and interactional features of language and meaning. As Rommetveit (1983) argues, "The locus of literal meaning ... [is] neither the individual human brain nor language as an idealised and super-individual system, but the intersection of the individual human mind and the collectivity which constitutes the matrix and precondition for ordinary language" (pp. 102–103). Perhaps we may characterize this position as calling for a fully situational (rather than an absolute) theory of meaning (cf. Wintermantel, 1983).

The second, alternative position on the interdependent nature of language and situation is essentially cognitivist. It does not reject the Cartesian idea that language embodies invariable meanings, but simply assumes that these meanings are modulated by cognitive processes and internal representations of contextual features. In order to correctly qualify the meaning of a message, the sender and the receiver must share to some extent an internal model of the social situation, and use similar processes to encode and decode the impact of that situation on their messages. This view, although in essence nonsocial, is consonant with the implicit assumptions and methods of individualistic psychology and has been by far the more influential in stimulating empirical research. Several contributions to this volume illustrate the fruitfulness of using such an approach (e.g., Chapter 4, van Dijk; Chapter 5, Hoppe-Graff, et al.; Chapter 6, Gibbs, Chapter 9, Gallois & Callan; Chapter 11, Bavelas).

It lies beyond the objectives of this collection to take sides in this debate. We are mainly interested here in establishing that social situations influence not only the meaning of verbal messages, but indeed, that all language use is intricately tied to the requirements of the surrounding social context. Whether this relationship necessitates a situationist approach to semantics, or whether it can be adequately handled by the cognitivist, information-processing paradigm based on Cartesian principles is of secondary importance for the moment. First we need to find out very much more about how language and social situations are interconnected. The individualist cognitive position may well provide us with the most suitable methodology and research approach for the time being. The accumulation of empirical data may be a necessary prerequisite for a more radical, fully developed situational theory of meaning to eventually emerge.

Methodological Eclecticism

The absence of an agreement about this basic conceptual issue is reflected in the eclectic nature of most research to date on language and situations. There have been many ways of approaching this problem, ranging from the experimental to the purely descriptive. Almost all empirical research to date on language and situations implicitly or explicitly rests on a cognitivist conceptualization of situations: People are able to vary their language strategies by virtue of their ability to perceive, cognitively represent, and evaluate situational requirements. Even analyses of cultural characteristics (e.g., in this volume, Chapter 7, Blum-Kulka; Chapter 8, Wetzel; Chapter 9, Gallois & Callan) must ultimately make this implicit assumption.

One methodological means of dealing with this necessary assumption is to develop psychological, information-processing models that will adequately simulate the way that situational knowledge impinges upon language use (e.g., Chapter 4, van Dijk and Chapter 5, Hoppe-Graff, et al.). Perhaps not surprisingly, these approaches are most closely related to the traditional concerns of experimental cognitive psychology. Another methodological alternative is linguistic in orientation: By studying everyday language use, we can acquire useful insights into the features of the social situations that affect language production and comprehension strategies (e.g., Chapter 7, Blum-Kulka, et al., and Chapter 8, Wetzel). These methods bear some affinity to the traditional research strategies of linguists, although they are increasingly relying on quantitative techniques instead of the ubiquitous "native speaker of the language" for their evidence.

Techniques common in social psychological experimentation can also be brought to bear on this problem. Through the creation of controlled and

manipulated situational contexts and language alternatives, a better understanding of the links between these two classes of variables may be reached
(e.g., Chapter 6 by Gibbs; Chapter 9, Gallois & Callan; Chapter 11, Bavelas;
Chaper 13, Bergmann & Forgas). Quasi-experimental techniques, relying on
naturally occurring situations for their data (e.g., Chapter 3, Levin & Snow),
represent an important variant of this methodology. The useful consequences
of the cross-fertilization between social psychology and sociolinguistics have
been well documented elsewhere (Smith, 1983).

Finally, structured observation may be used as a suitable technique to study
situational influences on language use. The impressive research program by
Bruner that looks at how shared situational "formats" pave the way for the
acquisition of language in the early years is an excellent example of the
potency of this method. With adult speakers, observational methods have
been mainly used to investigate the "ethnography of speaking" (e.g., Chapter
10, Harré and Chapter 11, Heikkinen & Valo).

These various research strategies are rooted in disciplines such as linguistics,
psychology, and sociology. At present, we must see their contributions as
complementary rather than contradictory: We need descriptive linguistic
analyses just as much as we need controlled psychological experimentation.
The belief in methodological, and indeed, conceptual pluralism should serve
our enterprise well, just as it would serve some more established fields of social
psychological research (cf. Forgas, 1983c). However, there is every reason to
believe that quantitative, empirical techniques based on the methods of
cognitive and social psychologists will ultimately provide us with the most
suitable research strategy, a suggestion about which we shall have more to say
later.

The Search for a Theory Linking Language and Situations

Despite the rich background of research on situations in linguistics, psychology, and sociology, there are still very few theoretical models linking
language to situations. Apart from the essentially descriptive schemes
proposed by authors such as Hymes (1967, 1972) or Brown and Fraser
(1979), there are probably four major alternative avenues for the development
of language-situation models: Developmental, logical, cognitive, or social
psychological principles may be used as the basic integrating devices. Several
of the contributions to this volume illustrate the potentialities of these four
alternatives. In this section we shall briefly look at each of these possibilities.

The Developmental Approach

The growing evidence that children are quite sensitive to subtle situational
requirements well before they learn to use language suggests that developmental principles may provide a major explanatory device of the later links

between language and social situations. Bruner's chapter, reviewing an extensive research program spanning several years, provides strong evidence for the situational character of early language acquisition. Mothers and caretakers interact with infants in a highly patterned and even ritualistic fashion. Even with older children, caretakers subtly regulate their language use to fit in with situational requirements (cf. Chapter 3 by Levin & Snow). It is the very predictability and structure of these early encounters that prepare a child for the later systematicity of social encounters, and at the same time help him to understand the situated meanings of the various moves well before their verbal equivalents are mastered.

Bruner's work offers us a major alternative to the previously dominant and in themselves unsatisfactory nativist (cf. Chomsky) and learning theoretical (cf. Skinner) views of how language is acquired. The model is entirely consistent with the symbolic interactionist theory of Mead, who also emphasized the interdependence between language and situation representations. It remains a task for developmental psychologists to further explore the exact nature of the kind of situation schemas that infants and young children possess, and how these representations come to be elaborated later on. It is a promising hypothesis indeed that cognitive situation representation skills and linguistic skills might proceed hand in hand. To the extent that both cognitive representations of situations and the acquisition of linguistic competence are probably rooted in the same sort of experiences of structured social activities, such an interdependence would of course be less surprising than at first appears.

The Logical Approach

Logical principles suggest themselves as one of the possible bases for explaining situated language use. The language/situation theory developed by Herrmann (1982) based on the pars pro toto principle is essentially based on such logical principles. The central idea is that in any verbal utterance, only a small part of the total mental data is communicated. This part-message has to carry the whole meaning of the original representation. Situations mediate language use by influencing *which* part of the total propositional content is selected for transmission. The theory is thus clearly based on principles of logic: For particular utterance categories (e.g., naming objects, requesting, etc.), an analysis of possible alternative propositions is undertaken in order to define the population of utterances from which the speaker has to choose in the light of situational requirements.

According to Herrmann, the "selection of those components of propositional structures which—pars pro toto—are verbalized is probably determined by two major factors: (a) [the necessary] information (for the partner) and (b) instrumentality (for the achievement of the goal intended by the transfer of communication)" (1982, p. 130). In naming objects, for example, those features should be selected that distinguish an object from other possible objects present in the situation; if there are several such features, the "speaker is likely to emphasise those features of the intended object which mark off the object most clearly in the general context" (p. 135), and if several such features exist, the most conspicuous or salient one will be named. These are of course logical, and not merely psychological considerations.

Experiments with children, who for example had to name a particular car in a toy car park among other cars with different manipulated features (size, color, etc.) supported these postulates. In a similar vein, Herrmann (1982) suggests that choice of requests is influenced by three situational features: (1) the partner's understanding of the situation as assumed by the speaker, (2) the partner's willingness to carry out the request as assumed by the speaker, and (3) the assumed legitimacy of the request. Empirical work using a variety of procedures supported these postulates, as the overview of the program in Chapter 5 by Hoppe-Graff, et al. indicates.

Herrmann's theory is one of the very few comprehensive attempts to develop an integrated approach to the language/situation issue. Its major advantage is that it is systematically linked to a series of empirical studies demonstrating the validity of its (often intuitively based) postulates. In its most recent reformulation (cf. Chapter 5 by Hoppe-Graff, et al.), aspects of the theory are much more clearly specified in information-processing terminology. Ultimately, this model could be formally translated into computer programs, thus providing the first truly artificial intelligence model of situated language use. Recent work by Mangold and Herrmann (1984) suggests that this is indeed an achievable objective in the not too distant future.

A potential problem with the model is that an almost infinite array of additional logical postulates may exist which regulate language choices, and that such postulates can not explain why often logically unnecessary, misleading, or redundant messages are communicated. As Chapter 11 by Bavelas shows, equivocal, confusing, or evasive communication is not necessarily suboptimal. In some situations, such messages may be the best ones available. Logical models, such as Herrmann's, need to be (and indeed, currently are) expanded to be able to account for such vagaries in everyday discourse. Cognitive and social psychological models often have similar problems, as we shall presently see.

The Cognitive Approach

According to such models, cognitive processes of language production and comprehension are modulated by an individual's internal representations and understanding of the surrounding social situation. Such situation representation strategies in turn are triggered by certain critical factors present in the encounter. Bergmann and Forgas's preliminary model of how situational features may come to affect speech dysfluencies and stuttering (Chapter 13, this volume) provides an example of what such a model might look like.

The kind of language-situation model proposed by Giles and Hewstone (1982) described earlier provides another illustration of an essentially cognitive strategy. These authors propose that the subjective definition of a social encounter as an interindividual or an intergroup occasion (cf. Tajfel & Forgas, 1981), and the actor's cognitive representation of the encounter (cf. Wish, 1975; Forgas, 1982) will guide the choice of appropriate language behaviors. The theory is soundly based on empirical research on group categorization and episode perception. What remains to be done is the careful elaboration of the exact links between these variables and language behaviors into a workable and falsifiable system of hypotheses.

Another example of a cognitive language-situation model is van Dijk's (Chapter 4, this volume) theory. This approach is linked to cognitive models of discourse production and comprehension, which are further elaborated by taking the role of situation schemas explicitly into account. Concern with the associated encoding and recall mechanisms, and the nature of the cognitive representational structures are also hallmarks of this approach. Van Dijk's analysis of how, for example, prototypical ethnic situation models shape and mould the story-telling activities of his subjects is at the same time profoundly social psychological. The model represents a genuine merger between cognitive and social psychological concerns, and offers a stimulating foundation for further empirical research.

We should also consider here the increasingly important contributions of artificial-intelligence researchers, particularly those from the Yale group (Lehnert & Ringle, 1982). This approach has been noticeably successful in recent years in constructing computer simulation models of discourse processing that rely heavily on input about everyday interaction situations or "scripts" for their effectiveness. While the epistemological status of artificial-intelligence research as an avenue to understanding human cognitive processes remains controversial (Sharkey, 1984), the opportunities it provides for clarifying the links between situational features and discourse are extremely important. A common criticism of such cognitive approaches is that they are asocial: Neither the cultural, nor the interactive, negotiated aspects of communicative behavior are taken into account in these individualistic models, except as they may be represented in the cognitive system of individuals. Social psychological models seek to overcome some of these problems.

The Social Psychological Approach

Although social psychological factors such as the participants' feelings, expectations, and attitudes toward each other play an important role in the linguistic choices they make, this simple fact has often been ignored in the past. As the work by Bavelas shows, such social psychological factors can play a major role in explaining the rationale behind what might at first appear to be nonsensical or evasive communications. Lewinian field theory offers a particularly promising framework for taking such social psychological variables into consideration.

Another example of a social psychological model is speech accommodation theory, which, at the simplest level, asserts that "when interlocutors desire each other's approval, they will converge their speech patterns, whereas when they wish to differentiate from each other socially, they will diverge them" (Thakerar, Giles, & Cheshire, 1982, p. 205). Persons with a high need for approval (Natale, 1975) and members of groups with lower status or power accommodate their speech more than do dominant or powerful groups. Other situational factors, such as competitive versus cooperative, friendly versus unfriendly, formal versus informal social episodes, may also selectively facilitate converging or divering speech styles.

It is perhaps unfortunate that speech accommodation theory has been more often used to explain cross-situational regularities rather than situational differences in language behaviors. This model would have considerable potential for predicting situation-contingent language production and interpretation, as the research by Bond (in press), and the empirical work presented in Chapter 9 by Gallois and Callan so clearly illustrate. The theory is particularly useful when it comes to explaining the language choices of people who meet each other in what Giles and Hewstone (1982) called intergroup rather than interindividual encounters. These are situations when the group identity of the interlocutors is particularly salient—many first encounters, as well as most interethnic or intercultural interaction episodes, are of this kind. Gallois and Callan's work provides us with an illustration of the potential usefulness of this model.

Another social psychological approach linking language and social situations is ethogenic theory. Harré (1981) firmly believes that "talk" is not only the primary data of social psychology, but that the analysis of the situational, normative, and moral concommittants of everyday talk and explanations is the only way to truly understand social behavior. Harré originally distinguished between routine and "enigmatic" episodes, and later developed a full set of criteria for analyzing everyday talk as "accounting." An important element in Harré's analyses, which goes beyond Goffman's microsociology, is the notion of a "moral order" within which people seek to establish their personas as worthy individuals. Such "moral order" may be nationwide, as the study by Wetzel of the Japanese indicates, or limited to a small group or subculture.

Chapter 10 by Harré suggests that there are many kinds of language behaviors that can (and perhaps should) be analyzed from this perspective. Our choice of words and phrases apparently says quite a lot about the situated morality of the groups we belong to, whether it is a bunch of football hooligans, psychiatrists, or academic psychologists. The interaction templates or episode representations of social actors play a central role in explaining their verbal accounts. Despite its problems, many of them methodological (Schlenker, 1977), ethogenic analysis offers a stimulating theoretical basis for studying the situational dimension of language that is profoundly social psychological in orientation. Perhaps it is not too daring to hope that one day these stimulating descriptive analyses will be amenable to the empirical methodology of cognitive social psychologists.

Prospects for a Theory of Situated Language Use

As this review clearly shows, there are several alternative theoretical formulations linking situations to language use. The approaches mentioned here rely on developmental, cognitive, logical, or social psychological principles to establish such links. Although some recent models make use of empirical studies of situational characteristics, the exact links between situations and language usually remain unspecified. There is a clear need to develop more specific models of how situational features are linked to language behaviors, a task that will most likely be undertaken on the basis of cognitive models of situation perception and social information processing.

Two developments in psychology serve as the basis for this proposition. The first one is the considerable success of psychologists in recent years in constructing reliable and valid representations of social interactions. Much of everyday social life consists of the cooperative enactment of familiar, recurring interaction routines, or "social episodes" (Forgas, 1979, 1982, 1983a). A relatively limited number of connotative attribute dimensions, such as self-confidence, intimacy, evaluation, and formality, serve as the basis for perceptions of such encounters by individuals from quite different cultural and subcultural groups, such as American, British, Australian, and Swedish students, housewives, sports teams, or academics (Battistich & Thompson, 1980; Forgas, 1976, 1979, 1982; Pervin, 1976; Wish, 1975; etc.). These findings enable us for the first time to empirically describe social situations in terms of individuals' perceptions of them, a necessary prerequisite for studying situation-contingent language behavior.

The second relevant development is the emergence of social cognition as a new integrative paradigm in psychology, and the growing use of information-processing models to account for many kinds of social behaviors. The study of situated language use lends itself admirably to such a cognitive approach (see, for example, van Dijk, this volume). We will probably need to distinguish between at least two basic kinds of situation-dependent language production strategies: highly routinized *automatic* production, typical of well-rehearsed episodes; and highly monitored *controlled* processing, typical of strategic interactions. Such cognitive models are now in the process of development, although by and large there still seems to be very little awareness in language research of the potential contribution of cognitive social psychology to this problem. It is thus not surprising that most existing research on language and situations is essentially descriptive, as we have seen in the introductory chapter.

Conclusions

This necessarily brief review of the links between social situations and language suggests that the field may be approaching something like a paradigmatic shift. As the research reviewed in the first chapter amply suggests, ideas of situational effects on language were in the past often based on speculative, descriptive systems of situational classification. Most such taxonomic schemes say little about how social actors themselves subjectively perceive and interpret the situations confronting them. Yet it is such cognitive representations and interpretations that must ultimately determine our language behaivors. We thus find that past research on situational variations in language use has been seriously restricted by confusion about exactly what a "situation" is, and by the lack of empirical techniques for analyzing situations. The contributions to this volume point the way toward a new, different conceptualization.

Despite such difficulties, there has been no shortage of prior empirical research illustrating various aspects of situational influences on language use. Many of these undoubtedly interesting studies are ethnographic or anthropological in orientation—they tell us more about the "ethnography of speaking" than about the psychological processes involved in interpreting social situations, and the selection of appropriate linguistic alternatives. They illustrate prevailing cultural practices, as it were, instead of explaining how social actors manage to perform the complex psychological task of perceiving and interpreting social episodes and selecting from their linguistic repertoire the appropriate response. Many of the chapters included here go a considerable way toward achieving this objective. As suggested earlier, the existing state of affairs is likely to undergo further rapid change in the future, for at least two reasons.

Firstly, the recent development of reliable empirical techniques to deal with subjective perceptions of situations represents a major development in cognitive social psychology, which must have its consequences in research on the social psychology of language. Most of the ad hoc situational taxonomies considered here should eventually be replaced by empirical schemes of classification. But how can we establish the links between such situation perception variables and language choices? A second development in psychology, the emergence of a genuinely social approach to cognition, is likely to provide an answer. The idea that people may be understood as individually (Forgas, 1981, 1983c) and collectively (Moscovici, 1981) processing environmental information to regulate their actions firmly focuses attention on the links between internal information processing and external "social representations."

As distinct from the earlier behaviorist paradigm which sought to dismiss as irrelevant all that occurred within the "black box" of our minds, the social cognition approach seeks to discover both the internal knowledge structures and the information-processing strategies we use to deal with the social environment. Social cognition has been a major integrative influence, establishing a common vocabulary and methodology between various branches of pscyhology. Social, developmental, personality, clinical, and cognitive psychologists have discovered their common interests for the first time in decades. The social psychology of language cannot but be influenced by these developments. Considerable research already exists showing that cognitive representations of recurring behavioral sequences, or "scripts," influence the way that we think about, remember, predict, and assoicate information, and in particular, information about social events (Abelson, 1980; Bower, Black, & Turner, 1979). Chapters 4, 5, 6, 9, and 12 by van Dijk, Hoppe-Graff, Gibbs, Gallois and Callan, and Bavelas respectively, and others illustrate the way that such an approach can be translated into language research.

It is but a small step from existing empirical models of episode representations (cf. Forgas, 1979, 1982, 1983b) to the study of how such representations influence language choices. Several projects are at the threshold of accomplishing this task. Herrmann's most recent model of situated language use takes the form of an information-processing flow chart. Furnham (1982) manipulated ad hoc episode features to establish their effects on preferred communicative strategies. Studies such as the research presented here by Blum-Kulka, et al. (Chapter 7) and by Wetzel (Chapter 8) offer a way of analyzing the sociocultural context of an individual's language choices. By constructing taxonomies of naturally occurring episodes, it should be possible to establish empirical links between the cultural and the individual domains. The important conceptual scheme developed by van Dijk already proposes the incorporation of cognitive taxonomies of episodes into studies of language. And several experiments by Forgas (1982) have assessed the links between episode representations and a range of social behaviors and cultural variables.

The eventual emergence of an all-inclusive social cognitive model will thus not mean that traditional linguistic or ethnographic research on language and social situations will be superseded. We will continue to need the kind of research represented here by Chapters 7, 8, and 10, by Blum-Kulka, Wetzel, and Harré respectively to give us the necessary information about the links between macrolevel cultural and social variables and language use. But it is the emerging social cognition paradigm that is most likely to provide the much needed integrative theory linking language and cognitive representations of social situations in a single theoretical scheme. Such a model should in turn provide a new stimulus for empirical research that goes beyond the hitherto dominant ethnographic strategies. This volume could do little more but to point to some of the reasons for this development. We hope that by surveying some of the ideas and trends in the study of situational influences on language use, the present volume will also provide stimulation for further investigations in this exciting field.

References

Abelson, R. P. (1980). *The psychological status of the script concept* (Tech. Rep. No. 2). New Haven, CT: Yale University, Cognitive Science.

Battistich, V. A., & Thompson, E. G. (1980). Students' perceptions of the college milieu. *Personality and Social Psychology Bulletin, 6*, 74–82.

Bell, R. T. (1976). *Sociolinguistics*. London: Batsford.

Bond, M. (in press). How language variation affects inter-cultural differentiation of values by Hong Kong Bilinguals. Hong Kong: The Chinese University.

Bower, G. H., Black, J. B., & Turner, T. J. (1979). Scripts in memory for text. *Cognitive Psychology, 11*, 177–220.

Brown, P., & Fraser, C. (1979). Speech as marker of situation. In K. R. Scherer & H. Giles (Eds.), *Social markers in speech*. Cambridge: Cambridge University Press.

Chomsky, N. (1965). *Aspects of the theory of syntax*. Cambridge, MA: MIT Press.

Forgas, J. P. (1976). The perception of social episodes: Categorical and dimensional representations in two different social milieus. *Journal of Personality and Social Psychology, 33*, 199–209.

Forgas, J. P. (1979). *social episodes: The study of interaction routines*. London: Academic Press.

Forgas, J. P. (Ed.) (1981). *Social cognition: Perspectives on everyday understanding*. London: Academic Press.

Forgas, J. P. (1982). Episode cognition: Internal representations of interaction routines. In L. Berkowitz (Ed.), *Advances in experimental social psychology*. New York: Academic Press.

Forgas, J. P. (1983a). Episode cognition and personality: A multidimensional analysis. *Jouranl of Personality, 51*, 34–47.

Forgas, J. P. (1983b). Social skills and episode perception. *British Journal of Clinical Psychology, 22*, 195–207.

Forgas, J. P. (1983c). What is social about social cognition? *British Journal of Social Psychology, 22*, 129–144.

Furnham, A. (1982). The message, the context and the medium. *Language and communication, 2*, 33–47.

Giles, H., & Hewstone, M. (1982). Cognitive structures, speech and social situations: Two integrative models. *Language Sciences, 4*, 188–219.

Harré, R. (1981). Rituals, rhetoric and social cognition. In J. P. Forgas (Ed.), *Social cognition: Perspectives on everyday understanding*. London: Academic Press.

Herrmann, T. (1982). Language and situation: The pars pro toto principle. In C. Fraser & K. Scherer (Eds.), *Advances in the social psychology of language*. Cambridge: Cambridge University Press.

Hymes, D. (1967). The anthropology of communication. *Social Research, 34*, 632–647.

Hymes, D. (1972). Models of the interaction of language and social life. In J. J. Gumperz & D. Hymes (Eds.), *The ethnography of communication*. New York: Holt, Rinehart & Winston.

Lehnert, W. G., & Ringle, M. H. (1982). *Strategies of natural language processing*. Hillsdale, NJ: Erlbaum.

Mangold, P., & Herrmann, T. (1984). *Zur maschinellen Klassifikation von Aufforderungen*. Arbeiten der Forschergruppe Sprechen und Sparchverstehen im sozialen Kontext, Heidelberg-Mannheim.

Mead, G. H. (1934). *Mind, self and society*. Chicago: University of Chicago Press.

Moscovici, S. (1981). Social representations. In J. P. Forgas (Ed.), *Social cognition: Perspectives on everyday understanding*. London: Academic Press.

Natale, M. (1975). Convergence of mean vocal intensity in dyadic communication as a function of social desirability. *Journal of Personality and Social Psychology, 32,* 790–804.

Pervin, L. A. (1976). A free response description approach to the study of person-situation interaction. *Journal of Personality and Social Psychology, 34,* 465–474.

Rommetveit, R. (1983). Prospective social psychological contributions to a truly interdisciplinary understanding of ordinary language. *Journal of Language and Social Psychology, 2,* 89–105.

de Saussure, F. (1915). *Cours de linguistique generale.* Paris: Payot.

Schlenker, B. (1977). On the ethogenic approach: Etiquette and revolution. In L. Berkowitz (Ed.), *Advances in experimental social psychology.* New York: Academic Press.

Sharkey, N. (1984). Cognitive psychology and artificial intelligence research. Unpublished manuscript, Stanford University.

Smith, P. M. (1983). Social psychology and language: a taxonomy and overview. *Journal of Language and Social Psychology, 2,* 163–183.

Tajfel, H., & Forgas, J. P. (1981). Social categorisation: cognition, values and groups. In J. P. Forgas (Ed.), *Social cognition.* London: Academic Press.

Thakerar, J. T., Giles, H., & Cheshire, J. (1982). Psychological and linguistic parameters of speech accommodation theory. In K. Fraser & K. Scherer (Eds.), *Advances in the social psychology of language.* Cambridge: Cambridge University Press.

Wintermantel, M. (1983). Subjective word knowledge and language in use. Paper presented at the 2nd International Conference on Language and Social Psychology, Bristol.

Wish, M. (1975). Subjects' expectations about their own interpersonal communication. *Personality and Social Psychology Bulletin, 1,* 11–20.

Wurm, S. A. (1976). Summary of discussion. In W. C. McCormack & S. A. Wurm (Eds.), *Language and man.* The Hague: Mouton.

Author Index

Subject Index

Springer Series in Social Psychology

Springer Series in Social Psychology

The Social Construction of the Person
Kenneth J. Gergen/Keith E. Davis (Editors)

Entrapment in Escalating Conflicts: A Social Psychological Analysis
Joel Brockner/Jeffrey Z. Rubin

The Attribution of Blame: Causality, Responsibility, and Blameworthiness
Kelly G. Shaver

Language and Social Situations
Joseph P. Forgas (Editor)

Power, Dominance, and Nonverbal Behavior
Steve L. Ellyson/John F. Dovidio (Editors)

Changing Conceptions of Crowd Mind and Behavior
Carl F. Graumann/Serge Moscovici (Editors)